新维度外语系列教程

商学导论英语教程

An English Course of Introduction to Business

丛书主编　谢　群　陈立华
主　　编　袁　奇
编　　者　郭梦云　杨珍珍　胡雨洪

北京理工大学出版社
BEIJING INSTITUTE OF TECHNOLOGY PRESS

版权专有　侵权必究

图书在版编目（CIP）数据

商学导论英语教程 / 袁奇主编. —北京：北京理工大学出版社，2012.8（2022.9 重印）

新维度外语系列教程 / 谢群，陈立华主编

ISBN 978-7-5640-6528-7

Ⅰ. ①商…　Ⅱ. ①袁…　Ⅲ. ①商务-英语-高等学校-教材　Ⅳ. ①H31

中国版本图书馆 CIP 数据核字（2012）第 186488 号

出版发行 / 北京理工大学出版社
社　　址 / 北京市海淀区中关村南大街 5 号
邮　　编 / 100081
电　　话 / (010)68914775(办公室)　68944990(批销中心)　68911084(读者服务部)
网　　址 / http://www.bitpress.com.cn
经　　销 / 全国各地新华书店
印　　刷 / 北京虎彩文化传播有限公司
开　　本 / 710 毫米×1000 毫米　1/16
印　　张 / 17　　　　　　　　　　　　　　　　　　责任编辑 / 武丽娟
字　　数 / 298 千字　　　　　　　　　　　　　　　　　　　　　 梁铜华
版　　次 / 2012 年 8 月第 1 版　2022 年 9 月第 5 次印刷　　责任校对 / 周瑞红
定　　价 / 46.00 元　　　　　　　　　　　　　　　　　　责任印制 / 王美丽

图书出现印装质量问题，本社负责调换

(Preface)

　　随着中国经济与世界经济接轨的步伐逐步加快,英语专业教学的内容、方法和模式都需要进行不断的创新、嫁接与融合,只有如此,学生的知识和能力才能得到丰富和加强,才能在竞争激烈的就业市场拥有广阔的就业空间,英语专业教学才能符合经济社会发展的需要。传统的英语语言文学专业只注重英语语言文学知识和语言能力的培养,课程的设置都是围绕语言知识的获得和英语语言一般使用能力的培养来进行。照此模式培养的学生一旦走上工作岗位就会发现,单一的语言知识和不涉及专业的语言能力远远不能满足不同行业对专业知识的要求。

　　商务英语是商务和语言的相互融合,是英语的一种应用变体。随着经济发展的全球化,中国已更广泛、更深入地融入了国际商务活动,社会对具备商务英语专业技能的人才需求也呈不断上升趋势。教育部于 2007 年首次批准在对外经济贸易大学设立中国第一个商务英语本科专业,这标志着商务英语经过 50 多年的发展,第一次在中国高等教育专业序列中取得了应有的学科地位。根据《高等学校商务英语专业教学要求》,商务英语专业知识与能力由语言知识与技能、商务知识、跨文化交际能力和人文素养 4 个模块构成。其中商务英语专业知识类课程是商务英语专业人才培养方案中的一个重要组成部分。

　　基于以上认识编写了本书,旨在让学生置身于实际的商务情境,通过学习商务基础理论和知识,直接进行商务实践的训练,从而为将来的职场竞争打好基础。

　　全书分为 15 个单元,每单元设置一个主题,以基本的商业行为为主线,从企业的开始创建到经验管理,系统地培养学习者对各种商业情境的认知和理解,训练其从事相关商务活动的基本能力。这 15 个单元包括商业环境、企业家精神、发现商机、创建企业、组织结构、员工招聘与培训、员工激励、企业文化、生产与产品、市场营销、财务管理、企业融资、企业社会责任、进入国际市场、电子商务。

在编写本书时，为了提高学习效果，编者对每个单元的结构进行了特别的安排。

第一，在每个单元开头都有一段英文导读（Lead-in），简要介绍本单元所涉及的商务活动或内容，并设计了关于该单元内容的思考题（Warm-up Questions/Discussion），以激发读者的兴趣。

第二，每个单元包括一篇课文和一篇补充阅读材料。通过阅读课文，学生不仅能够熟悉专业词汇和特殊表达方式，还能够了解该领域内的主要概念。课文页面标出了文中的关键词汇，并给出了中英文解释。这样的安排能够便于学习者快速地理解和记忆词汇，同时也有助于他们对课文的理解。补充阅读材料意在扩大学生相关的知识面。

第三，每个单元课文后面都设计了一些课后练习，包括针对课文的问答题（Reviewing Questions）、完形填空（Cloze）、句子翻译（Translation）。每个单元还提供了一个案例分析（Case Study），让读者能够运用本单元所学词汇来分析问题，进行讨论。最后布置了两类任务——商务报告（Business Report）和观点陈述（Presentation），让学习者做一些实地调研活动，或者进行发散性思考，并且口头宣讲其调查结果，从而达到巩固其商务专业知识的目的，还可以锻炼其在商务领域的英语运用能力。

由于编者水平有限，编写中肯定存在不少疏漏和欠妥之处，欢迎读者批评指正。

编　者

Unit 1	Business Environment	1
Unit 2	Entrepreneurship	18
Unit 3	Discovering Business Opportunities	34
Unit 4	Establishment of a Business	50
Unit 5	Organizational Structure	66
Unit 6	Recruiting and Training Employees	83
Unit 7	Employee Motivation	99
Unit 8	Corporate Culture	118
Unit 9	Production and Product	134
Unit 10	Marketing	151
Unit 11	Financial Management	168
Unit 12	Financing	186
Unit 13	Corporate Social Responsibility	202
Unit 14	Going to the International Market	219
Unit 15	E-business	236

Unit 1

Business Environment

 Learning Objectives

After learning this unit, you should be able to:
1. Explain the concept of business environment.
2. Describe the importance of understanding business environment.
3. Differentiate the internal and external environment.
4. Describe the various components of the internal and external environment.
5. Describe the various components of the micro and macro environment.

 Lead-in

Understanding the environment within which the business has to operate is very important for running a business unit successfully at any place. Because, the environmental factors influence almost every aspect of business, such as its nature, its location, the prices of products, the distribution system, and the personnel policies. Hence it is important to learn about the various components of the business environment, which consists of the economic aspects, the socio-cultural aspects, the political framework, the legal aspects and the technological aspects, etc.

Warm-up Questions/Discussion:
1. Could you give a brief explanation of business environment?
2. What factors will influence the operation of a business?
3. How can we classify the factors that influence the business operation?

Introduction to Business Environment[①]

The term business environment is composed of two words—"business" and "environment." In simple terms, the state in which a person remains busy is known as business. On one hand, the word "business" in its economic sense means human activities like production, extraction or purchase or sales of goods that are performed for earning profits. On the other hand, the word "environment" refers to the aspects of surroundings. Therefore, business environment may be defined as a set of conditions—social, legal, economical, political or institutional that is uncontrollable in nature and affects the functioning of organization.

The economic environment of business is affected by internal and external factors. On one hand, an internal factor that affects the business environment is the costs of labor, materials, processes and procedures. Internal factors can be improved through company projects. On the other hand, external factors can also affect a company's business environment and the business has less control over these factors.

Internal Environment

An organization's internal environment is composed of the elements within the organization, including current employees, management, and especially corporate culture, which defines employee behavior. The following sections describe some of the elements that make up the internal environment.

(1) Organizational mission statement

An organization's mission statement[②] describes what the organization stands for and why it exists. It explains the overall purpose of the organization and includes the attributes that distinguish it from other organizations of its type. Effective mission statements lead to effective efforts. In today's quality-conscious and highly competitive environments, an effective mission statement's purpose is centered on serving the needs of customers.

(2) Company policy

Company policies are guidelines that govern how certain organizational situations are addressed. Just as colleges maintain policies about disciplines,

---

① The text is excerpted from www.thegeminigeek.com with abridgment.
② mission statement（目标宣言）：An official statement of the aims and objectives of a business or other organization.

companies establish policies to provide guidance to managers who must make decisions about circumstances that occur frequently within their organizations. Company policies are an indication of an organization's personality and should coincide with its mission statement.

(3) Formal structure

The formal structure of an organization is the hierarchical① arrangement of tasks and people. This structure determines how information flows within the organization, which departments are responsible for which activities, and where the decision-making power rests. Some organizations use a chart to simplify the breakdown of its formal structure. This organizational chart② is a pictorial③ display of the official lines of authority and communication within an organization.

(4) Organizational culture

The organizational culture is an organization's personality. Just as each person has a distinct personality, so does each organization. The culture of an organization distinguishes it from others and shapes the actions of its members. Corporate culture is based on the shared values, heroes, rites and rituals and the social network among the staff. Values are the basic beliefs that define employees' successes in an organization. A hero is an exemplary④ person who reflects the image, attitudes, or values of the organization and serves as a role model to other employees. A hero is sometimes the founder of the organization. However, the hero of a company doesn't have to be the founder; it can be an everyday worker who had a tremendous impact on the organization. Rites and rituals are routines or ceremonies that the company uses to recognize high-performing employees. The social network is the informal means of communication within an organization. This network, sometimes referred to as the company grapevine⑤, carries the stories of both heroes and those who have failed. It is through this network that employees really learn about the organization's culture and values.

(5) Organizational climate

A byproduct of the company's culture is the organizational climate. The overall

---

① hierarchical（等级体系的）：Classified according to various criteria into successive levels or layers.

② organizational chart（组织结构图）：A diagram representing the management structure of a company, showing the responsibilities of each department, the relationships of the departments to each other, and the hierarchy of management.

③ pictorial（用图画表示的）：Relating to, characterized by, or composed of pictures.

④ exemplary（可做模范的）：Serving as a model.

⑤ grapevine（消息传播途径）：An unofficial means of relaying information, esp. from person to person.

tone of the workplace and the morale of its workers are elements of daily climate. Workers' attitudes dictate the positive or negative "atmosphere" of the workplace. The daily relationships and interactions of employees are indicative of an organization's climate.

(6) Resources

Resources are the people, information, facilities, infrastructure, machinery equipment, supplies, and finances at an organization's disposal. People are the paramount① resource of all organizations. Information, facilities, machinery equipment, materials, supplies, and finances are supporting, nonhuman resources that complement workers in their quests② to accomplish the organization's mission statement. The availability of resources and the way that managers value the human and nonhuman resources impact the organization's environment.

(7) Managerial philosophies

Philosophy of management is the manager's set of personal beliefs and values about people and work and as such, is something that the manager can control. These managerial philosophies then have a subsequent effect on employees' behavior, leading to the self-fulfilling prophecy③. As a result, organizational philosophies and managerial philosophies need to be in harmony.

(8) Managerial leadership styles

The number of coworkers involved within a problem-solving or decision-making process reflects the manager's leadership style. Empowerment means delegating to subordinates decision-making authority, freedom, knowledge, autonomy, and skills. Fortunately, most organizations and managers are making the move toward the active participation and teamwork that empowerment entails.

External Environment

A business does not function in a vacuum④. It has to act and react to what happens outside the factory and office walls. These factors that happen outside the business are known as external factors or influences. These factors are government and legal factors, geo-physical factors, political factors, socio-cultural factors, demographical factors, etc. They will affect the main internal functions of the

---

① paramount（最重要的）：Of chief concern or importance.
② quest（追求）：The act or an instance of seeking or pursuing something.
③ prophecy（预言）：A statement made about the future.
④ vacuum（真空）：A state of being sealed off from external or environmental influences; isolation.

business and possibly the objectives of the business and its strategies. External environment is of two types: micro/operating environment and macro/general environment.

(1) Micro/operating environment

The environment which is close to business and affects its capacity to work is known as micro or operating environment. It consists of suppliers, customers, market intermediaries, competitors and public.

① Suppliers: They are the persons who supply raw materials and required components to the company. They must be reliable and businesses must have multiple suppliers, i.e. they should not depend upon only one supplier.

② Customers: Customers are regarded as the king of the market. Success of every business depends upon the level of their customers' satisfaction. Types of customers include wholesalers, retailers, industries, government, other institutions and foreigners.

③ Market intermediaries: They work as a link between business and final consumers including the middlemen, marketing agencies, financial intermediaries[①], and physical intermediaries.

④ Competitors: Every move of the competitors affects the business. Business has to adjust itself according to the strategies of the competitors.

⑤ Public: Any group who has actual interest in a business enterprise is termed as public, e.g. media and local public. They may be the users or non-users of the product.

(2) Macro/general environment

Macro/general environment includes factors that create opportunities and threats to business units. The following are the elements of macro environment.

① Economic environment: The larger economic environment of a society is a factor that can affect a company's business environment. During a recession, consumers spend less on optional items such as cars and appliances. As a result, the business environment suffers. On the other hand, if the economic environment is one of prosperity, consumers are more likely to spend money, not just on necessities, but larger items as well.

Economic environment is very complex and dynamic in nature that keeps on changing with the changes in policies or political situations. It has three elements:

---

① intermediary (中介): One that acts as an agent between persons or things; a means.

economic conditions of public, economic policies of the country, and economic system. It also includes other economic factors like infrastructural facilities, banking, insurance companies, money markets, capital markets, etc.

② Political environment: Political environment includes factors like the nature of government policies, particularly those related to taxation, industrial relations, regulation of internal business and industry, and foreign trade regulations. It also relates to the stability of the government in power and risk of major political disturbances.

The political environment can affect the economic environment of businesses. Legislators at different levels may provide incentives or tax breaks[①] to companies or they can impose regulations that restrict business transactions. For example, if a political body states that a company must include a certain chemical in its product, the cost of the product differs. The company passes those costs on to the customer in the form of higher prices. The customer must determine whether he wants to purchase that product. If he does not purchase the product, then the company does not receive the revenue. If a large number of customers decide not to purchase the product, the company may need to layoff employees.

③ Socio-cultural environment: Influence exercised by social and cultural factors, not within the control of business, is known as socio-cultural environment. Socio-cultural factors cover the nature of the life style, culture, attitude and other such common factors that influence and describe the behavioral characteristics typical of the people. These factors include: attitude of people to work, family system, caste system, religion, education and marriage, etc.

Social factors that affect the economic environment of a business are the cultural influences of the time. For example, a fashion designer that creates bell bottom, striped pants, will not succeed in an environment where straight-leg, solid colored pants are desired. A social environment that tends to be more conservative will not support styles that appear to be trendy. The fashion designer's business will suffer if he does not change the clothing style. The same would apply to the manufacturers that produce and stores that sell these wares.

④ Technological environment: A systematic application of scientific knowledge to practical task is known as technology. Innovation and technology affect business

---

① tax break（减税）: A tax deduction that is granted in order to encourage a particular type of commercial activity.

environments. Technological dimension covers the nature of technology available and used by an economy or industry in general. It also covers the extent to which development in technologies are likely to take place. This may be reflected by factors like expenditure on R&D and rate of obsolescence①.

Every day there have been vast changes in products, services, lifestyles and living conditions, therefore these changes must be analyzed by every business unit. As technology advances, a business is forced to keep pace. For example, when computers were first invented, they were the size of a room. Users were forced to employ punch cards to perform basic functions. Today, computers that are much more powerful can fit into the palm of a hand. Businesses that do not keep up with technology risk increased costs of production and higher prices. If the company's cost to produce a product or service outpaces the competitors, the company may soon find itself out of business.

⑤ Natural environment: Natural environment refers to the physical or geographical environment affecting the business. It includes natural resources, weather, climatic conditions, port facilities, topographical② factors such as soil, sea, rivers, rainfall, etc. It also includes the considerations like environmental pollution. Every business unit must look for these factors before choosing the location for their businesses.

⑥ Demographic environment: It is a study of the perspective of population, i.e. its size, standard of living, growth rate, age-sex composition, family size, income level (upper level, middle level and lower level), education level, etc. Every business unit must see these features of population and recognize their various needs and produce accordingly.

⑦ International environment: International environment is particularly important for industries directly depending on imports or exports. The international factors that affect the business are globalization, liberalization, foreign business policies, and cultural exchanges.

As stated above, business enterprises cannot remain independent of the society and the institutions. So whatever decision they make has to be in tune with③ the requirements of society and the dictums④ of the institutions. A business

---

① obsolescence（陈旧过时）：Being in the process of passing out of use or usefulness; becoming obsolete.
② topographical（地形的）：Concerned with the surface features of a place or region.
③ in tune with（符合）：In agreement with someone or something.
④ dictum（官方宣言）：A formal or authoritative statement or assertion; pronouncement.

organization has to continuously monitor the environment so as to identify the business opportunities and threats. By exploring its strengths and minimizing its weaknesses, if the organization can capitalize these opportunities and effectively thwart① the threats, then it would be able to grow.

 Exercises

I. Reviewing Questions
Answer the following questions according to the text.
1. How can we define business environment?
2. How can we define an organization's internal environment?
3. How can we define an organization's external environment?
4. What are the internal factors that affect the economic environment of a business?
5. What are the external factors that affect the economic environment of a business?
6. How can we define an organization's micro environment?
7. How can we define an organization's macro environment?
8. What are the elements of an organization's micro environment?
9. What are the elements of an organization's macro environment?
10. Why is it important for businesses to scan the business environment?

II. Cloze
Read the following passage and fill in the blanks with the words given below. Change the form where necessary.

| predict | competitive | category | adopt | dynamic |
| scanning | framework | affect | operation | confusing |

Business firms wishing to ___1___ an open system of management approach find it difficult to define the business environment. The management has to limit its consideration of the environment, only to those aspects of the outside world which are of major importance to the success of an organization. The concept of business environment is too broad and it would be hopelessly ___2___ to consider each and every aspect in it. Customers, competitors, government units, suppliers, financial institutions and labor pool are part and parcel of the external environment, and available resources, be it physical or human, behavior, synergy, strengths and

---
① thwart（阻止）: To oppose successfully or prevent.

weaknesses and distinctive competence determine the nature of the internal environment of a business firm.

Further, you can divide the business environment into two ___3___, the direct-action environment that has an immediate effect and influence on the organization's decisions, say, government regulations, labor unions, suppliers, customers and competitors. The other category, namely, the indirect environment does not have a direct effect, but nevertheless influences the operations of a firm. These would include factors such as technological, economical, socio-cultural and political, to name a few.

Each and every organization is bound to form its own strategies to define the scope or network of operations, in a business environment. What is a general environmental factor may be specific for another. Precisely speaking, a firm has to consider both the macro and micro environments that ___4___ its life and development. Corporate strategists must be aware of the fundamental features of the current environment to plan accordingly.

SWOT analysis or environmental ___5___, is the basic monitoring system that helps a firm to compile, process and forecast the necessary information gathered from the external environment. This is also helpful in determining the opportunities available for the success of the firm in the market, and gives a clear picture about the threats to be handled. As the business environment is highly ___6___ and volatile, it is inevitable for a business organization to visualize and perceive the opportunities and constraints in store for it.

While SWOT analysis is a tool that helps in scanning the external environment, using the value chain in internal analysis proves to be a useful approach to determine the organization's strengths and weaknesses. It is equally important that a firm must be competent both externally and internally. Adoption of a disintegrated view of the firm helps in diagnosing a company's key strengths and weaknesses. The value chain is a ___7___ that disintegrates a firm into its strategically relevant activities, to understand the behavior of the company's cost and potential sources of differentiation.

A firm gains ___8___ advantage by performing these key internal factors or strategically important activities, in an efficient manner than its competitors. Identifying the primary activities of a firm such as inbound logistics, operations, outbound logistics, marketing and sales, followed by service, denotes the distinct activities that are performed to design, produce, market, deliver and support its product.

The support activities such as procurement, technology development, human resource management and the infrastructure of the firm should not be overlooked, since they are the ones that are essential throughout the entire chain of ___9___.

It is therefore an indispensable fact that, the management should attempt to ___10___ changes in different environmental forces and discern the opportunities and threats emanating from the environment.

III. Translation

1. Just as colleges maintain policies about disciplines, companies establish policies to provide guidance to managers who must make decisions about circumstances that occur frequently within their organization. Company policies are an indication of an organization's personality and should coincide with its mission statement.

2. The formal structure of an organization is the hierarchical arrangement of tasks and people. This structure determines how information flows within the organization, which departments are responsible for which activities, and where the decision-making power rests. Some organizations use a chart to simplify the breakdown of its formal structure. This organizational chart is a pictorial display of the official lines of authority and communication within an organization.

3. Philosophy of management is the manager's set of personal beliefs and values about people and work and as such, is something that the manager can control. These managerial philosophies then have a subsequent effect on employee's behavior, leading to the self-fulfilling prophecy. As a result, organizational philosophies and managerial philosophies need to be in harmony.

4. A fashion designer that creates bell bottom, striped pants will not succeed in an environment where straight-leg, solid colored pants are desired. A social environment that tends to be more conservative will not support styles that appear to be trendy. The fashion designer's business will suffer if he does not change the clothing style. The same would apply to the manufacturers that produce and stores that sell these wares.

5. When computers were first invented, they were the size of a room. Users were

forced to employ punch cards to perform basic functions. Today, computers that are much more powerful can fit into the palm of a hand. Businesses that do not keep up with technology risk increased costs of production and higher prices. If the company's cost to produce a product or service outpaces the competitors, the company may soon find itself out of business.

IV. Case Study

Business Climate "Tougher"

by Wei Tian

Chinese companies are facing even tougher business conditions now than during the 2008 global crisis, according to a survey of more than 4,000 companies. The findings resulted in experts calling for less government intervention and more support for the private sector to improve the business environment.

Among the seven sub-categories of the research, conditions for companies in the fields of human resources, financial services, the legal environment, government administration, and infrastructure have worsened.

However, progress has been made in intermediary services and the social environment, according to the Business Environment Index for China's Provinces 2011 Report.

The findings follow a three-part survey of businesses nationwide, conducted in 2006, 2008 and 2010. More than 90 percent of the 4,230 companies interviewed in 2010 were small and medium-sized enterprises (SMEs).

Non-State-owned enterprises contributed more than 90 percent of the sample, and more than 70 percent of the companies surveyed operate in the manufacturing sector.

The survey is based on both the operational data from companies and the opinions of business owners, who were asked to grade each category from one to five, with five being classified as "very good." The average score improved significantly between 2006 and 2008, but declined in 2010.

Some of the problems highlighted include supplementary levies charged by local governments, regional protectionism and difficulty in obtaining support for financing, said Fan Gang, director of the National Economics Research Institute at the China Reform Foundation, who helped compile the report.

"The competitiveness of Chinese companies is highly related to the policy environment, thus less government intervention in the market and a better relationship between businesses and the authorities will be the direction of our next step in economic reform," Fan said at a forum to introduce the findings earlier this week.

The report ranked the country's regional business climate on a provincial basis, with Shanghai topping all three of the surveys. Provinces in the Yangtze River Delta and coastal areas also ranked high in the table.

"Shanghai provides a more regulated environment for companies, especially for smaller businesses. There is an evolving support system which will be hard for many other cities to catch up with," said Song Xiaohui, an officer of the Shanghai SME Development and Service Center.

However, the opinions of small business owners in Zhejiang province, where the private sector is the most vibrant in China, reflect the poor conditions faced by SMEs, including a challenging external environment and inadequate government supports.

"The situation for the traditional manufacturing sector allows no optimism, because we are facing the dilemma of shrinking loans and increasing costs. And we are in an inferior position to State-owned enterprises," said Ye Mingchun, the owner of a shoe factory in Zhejiang.

"The local government may have adopted some policies to support SMEs but it will take time for them to become effective," Ye said.

"SMEs now have to face the challenges of providing higher quality goods in the domestic market and of weak demand overseas, so an upgrading of the product is the only way to go," said Wang Shibin, who manages a company that produces household goods.

But it's difficult for small businesses to carry out technical innovation on their own, and Wang hopes the government will offer more support in this area while adopting stricter policies on the protection of intellectual property.

Liu Shijin, deputy director of the Development Research Center of the State Council, said "the development of small businesses will be an essential element in helping China emulate the high incomes and living standards seen in developed economies."

"In countries like Brazil and Mexico, where monopolies still have a strong foothold, per capita GDP still lags behind the levels in high-income countries, whereas people in Japan and South Korea enjoy a higher level of personal income because of a boom in private enterprises," Liu said.

He suggested that the government should encourage more competition, especially in basic industries and the service sectors.

(The text is excerpted from www.chinadaily.com.cn)

Questions for discussion:
1. How did people get the conclusion that China's business climate is getting "tougher"?
2. How does the "tougher" business environment affect businesses' operations?
3. What can be done to improve the business environment of China according to the experts' opinions? Could you give some suggestions?

V. Supplementary Reading

Business Environment of China

With a huge market, continuing strong economic performance and an increasing trend for consumer spending, China remains one of the world's most attractive destinations for foreign capital investment. Lack of transparency in the regulatory framework, corruption as well as skills shortages, however, continue to be challenges for investors into the country.

1. Economic Stability: Continuing strong economic performance

Despite a slowdown amidst the global economic crisis of 2008-2009, China remains the world's fastest growing economy. China's exceptional economic growth as well as its impressive growth potential continues to attract a large number of investors to the country. The Chinese government generally welcomes foreign investment and implements a wide range of incentive policies to foreign businesses. However, investors continue to complain about a complicated business environment with a lack of transparency, inconsistent law enforcement as well as protective policies for local firms. In 2009, the Chinese government increased its support for the export sector, imposed restrictions on government procurement from foreign companies, used its new anti-monopoly law to block foreign investment and came under pressure from trade partners for its "dumping" practices. Despite these challenges, China's economy remains competitive and the country is one of the main destinations for foreign capital investment.

2. Ease of Doing Business: Complex business environment

China ranks 89th out of 183 economies in the World Bank's Ease of Doing Business 2010 Report, representing a downgrade of three places compared to the 2009 Report. The process of starting a business in China involves complex administrative procedures. It requires 14.0 procedures, takes 37.0 days, and costs 4.9% of gross national income per capita to set up and run a local limited liability company compared to an average of 8.1 procedures required in East Asia & Pacific.

Access to credit remains a constraint for small and medium-size businesses (SMEs) in China. While bank credit has been expanding rapidly, it has been weighted towards large, state-owned companies which continue to play a dominant role in the economy. Due to a lack of adequate credit information on borrowers, personal connections remain an important source of getting credit in China. The slowdown of the economy since 2008 has also an impact on credit availability in China and the government has since then announced measures to enhance the access of SMEs to bank credit.

3. Government Regulations and Trading Across Borders: Lack of transparency still a major concern

China's investment laws have gradually been improved since the country's accession to the World Trade Organization (WTO) in 2001 in order to conform to WTO investment requirements. In practice, the Chinese government favors investment that meets the country's development goals such as those in higher value-added sectors and advanced rather than basic manufacturing. Its investment objectives are outlined in the Foreign Investment Catalogue, which divides sectors of the economy where foreign investment is encouraged, restricted or prohibited. Sectors which are "prohibited" for foreign investment include media-related industries and compulsory basic education. In order to protect local companies, the government also implements administrative measures to limit foreign investors' ability to participate in the domestic markets.

4. Taxes: Improved tax system

China's tax system is complicated with 26 types of taxes being classified into seven categories. According to the World Bank's Ease of Doing Business 2010

Report, it takes 504 hours for an enterprise to prepare, file and pay taxes in China, higher than India's 271 hours but lower than Brazil's 2,600 hours.

Since January 1st, 2008, China has applied a unified corporate income tax rate of 25.0% on both Chinese and foreign firms, while small-scale companies can enjoy a tax rate of 20.0% in certain cases. The government offers a three-year tax exemption for environmental protection, water and energy efficiency projects. The new tax law is one of the measures to improve tax governance and to level the playing field between local and foreign firms in China.

In 2009, the standard value added tax (VAT) rate stood at 17.0%. There is a reduced VAT rate of 13.0% being applied to certain goods including agricultural products and books. Taxes on labor are included in income taxes of employees and payroll taxes of employers. In order to boost the economy during economic slowdown, the Chinese government has, since 2008, offered tax cuts to a number of sectors including automobile, real estate and environmental protection.

5. Labor and Skills: Competitive labor costs while there is a shortage of the right skills

Despite China's high adult literacy rate of 94.5% in 2009, the country's huge labor force faces difficulty in providing the right skills needed to support China's rapid economic growth. Due to inadequate and out-of-date university training, graduates often do not possess the required skills including computer literacy and foreign languages. Foreign investors have raised their concerns about the difficulty in finding skilled staff. In order to cope with skills shortage problem, the government has implemented measures to attract foreign talent as well as Chinese living overseas to come to China to work.

Cheap labor costs have long been China's advantage over other developing countries which enhance the country's competitiveness in attracting FDI. Minimum working wage regulation varies from city to city. In prosperous cities such as Shanghai, Beijing and Shenzhen, the minimum wage is often higher than other areas. As the economy has shown signs of recovery and inflation has been on the rise since early 2010, China's local governments plan to raise their minimum wage levels.

6. Consumer Markets and Demographics: Robust growth of consumer spending

With a total population of 1.3 billion people as of 2009, China's consumer market is the largest in the world. As annual disposable income has been rising, Chinese consumers have enjoyed growing spending power. The preference to save among Chinese consumers, however, remains high. In 2009, the country's savings rate reached 39.3% of total disposable income, higher than its peer countries such as Russia (12.1%) and India (28.5%).

Consumer expenditure has been rising significantly in China. In 2009, total consumer expenditure accounted for 34.0% of total GDP and grew by 8.0% in real terms over the previous year. Sectors which saw a rise in consumer spending include telecommunications, transport as well as health goods and medical services.

China's consumer market represents great business opportunities for investors and exporters. As a result of the "one child" policy, China is facing population aging. This will lead to an increasing demand for medical products and health care services, providing great opportunities for businesses in these sectors. At the same time, rapid urbanization is resulting in a growing demand for housing. With rising income, Chinese urban youth is becoming more affluent and the consumption of upmarket products including luxuries continues to be an increasing trend.

Reading Comprehension

Choose the best answers to the following questions.

1. Due to its exceptional economic growth, China has attracted a large number of foreign investments. However, investors continue to complain about _____ China.

   A. the complicated business environment with a lack of transparency

   B. the inconsistent law enforcement

   C. the protective policies for local firms

   D. all of the above

2. Access to credit remains a constraint for small and medium-size businesses in China. Due to a lack of adequate credit information on borrowers, _____ remain an important source of getting credit in China.

   A. the government institutions

   B. the state-owned banks

   C. the private banks

   D. personal connections

3. China's investment laws have gradually been improved since the country's accession to the WTO in 2001. Chinese government favors the following foreign

investments except _____.
   A. investment in higher value-added sectors
   B. investment in advanced manufacturing
   C. investment in basic manufacturing
   D. investment that meets the country's development goals
4. All of the following are correct descriptions of China's tax system except _____.
   A. There is a three-year tax exemption for environmental protection, water and energy efficiency projects
   B. The new tax law is one of the measures to improve tax governance
   C. The new tax law is one of the measures to level the playing field between local and foreign firms in China
   D. Due to an efficient tax collection system, tax evasion is not a problem in China
5. China's consumer market represents great business opportunities for investors and exporters. According to the passage, the consumption of the following goods or services will continue to be an increasing trend except _____.
   A. education
   B. medical products and health care services
   C. housing
   D. upmarket products including luxuries

VI. Assignment
1. Interview the manager of a state-owned enterprise, the manager of a foreign company, and the manager of a small Chinese company. Ask them about their opinions of the business environment of China. Do they feel the business environment of China is getting better or worse? Write a report with about 200 words.
2. Please prepare a ten-minute presentation to introduce the measures taken by the Chinese government for the purpose of improving the business environment.

Unit 2

Entrepreneurship

 Learning Objectives

After learning this unit, you should be able to:
1. Understand the concept of entrepreneurship.
2. Define entrepreneurship and entrepreneurs.
3. Describe entrepreneurs' general personalities.
4. Describe entrepreneurs' behaviors.
5. Know the relation of entrepreneurship and leadership.

 Lead-in

Entrepreneurship is the act of being an entrepreneur, which can be defined as "one who undertakes innovations, finance and business acumen in an effort to transform innovations into economic goods." This may result in new organizations or may be part of revitalizing mature organizations in response to a perceived opportunity. The most obvious form of entrepreneurship is that of starting new businesses; however, in recent years, the term has been extended to include social and political forms of entrepreneurial activity.

Warm-up Questions/Discussion:
1. Could you name some successful entrepreneurs and tell their stories?
2. What is the entrepreneurs' role in the development of companies and the whole economy?
3. What qualities should an entrepreneur possess?

Introduction to Entrepreneurship[①]

An entrepreneur is one who organizes a new business venture in the hopes of making a profit. Entrepreneurship is the process of being an entrepreneur, of gathering and allocating the resources—financial, creative, managerial, or technological—necessary for a new venture's success. One engages in entrepreneurship when one begins to plan an organization that uses diverse resources in an effort to take advantage of the newly found opportunity. It usually involves hard work, long hours, and, usually with the hope of significant financial return. More importantly, entrepreneurship is characterized by creative solutions to old or overlooked problems; ingenuity[②] and innovation are the entrepreneur's stock in trade. By taking a new look at difficult situations, the entrepreneur discerns[③] an opportunity where others might have seen a dead end.

Entrepreneurship is also a source of more entrepreneurship. Societies around the world have always been fueled[④] by the innovations and new products that entrepreneurs bring to the market. All big businesses started out small, usually as one man or woman with a good idea and the willingness to work hard and risk everything. While it is true that many new businesses fail, the ones that succeed contribute a great deal to the creation of other new ventures which leads, in turn, to a dynamic national economy. Indeed, today's economists and business researchers cite entrepreneurship as a key component of future economic growth around the world.

Successful entrepreneurship depends on many factors. Of primary importance is a dedicated, talented, creative entrepreneur. The person who has the ideas, the energy, and the vision to create a new business is the cornerstone to any start-up. But the individual must have ready access to a variety of important resources in order to make the new venture more than just a good idea. He or she needs to develop a plan of action, a road map that will take the venture from the idea stage to a state of growth and institutionalization[⑤]. In most instances, the entrepreneur needs to put together a team of talented, experienced individuals to help manage the new

---

① The text is excerpted from www.answers.com with abridgment.
② ingenuity（智力，创造力）: Inventive skill or imagination; cleverness.
③ discern（分辨，识别）: To recognize or perceive clearly.
④ fuel（推动，促进）: To support or stimulate the activity.
⑤ institutionalization（制度化）: To make part of a structured and usually well-established system.

venture's operations. Entrepreneurship also depends on access to capital, whether it is human, technological, or financial. In short, entrepreneurship is a process that involves preparation and the involvement of others in order to exploit an opportunity for profit.

1. Definition of Entrepreneurship

The multiplicity of the entrepreneur's motivations and goals leads to questions aimed at distilling① the essence of entrepreneurship. To what or to whom does one refer when one uses the word? Is there any difference between a person who opens yet another dry cleaning establishment, sandwich shop, or bookstore and the entrepreneur? If so, what is it that separates the two? What characteristics define an entrepreneur and entrepreneurship itself? Historians and business writers have struggled with providing the answers. Even today, there is no widely accepted definition, but the variety of possibilities provide important clues as to what makes entrepreneurship special.

Harvard professor Joseph Schumpeter, for example, argued that the defining characteristic of entrepreneurial ventures was innovation. By finding a new "production function" in an existing resource—a previously unknown means through which a resource could produce value—the entrepreneur was innovating. The innovation was broadly understood; an innovation could take place in product design, organization of the firm, marketing devices, or process design. Nevertheless, innovation was what separated the entrepreneur from others who undertook closely related endeavors. Other researchers, such as Professor Arthur Cole, defined entrepreneurship as purposeful activity to initiate, maintain, and develop a profit-oriented business. The important part of this definition is the requirement that individuals must create a new business organization in order to be considered entrepreneurial. Cole's entrepreneur was a builder of profit-minded organizations.

Still other observers, such as Shapero and Sokol, have argued that all organizations and individuals have the potential to be entrepreneurial. These researchers focus on activities rather than organizational make-up② in examining entrepreneurship. They contend③ that entrepreneurship is characterized by an individual or group's initiative taking, resource gathering, autonomy, and risk taking.

---

① distill（提炼）: To separate or extract the essential elements of something.
② make-up（结构）: The way in which something is composed or arranged; composition or construction.
③ contend（主张，声称）: Have an argument about something.

Their definition could theoretically include all types and sizes of organizations with a wide variety of functions and goals.

In his book *Innovation and Entrepreneurship*, Peter F. Drucker took the ideas set forth by Schumpeter one step further. He argued that Schumpeter's type of innovation can be systematically undertaken by managers to revitalize business and non-business organizations. By combining managerial practices with the acts of innovation, Drucker argued, business can create a methodology of entrepreneurship that will result in the institutionalization of entrepreneurial values and practice. Drucker's definition of entrepreneurship—a systematic, professional discipline available to anyone in an organization—brings our understanding of the topic to a new level. He demystified① the topic, contending that entrepreneurship is something that can be strategically employed by any organization at any point in their existence, whether it is a start-up or a firm with a long history. Drucker understood entrepreneurship as a tool to be implemented by managers and organizational leaders as a means of growing a business.

2. The Entrepreneurs' Personalities

Many business people believe that entrepreneurs have a personality that is different from those of "normal" people. Entrepreneurs are seen as having "the right stuff." But defining the various characteristics and qualities that embody② entrepreneurial success can be an elusive③ task since today's entrepreneurs are big and tall, and short and small. They come from every walk of life, every race and ethnic setting, all age groups, male and female, and from every educational background. There is no mould④ for the entrepreneur. Entrepreneurs make their own mould.

But while it is hard to generalize about what it takes to be a successful entrepreneur, some personality traits seem to be more important than others. While many authors and researchers have disagreed on the relative significance of individual entrepreneurial traits, all agree on one quality that is essential to all entrepreneurs, regardless of definition. That quality is "commitment;" it is self-motivation that distinguishes successful entrepreneurs from those that fail. It is

---

① demystify (使非神秘化): Make less mysterious or remove the mystery from...
② embody (包含, 代表): To be an example of or express (an idea, principle, etc.).
③ elusive (难捉摸的): Difficult to define or describe.
④ mould (模子): A frame on which something may be shaped.

the common thread in the lives and biographies of those that have succeeded in new enterprises. It is the one quality that entrepreneurs themselves admit as critical to the success of their initiatives.

Other traits commonly cited as important components of entrepreneurial success include business knowledge (business planning, marketing strategies, asset management, etc.), self-confidence, technical and other skills, communication abilities, and courage. But there are other, less obvious, personality characteristics that an entrepreneur should develop as a means of further ensuring their successes. It has been indicated that some additional traits help entrepreneurs build thriving organizations, including creativity and the ability to tolerate ambiguous situations.

Creative solutions to difficult problems may make or break the young and growing business; the ability of an entrepreneur to find unique solutions could be the key to his or her success. One of the most **vexing**① situations entrepreneurs face is the allocation of scarce resources. For instance, owners of new ventures need to be able to decide how to best use a small advertising budget or how to best use their limited computer resources. Furthermore, they must be creative in their ability to find capital, team members, or markets. Entrepreneurial success is often directly predicated② on the business owner's ability to do with the limited resources available to him or her.

In addition to being creative, an entrepreneur must be able to tolerate the ambiguity and uncertainty that characterize the first years of a new organization. In nearly all cases, business or market conditions are bound to change during the first few years of a new business's life, causing uncertainty for the venture and for the entrepreneur. Being creative enables entrepreneurs to more successfully manage businesses in new and ambiguous situations, but without the ability to handle the pressure that uncertainty brings upon an organization, the entrepreneur may lose sight of his or her purpose.

Finally, environmental factors often play a significant part in influencing would-be entrepreneurs. Often, personal or work history has led individuals to be more open to take the risks involved with undertaking a new venture. <u>For instance, individuals who know successful entrepreneurs may be stimulated to try their hands at running their own businesses. The successful entrepreneurs act as role models for</u>

---

① vexing（使人烦恼的）: Extremely annoying or displeasing.
② predicated（基于）: To base or found.

those thinking about undertaking a new venture, providing proof that entrepreneurship does not always end in bankruptcy.

In addition, work experience can provide entrepreneurs with invaluable experience and knowledge. First and foremost, entrepreneurs should have experience in the same industry or a similar one. Starting a business is a very demanding undertaking indeed. It is no time for on-the-job training. If would-be entrepreneurs do not have the right experience, they should either get it before starting their new ventures or find partners who have it.

3. The Process of Entrepreneurship

The myths that have grown up around the great entrepreneurs in America have focused more on the personality of the individual than on the work that he or she did to create a prosperous organization. What sticks in our memories are the qualities of a great entrepreneur, those personality traits that "make" a great business person. Successful entrepreneurs, however, work hard to build their organizations, starting from little and undertaking a process that results in a thriving① business. Even the best ideas become profitable only because the entrepreneur went through the steps necessary to build a company from the ground up. Successful new ventures do not appear magically out of the swirl② of the marketplace; they are planned, created, and managed.

It is important to understand some of the stages a business person must go through in order to create a successful entrepreneurial venture. All entrepreneurs go through three very general stages in the process of creating their ventures: a concept formation stage where ideas are generated, the innovation and opportunity are identified, and the business begins to take shape; a resource gathering stage where necessary resources are brought together to launch the new business; and a stage where the organization is actually created.

4. Entrepreneurship and Leadership

Entrepreneurs must also be able to balance their managerial duties with leadership activities. In other words, they have to be able to handle both the day-to-day operations of the business as well as decision making obligations that

---

① thriving (繁荣的,兴旺的): Making steady progress; prosperous.
② swirl (复杂局面): Confusion or disorder.

determine the organization's long-term direction, philosophy, and future. It is a precarious① relationship, but entrepreneurs must be both managers and visionaries② in order to build their organizations. Indeed, researchers contend that many otherwise talented entrepreneurs have failed because they were unable to strike an appropriate balance between details of management and the larger mission that guides the new venture. Many entrepreneurs eventually reach a point where they realize that these twin obligations can not be fully met alone. It is at this point that staffing decisions can become a critical component of a long-term business success. In general, entrepreneurs should search for ways to delegate③ some of their management tasks rather than their leadership tasks. After all, in most cases the new business has long been far more dependent on its founder's leadership and vision than on his or her ability to monitor product quality or select new computers.

The mission of the new venture can only be fulfilled if the entrepreneur remains entrepreneurial throughout the life of the organization. That is, innovation has to be a primary strategy of the venture. The venture must be receptive to innovation and open to the possibilities inherent in change. Change must be seen as positive for a business to remain entrepreneurial. Therefore, management of an entrepreneurial organization requires policies that encourage innovation and reward those who innovate. If the venture is to remain dedicated④ to entrepreneurship, management has to take the lead in establishing the patterns that will lead to a dynamic, flexible, and vital organization.

Exercises

I. Reviewing Questions

Answer the following questions according to the text.

1. What kind of person can be considered as an entrepreneur?
2. How will an entrepreneur influence other businessmen?
3. What factors does successful entrepreneurship depend on?
4. What are Joseph Schumpeter and Arthur Cole's definitions of an entrepreneur?
5. What are Shapero and Sokol's definitions of an entrepreneur?
6. What is Peter Drucker's definition of an entrepreneur?

---

① precarious（不稳定的）：Subject to chance or unknown conditions.
② visionary（好幻想的人）：One who is given to impractical or speculative ideas; a dreamer.
③ delegate（授权）：Give power or authority to someone.
④ dedicated（致力于）：Wholly committed to a particular course of thought or action.

7. What personality traits are important for an entrepreneur?
8. What are the stages a businessperson must go through in order to create a successful entrepreneurial venture?
9. What is the relation of entrepreneurship and leadership?
10. What policies are required in the management of an entrepreneurial organization?

II. Cloze
Read the following passage and fill in the blanks with the words given below. Change the form where necessary.

rank	traditional	vital	foundation	agreement
make	despite	prior	willingness	trait

Despite decades of academic research into the subject, there is still little ___1___ over the precise definition of entrepreneurship. Entrepreneurial leaders are variously described as risk-takers, innovators, bold opportunists or restless agents of change. Some commentators have even argued that entrepreneurial leaders are born with a unique set of characteristics that will always set them apart from more ___2___ corporate managers.

In reality, there is no single entrepreneurship gene. But there are ___3___ and experiences that make it more likely that an individual will choose the path of entrepreneurship and, crucially, succeed over the long term.

The set of management behaviors that characterize many entrepreneurial leaders lies along a spectrum, which includes factors such as a ___4___ to take risks and seize opportunities, and openness to changing. Successful entrepreneurial leaders will often fall toward one end of that spectrum in at least one of those factors, but they will also draw upon a variety of other life experiences to create the finished product.

Entrepreneurial leaders may be ___5___ rather than born, but a large majority of the most successful embarked on their first ventures at a young age. Among a survey of 685 leading entrepreneurial leaders conducted for this report, more than half started their first company before the age of 30.

___6___ starting at a relatively young age, most entrepreneurial leaders do not launch straight into their ventures from higher education. More than half of the entrepreneurial leaders in the survey describe themselves as "transitioned"—meaning that they had some experience outside of the world of entrepreneurship before launching their ventures. Although there are notable examples of entrepreneurial leaders who left college to form hugely successful businesses, such as Bill Gates of Microsoft or Mark Zuckerberg of Facebook, these are very much in the minority. According to some entrepreneurs, a form of business experience is a vital ___7___ that increases the chances of future entrepreneurial success.

Many entrepreneurs cite experience in a corporate environment as an important training ground. When asked to rank the factors that contributed to their ventures' success in order of importance, the entrepreneurs are most likely to select "experience as an employee" as having the greatest impact. And if experience is the best education, the classroom is not far behind. Higher education was ___8___ the number one factor by almost one-third of respondents, just behind employee experience.

Over time, however, corporate experience and progression through the ranks can reduce the chances that would-be entrepreneurial leaders strike out on their own. As they climb the corporate ranks and take on greater personal responsibilities, perhaps with a family to support, the perceived risk of abandoning the security of a salaried corporate position grows.

The challenge of finding the right time to make the transition is one that resonates with Yulisianne Sulistiyawati, founder of PT Pazia Pillar Mercycom, an IT company based in Indonesia. ___9___ to forming her company, Ms. Sulistiyawati spent 15 years working in the IT industry. "When I became an entrepreneur for the first time, it was a big decision because I was already in the comfort zone of having had a professional career," she explains. "Many professionals find it difficult to become entrepreneurial leaders because they think they are risking too much. But the experience that professionals gain early in their career is vital and cannot be bought."

Despite the need to make timely decisions about career direction, a long-term focus is ___10___ for successful entrepreneurial leaders. You need to make decisions at least for the next 5 to 10 years and be brave about planning for your future.

III. Translation

1. Successful entrepreneurship depends on many factors. Of primary importance is a dedicated, talented, creative entrepreneur. The person who has the ideas, the energy, and the vision to create a new business is the cornerstone to any start-up.

Unit 2　Entrepreneurship

But the individual must have ready access to a variety of important resources in order to make the new venture more than just a good idea.

2. These researchers focus on activities rather than organizational make-up in examining entrepreneurship. They contend that entrepreneurship is characterized by an individual or group's initiative taking, resource gathering, autonomy, and risk taking. Their definition could theoretically include all types and sizes of organizations with a wide variety of functions and goals.

3. Drucker's definition of entrepreneurship—a systematic, professional discipline available to anyone in an organization—brings our understanding of the topic to a new level. He demystified the topic, contending that entrepreneurship is something that can be strategically employed by any organization at any point in their existence, whether it is a start-up or a firm with a long history.

4. Entrepreneurs are seen as having "the right stuff." But defining the various characteristics and qualities that embody entrepreneurial success can be an elusive task since today's entrepreneurs are big and tall, and short and small. They come from every walk of life, every race and ethnic setting, all age groups, male and female, and from every educational background. There is no mould for the entrepreneur. Entrepreneurs make their own mould.

5. For instance, individuals who know successful entrepreneurs may be stimulated to try their hands at running their own businesses. The successful entrepreneurs act as role models for those thinking about undertaking a new venture, providing proof that entrepreneurship does not always end in bankruptcy.

IV. Case Study

Brian Scudamore of 1-800-GOT-JUNK?

by Scott Allen

1-800-GOT-JUNK? is a full-service junk removal company with 200 franchises in Canada, the United States and Australia. On average, up to 60% of the junk that is hauled is diverted from the landfill and is then either recycled or donated to charity and non-profit organizations.

Brian Scudamore started his company 1-800-GOT-JUNK? in 1989 straight out of high school with $700 and a beat-up old pick-up truck. Today they have 95 franchise partners across North America with a true national presence—they are in 47 of North America's top 50 cities.

Scudamore was a risk-taker, but firm in his vision. "With a vision of creating the FedEx of junk removal," says Scudamore, "I dropped out of University with just one year left to become a fulltime JUNKMAN! Yes, my father, a liver transplant surgeon, was not impressed to say the least." He chuckles, "He is onside now."

Many entrepreneurs minimize their risks by outsourcing to contractors. Scudamore chose a different route.

"I hired my first employee a week after I started. I knew I needed the help. His name was David Sniderman—a good friend of mine. I really didn't know yet how to hire so I just asked a buddy." It may have started as a matter of simply not knowing what else to do, but it became a philosophical issue for him. "On a bigger level, I always believed in hiring people vs. contract or consultants. I felt that if I weron't willing to make the investment then I was questioning my own faith in the business."

On the other hand, he's a big believer in letting other people share some of the risk. His choice of franchising as a business model allowed him rapid growth without having to turn to outside investors or other funding sources.

"It's the ultimate leverage model. People pay you a fee up-front to help them grow. Rather than lose control of my vision by going public—I chose franchising. It's the ultimate growth model."

Their recipe for success has been simple. Take a fragmented business, add clean shiny trucks that act as mobile billboards, uniformed drivers, on-time service and up-front rates, and then mix in with a culture that is young, fun and completely focused on solid, healthy growth. He has managed to retain 100% ownership and bootstrapped the business solely out of cash flow—something that is very rare these days.

Although this is a simple business, they couldn't possibly have grown this quickly without technology. Taking a low tech business and putting a high tech spin on it allowed them to rapidly distinguish themselves from their competition. All calls come into a central 1-800-GOT-JUNK? call center where they do all the booking and dispatch for their franchise partners. Franchise partners then assess all of their real time reports, schedules, customer info, etc., off of JUNKNET, their corporate intranet. This allows franchise partners to get into business quickly, and to focus solely on growth—working on the business vs. working in the business.

(The text is excerpted from entrepreneurs.about.com)

Questions for discussion:
1. What kind of person is Brian Scudamore? When and how did he start his business?
2. What is Brian 1-800-GOT-JUNK?'s recipe for success?
3. What have you learned from Brian Scudamore's case?

V. Supplementary Reading

The Boom of Start-ups in China

Kevin Cang graduated from a top university in China four years ago. After working three months for Pricewaterhouse Coopers（普华永道会计师事务所）, he left to start Looker, a career training and consulting services company, with several partners at his own age. Over the past three years, Cang has received funding from an angel investor, argued with partners who subsequently quit, shifted his product portfolio, and merged with another similar small business. He and the founder of that business are now partners and the only full-time employees of their company, which pulls in 1 million RMB (about US$150,000) in annual revenue—and a profit.

Cang isn't unique. After seeing big-name multinational companies downsize significantly, one after another, young professionals are realizing that the "Iron Rice Bowl" has disappeared since China opened its doors to the West in the 1980s. Then the economic tsunami of 2008 made the nation's economy even shakier. Recent college grads are asking, "Why should we work so hard, day in and day out, to pursue non-existent job security? If we have to gamble on success, why not spend our precious youth doing something that we can control and that has a chance to grow into a lifetime business"? Good questions. Their answer, increasingly, is to start their own businesses.

The government is providing more and more entrepreneurial opportunities to the six million students who graduate from college in China every year, partly to ease employment tension across the nation. In 2009, China's central government announced a preferential policy that allows graduates to register a company with "zero" capital up front; whatever money they pledged to fund their start-up may be paid within two years after the company is established. Passionate youngsters applaud the new policy and have shown great zeal of taking advantage of the opportunity.

A Game of Resources

Some Chinese entrepreneurs prefer to use their own investment capital to get their operations off the ground. "It's a game of resources," Cang explains. "Investors own the money, but we entrepreneurs make real-life decisions. It works well if both parties are on the same track; otherwise, the conflict can go wild." Cang, who had an unpleasant experience dealing with several initial investors in the early phase of his start-up, eventually bought all of his company's shares back.

In addition to college grads, a group known as the "Rich Second Generation" has emerged. These 20-something professionals are either children of high-level government officials with strong local connections, or kids born to wealthy first-generation entrepreneurs. Their deep pockets generally make them less concerned about finding initial investments and evaluating risks than others, and more focused on experimenting with ideas that interest them. Money, of course, isn't the only resource that entrepreneurs need. Customers, partners, and social networks can help take a business to the next level and give it a competitive edge. In China, people tend to rely mostly on their personal networks to reach out for help. This explains why a few entrepreneurs say they'd rather wait to start businesses until they're in their 30s and 40s, after they've accumulated contacts and experience. Younger people seem willing to take greater risks.

The Digital Generation

Technology does seem, after all, to be the future. Although the success of early pioneers in the late 20th century undoubtedly influences current dream chasers in China, times have changed. Tools have changed. Opportunity has drifted away from raw materials and manufacturing—and toward the digital world.

The majority of today's Chinese entrepreneurs grew up in the Internet boom as well-educated children. Computers and the Web, not to mention mobile devices (from touch-screen handsets to lightweight netbooks), are second nature to them. A friend of mine who runs a family business of ceramic bathroom products recently switched to HTC Hero, a touch-based Android phone, for the ease of using embedded Google services on-the-go. Likewise, Cang uses his mobile phone daily to check email and keep up with his contacts.

Besides being familiar with all kinds of new gadgets, this generation of entrepreneurs has a natural curiosity about software and online services. They were raised in an era of Internet heroes. They want the latest scoop from that magical Silicon Valley across the Pacific Ocean. To them, life is digital, from information search to bank transactions, whereas the older generation still holds doubt about the universality and security of the Matrix-ed world.

Thanks to technology, these young entrepreneurs put convenience, time-efficiency, and productivity before routines and procedures.

Emerging Behaviors

The behaviors of Chinese entrepreneurs are changing not only around new devices and e-commerce, but also around the concept of collaboration. Cang relies heavily on the Web-based tools offered by Zoho.com. "I benefit a lot from online real-time collaboration," he says. "We are a two-person company, but we have a broader network of student agents across various universities in Shanghai. With the multiuser online document application, we can work simultaneously with our agents on project plans and customer reports. It's very efficient and flexible."

This new generation of entrepreneurs is savvy about leveraging the Internet to market their ideas as well. As users of popular social networks themselves, young entrepreneurs intuitively make best use of these online communities. While large, well-known consumer brands have just started to spend big money on research and planning in the social media arena, many small business owners have actively grown their exposure in the white-hot space. In the case of Cang, he has his company page on Xiaonei, a China-version of Facebook, and has been messaging the activity updates on Fanfou, a China-version of Twitter, for almost two years.

Work is Life, Life is Work

Amid all of these 21st-century trends, Chinese entrepreneurs share one key trait with their predecessors: a penchant for hard work. No matter how many resources and tools a Chinese entrepreneur has, to become very successful, he or she usually has to go through an intense period of struggling to figure out the right business model and build a sustainable organization. To achieve that—and even after achieving that—an entrepreneur rarely stops to relax. Instead, he or she goes for the next goal.

Cang's daily schedule awed me. He gets up before 8 a.m. and works until after 9 p.m. Once he's home, he usually spends another hour on miscellaneous work, such as making PowerPoint presentations, because his office hours are too precious to spend creating slide shows. He says he needs to put the time when his customers are in "active mode" to better use. In Cang's calendar, there are seven Mondays in a week. Since he works for himself, he doesn't care to make Saturday more self-entertaining than any other day. He enjoys every workday; if he has any personal things to deal with, he usually doesn't wait for nights or weekends. To Cang, life is flexible, and he's in total control of it.

Reading Comprehension

Choose the best answers to the following questions.

1. All of the following are the reasons for Cang to start his own business except _____.
   A. that the "Iron Rice Bowl" has disappeared since China opened up to the outside world
   B. that he has worked very hard, but got nothing in return
   C. that he wants to spend his precious youth doing something that he can control
   D. that he wants to do something that has a chance to grow into a lifetime business

2. According to this passage, people tend to rely mostly on _____ to reach out for help in China.
   A. their personal networks
   B. the government's financial aid
   C. the investors' venture capital
   D. the bank loans

3. Why does the author consider today's Chinese entrepreneurs as "the Digital Generation"?
   A. Because the majority of today's Chinese entrepreneurs grew up in the Internet boom.
   B. Because these entrepreneurs are familiar with all kinds of new gadgets.
   C. Because these entrepreneurs have a natural curiosity about software and online services.
   D. All of the above.

4. What is the new generation of entrepreneurs' attitude towards the Internet?

   A. They often use the Internet in social communication.

   B. They often surf the Internet in order to collect information.

   C. They are trying to make full use of the Internet to market their ideas.

   D. They seldom use the Internet for business purpose.

5. One key trait Chinese entrepreneurs share with their predecessors is that _____.

   A. they are both very thrifty in their lives

   B. they are both risk-lovers

   C. they are both good at catching business opportunities

   D. they both have a preference for hard work

VI. Assignment

1. Interview some famous entrepreneurs who developed their businesses from scratch. Ask them about how they decided to start their businesses. Write a report with about 200 words.

2. Please prepare a ten-minute presentation to introduce the measures we can take to foster entrepreneurship in China.

Unit 3
Discovering Business Opportunities

 Learning Objectives

After learning this unit, you should be able to:
1. Understand the concept of a business opportunity.
2. Know the importance of identifying business opportunities.
3. Describe the process of discovering business opportunities.
4. Evaluate the quality of business opportunities.
5. Identify the potential risks at the initial stage of a business.

 Lead-in

A business opportunity may be defined simply as an attractive proposition that provides the possibility of a return for the investor or on the person taking the risk. Such opportunities are represented by customer requirements and lead to the provision of a product or service which creates or adds value for its buyer or end-user. Business opportunities are not equally obvious to everyone, but they are equally available to anyone with the experiences and the knowledge of discovering them.

Warm-up Questions/Discussion:
1. What are the sources of business opportunities?
2. Could you give a brief description of a good opportunity?
3. Have you discovered any good business opportunities in your life?

How Entrepreneurs Identify New Business Opportunities[①]

A key question that all would-be entrepreneurs face is finding the business opportunity that is right for them. Should the new startup focus on introducing a new product or service based on an unmet need? Should the venture select an existing product or service from one market and offer it in another where it may not be available? Or should the firm bank on[②] a tried and tested formula that has worked elsewhere, such as a franchise operation? We will discuss these questions and look into how entrepreneurs can identify new business opportunities and evaluate their potential and their risks.

How to find the opportunity that's right for you

There are many sources of new venture opportunities for entrepreneurs who are thinking of starting a new business or company. Clearly, when you see inefficiency in the market and have an idea of how to correct that inefficiency, and you have the resources and capability—or at least the ability to bring together the resources and capability needed to correct that inefficiency—that could be a very interesting business idea. In addition, if you see a product or service that is being consumed in a foreign market, and that product is not available in your market, you could perhaps import that product or service, and start that business in your home country.

Many sources of ideas come from existing businesses, such as franchises. You could license[③] the right to provide a business idea. You could work on a concept with an employer who, for some reason, has no interest in developing that business. You could have an arrangement with that employer to leave the company and start that business. You can tap[④] numerous sources for new ideas for businesses. Perhaps the most promising source of ideas for new business comes from customers—listening to customers. That is something we ought to do continuously, in order to understand what customers want, where they want it, how they want a product or service supplied, when they want it supplied, and at what price.

Obviously, if you work in a large company, employees might help you come

---

① The text is excerpted from www.wharton.upenn.edu with abridgment.
② bank on (指望，依靠)：To have confidence in; rely on.
③ license (颁发许可证，特许)：To grant a license to or for; authorize.
④ tap (开发，利用)：To take advantage of; make use of.

up with ideas. Indeed, you might want to listen to what they have to say. You could pursue these ideas by asking yourself some key questions such as, "Is the market real? Is the product or service real? Can I win? What are the risks? And is it worth it"?

Let's take E-Bay as an example. In the age of the Internet, there is no shortage of examples of entrepreneurs who started a company based on a perceived need. You could go back to the beginning of E-Bay①, where they saw an opportunity to connect people through launching a virtual flea market②. It offered a platform that connected buyers and sellers directly.

Other companies have found similar models. PayPal③ is a company providing people with the opportunity to pay online. Flycast④ is another company having started on the Internet. It addressed issues of advertising on-line. All of these companies have one thing in common. They addressed an unmet need in the marketplace.

<u>There is no substitute for understanding the unmet needs of customers. That will allow you to discover whether you are able to supply those needs, at the price customers want to pay, and if you can still make a profit.</u>

How to decide whether or not to pursue a business opportunity

<u>Once a would-be entrepreneur has identified what he or she thinks is a promising unmet need, he or she should evaluate and identify the risks that should be considered in deciding whether or not to pursue that business opportunity.</u>

The first step that everyone should go through is to ask the question, is the market real? In order to do so, the first thing you want to do is conducting a customer analysis. You can do that perhaps in a very technical way, by conducting surveys. Or perhaps, in a less technical way, you can attempt to answer the question, "Who is my customer? What does the customer want to buy? When does the customer want to buy? What price is the customer willing to pay? " So, asking the "W questions"—who, where, what, when—is the first step. At the end of the day,

---

① E-Bay（易趣网）: Founded in 1995, it is an American online auction and shopping website in which people and businesses buy and sell a broad variety of goods and services worldwide.

② flea market（跳蚤市场）: A type of bazaar where inexpensive or secondhand goods are sold or bartered.

③ PayPal（贝宝）: It is an E-commerce business allowing payments and money transfers to be made through the Internet, for which it charges a fee.

④ FlyCast（美国 FlyCast 公司）: It is a mobile broadcast network that delivers over 1,000 channels of music, talk, weather, and traffic to portable devices using wireless streaming technology.

the one thing every entrepreneur is looking for is revenue, and the revenue will come from customers. That is why you need to ask yourself, is there a market here?

The second thing you want to ask yourself is who else is supplying that particular market? That is competitor analysis. Ask yourself who else is in this market, and what are they doing for the customers. Are they supplying a similar substitute product or service as you have in mind? That is the second thing you have to establish, and by doing that, you can understand better what need is not met at the moment. That will also give you the opportunity to zero in① on the price points and feature points of where you can differentiate yourself from existing players in the market.

You also need to conduct a broader industry analysis to understand the attractiveness of the industry you're going to enter. Is the industry growing or shrinking? What power do the suppliers have in this industry? How many buyers are there? Are there substitute products? Are there any barriers to entry? If so, what are they? That is very important for you to understand, because it will help you realize whether the industry you're thinking of entering is attractive.

In addition, you may want to look at regulations that affect that industry. Are there any regulations that you would be subject to? This especially applies in the life sciences sector, where there are strict regulations that control the supply of products into the market. In the United States, the FDA, the Food and Drug Administration, is a significant regulator. Every country around the world has a regulator in the life science sector. So, these are the high level questions that you may want to ask yourself.

<u>Once you answer these questions, and you identify the need, given the competition and all the regulatory constraints that exist in that market, that will provide you with the opportunity to tailor② your service or product—or combination of the service and product—to that marketplace.</u> The logic we are suggesting here is to understand the need, and tailor the product and/or service to that need, as opposed to saying, "Well, I have an idea. And now let me think how I can shove③ it down the distribution channel." More often than not, the latter doesn't work. More often than not, the former approach works. This is the approach where you identify the need, do a rigorous analysis of understanding who else is out

---

① zero in (瞄准): Direct onto a point or target, especially by automatic navigational aids.

② tailor (调整使适合): To adapt so as to make suitable for something specific.

③ shove (用力推): To push someone or something with force.

there, and what constraints exist, and how you could differentiate yourself in a meaningful way. When you approach a new opportunity this way, when you introduce your product and/or service, you can expect to have substantial sales and growth for your company.

How to evaluate and identify the risks

In addition to conducting market analysis and competitive analysis, and also looking at the industry and government, there are some other risks that entrepreneurs should take into account. One way to think about the various risks an entrepreneur is faced with—or, for that matter, an investor in an entrepreneurial venture is faced with—is to break them down into several buckets.

Let's start with the first bucket, the company bucket. Well, here, the biggest sources of risk are the founders. Do they have the wherewithal① not just to start the company, but also grow the company? Individuals such as Bill Gates or Michael Dell, Steve Jobs can not only start companies, but also manage its growth. Experience has shown that the prevalence② of such individuals is relatively limited.

The second source of risk is technology risk. To the extent that your company employs technology, there are obvious issues of how long this technology will be the leading edge③. Secondly, are there any intellectual property④ issues that need to be addressed? Lastly, there exists the product risk. If you haven't developed a product yet, can you manufacture it? Will it work? All these issues are under the bucket of technology risk.

The third bucket for the sources of risk is the market for the product. You need to be aware of two big uncertainties. First, what is the customer's willingness to buy? And second, what is the pace, if you're successful, at which competitors will be able to imitate you? One of the things you have to think about when you enter that market is how you can create barriers to imitation, so that if you're successful, the competition won't be able to imitate you very quickly.

The fourth bucket consists of risks associated with the industry. Are there any factors in that industry that relate to availability of supply? In some cases, you need

---

① wherewithal（必要的资金）: The necessary means, especially financial means.
② prevalence（普遍，广泛）: The quality of prevailing generally; being widespread.
③ leading edge（领先地位）: The foremost position in a trend or movement.
④ intellectual property（知识产权）: Intangible property that is the result of creativity (such as patents or trademarks or copyrights).

to have certain raw materials that are in limited supply, and some suppliers might be able to take advantage of that. Barriers to entry might change. Regulations might change, and adversely or positively affect your business.

Lastly, there are financial risks. And here, the question is, will you be able to raise the money early on? At what valuation will you be able to do it? Will you be able to raise follow-up money? And then, from the investor's standpoint, obviously there's a risk if the company is not very successful. Most early stage companies don't work out, but for the few that do, when it is time for a public offering, will the public market be open? We have just gone through a substantial period of almost two years when IPOs① were few and far between. At the time you make the investment, you don't know what the state of the capital market will be in five to seven years from the date you make the investment. That's a big risk the investor is assuming. Obviously, it's a big risk for the entrepreneur to be able to have some liquidity, and perhaps realize the fruits of his investment, his time, talent, and in some cases some of the money he puts into that venture.

Advice to potential entrepreneurs

The most frequent mistake that entrepreneurs tend to make at the initial stage is to think everybody in the market is like them. If they like the product, everybody else will. Sometimes entrepreneurs, especially entrepreneurs with an engineering background, are too focused on the engineering features or technology features of the particular product, rather than on the need that they are trying to fulfill. Customers don't buy technology. Customers buy products that add value. Customers buy products that they need, in order to satisfy some need that they wish to satisfy. It is the services of the technology that matter, but not the technology. Very often, entrepreneurs—particularly smart entrepreneurs—are overwhelmed by the technological aspect, and they pay too little attention to what the customers want. This is the most frequent issue at the early stage that entrepreneurs are faced with.

Some potential entrepreneurs are very hesitant to start new businesses, because they think they don't have the characteristics of what would make for a successful entrepreneur. Also, it's too risky to be an entrepreneur. <u>Researches around the world</u>

---

① IPO（首次公开上市）：Abbreviation for initial public offering. A corporation's first offer to sell stock to the public.

have shown that there are no unique characteristics or traits that distinguish entrepreneurs from non-entrepreneurs, and successful entrepreneurs from unsuccessful entrepreneurs.

These potential entrepreneurs should bear it in mind that they have what it takes to be exceptionally successful. It is no more risky to start your own business than working for General Motors. As we can recall, General Motors has filed for bankruptcy. Therefore, the perception that working for a large company is somehow safer is not borne out① by the reality. Believe you have what it takes to be a successful entrepreneur; it is time to get started.

Exercises

I. Reviewing Questions

Answer the following questions according to the text.

1. How can we define business opportunities?
2. What are the sources for new business opportunities?
3. What can be learned from the cases of E-Bay, Paypal and Flycast?
4. What should be done while deciding whether or not to pursue a business opportunity?
5. How can we evaluate the attractiveness of a business opportunity?
6. Why is it important for companies to tailor their product and/or service to market need?
7. How can we evaluate the risks of a business opportunity?
8. What are the major risks an entrepreneur could be faced with?
9. What is the most frequent mistake that entrepreneurs tend to make?
10. Why are some potential entrepreneurs very hesitant to start new businesses? What should they do?

II. Cloze

Read the following passage and fill in the blanks with the words given below. Change the form where necessary.

| formula | franchise | suffering | consideration | demand |
| untapped | served | eventually | introduce | talents |

---

① bear out (证实，支持): To support with evidence or authority or make more certain or confirm.

There are so many business opportunities to get into these days. There are no limits because there are many new things to sell and resell. There is always the food industry. One can sell small time as homemade goodies are sold mostly to friends and referrals or one can go big time and open up a ___1___ of say McDonald's or Burger King. As for clothes, you can opt to come up with your own designs and offer services to your friends and relatives and then ___2___ expand. If you want to go mainstream, opening a store in the mall would already be a big step. So with all these choices, which business should you get into?

The first consideration you should have is to know yourself, most especially your skill and your ___3___. Look inside you. Study and observe your behaviors and achievements through the years. Ask the people closest to you when they saw you at your best.

Hopefully upon careful ___4___, you will stumble upon answers about your true skills and talents. These skills and talents are already in you so it is something that can be very bankable in any business that you will get into. There will also be your ___5___ inner resources. So ask mentors about these things. Most of the time it is mentors or elders that have seen you grow up and know your hidden abilities. Oftentimes, a person has various talents and skills and among the long list there are certain skills and talents that are most useful in pursuing chosen interests. Interests are hobbies that a person actually enjoys doing so if you have a knack for certain things, go for it. Usually it is this knack that will make you go for the top plum in any field you get into. The determination will follow because there is already that desire to do your best because you like excelling in that field.

After discovering your skills and interests, keep developing all these things and then finally choose the right business for you based on this evaluation. A good way to start is studying the market and investing in something that is already in ___6___. Make sure though that whatever this service or product in demand is not simply a fad. Otherwise you can also delve deeper and see the need of the greater number of population is not yet being ___7___.

There could be a product or service ___8___ from shortage in your state but there is an over supply of that same product or service in another state. Maybe you can be the one to bring in that product to your state. You can also create a need for a new product or service you want to ___9___ to the market. It is all about overall marketing. You should be able to have a marketing plan that will work for your product or service.

Tapping the right business opportunity is balancing what you already have and what you potentially can have. Getting the right combination is a sure ___10___ for success. Also keep in mind sustainability to make sure that you have long term goals for whatever business you want to get into. There is also that element of luck here being to wish you good luck on the next business opportunity you are planning to take on.

III. Translation

1. Clearly, when you see inefficiency in the market and have an idea of how to correct that inefficiency, and you have the resources and capability—or at least the ability to bring together the resources and capability needed to correct that inefficiency—that could be a very interesting business idea.

2. There is no substitute for understanding the unmet needs of customers. That will allow you to discover whether you are able to supply those needs, at the price customers want to pay, and if you can still make a profit.

3. Once a would-be entrepreneur has identified what he or she thinks is a promising unmet need, he or she should evaluate and identify the risks that should be considered in deciding whether or not to pursue that business opportunity.

4. Once you answer these questions, and you identify the need, given the competition and all the regulatory constraints that exist in that market, that will provide you with the opportunity to tailor your service or product—or combination of the service and product—to that marketplace.

5. Researches around the world have shown that there are no unique characteristics or traits that distinguish entrepreneurs from non-entrepreneurs, and successful entrepreneurs from unsuccessful entrepreneurs.

IV. Case Study

Virgin: Richard Branson's Story

by Evan Carmichael

"I don't go into ventures to make a fortune. I do it because I'm not satisfied with the way others are doing business."

Growing Up

Branson dropped out of school in 1967 at the age of 16 and started a magazine called *Student*. He hoped it would be a forum for politically-minded youth. He soon was publishing essays and interviews from such figures as Jean-Paul Sartre, James Baldwin, Alice Walker, and Robert Graves. Despite such a roster of great minds and literary figures, the magazine never made money and seemed bound to fail.

Starting the Business

Branson began marketing his next idea in the pages of *Student*; selling albums at a reduced rate through the mail. It rapidly became a more profitable business than the magazine itself. The staff of *Student* suddenly found themselves the employees of the Virgin discount record store. They used the name "Virgin" because no one had been in business before. Virgin had been going strongly but it was discovered Branson was dodging his tax payments. He was arrested and jailed.

Building an Empire

An out-of-court settlement was reached and, determined to keep the balance sheets carefully, Virgin Records was founded in 1973. Mike Oldfield's progressive "Tubular Bells" was the first record released through Virgin and became an international success. But, it was the signing of the Sex Pistols to his label in 1977 that truly established Virgin Records. Though the Pistols broke up soon after, Virgin became the largest indie label in the world. Bands like the Rolling Stone, Peter Gabriel and UB40 were signed to Virgin.

Over the next six years, Branson started over fifty different companies encompassing everything from filmmaking to air conditioner cleaning. Though he was making more than $17 million dollars from his various companies collectively, Branson insists that money is not the motivation behind his involvement in so many ventures. Rather, he enjoys attempting to do something more effectively than those who have tried before him.

In 1984, Branson started Virgin Atlantic Airlines—a company that would prove to be a great challenge as well as the cause of financial distress. Branson ignored discouraging comments that told him he could never compete with British Airways, and to look to the example of those who had failed before. The reason is that he had observed how airline companies did not look after their customers adequately enough, so he would be the one to bring affordable and enjoyable flights to the public. Virgin Air was immediately recognized for its service and luxury. In-flight massages, hydrotherapy baths and seat-back video screens were all part of the experience on-board a Virgin aircraft.

With fuel prices having doubled in the early 1990s, terrorist attacks making people afraid to fly, and BA launching a campaign to put Branson out of the airline business, Virgin Atlantic struggled to stay afloat. Branson was forced to sell Virgin Records in order to raise enough money to keep Virgin Atlantic and pay off his creditors. The sale of the company that gave him his start was a crushing blow.

From this point on, Branson developed a new approach to business called "branded venture capital." Through this method, Branson licenses the well-known Virgin name and logo in exchange for a controlling interest in the venture. Consequently, Branson has his company's name fixed to more than 200 different companies, among which are Virgin Bridal, Virgin Publishing, a blimp company and a modeling agency.

Branson is known for his unusual business practices (no central headquarters, no board meetings, and he can't operate a computer), his showy publicity stunts (like driving a tank into Times Square and buzzing over Big Ben in an Airbus jet), and his adventurous exploits (he was the first person to cross the Atlantic in a hot air balloon and has attempted three times to fly it around the world). It might be thought that such an approach to business could have ruined him, but Virgin is a towering $5 billion dollar giant. And Branson keeps dreaming for the future. In discussing the prospect of starting a shuttle service into space, Branson has said, "Why not? It's virgin territory."

Questions for discussion:
1. What was Branson's mindset when he started to do business?
2. What is the most basic drive for Branson when he is growing and expanding his business?
3. Could you give an explanation of the new approach of business developed by Branson, namely "branded venture capital"? What do you learn form Branson and his business?

V. Supplementary Reading

Government's Role in Encouraging Small Business

In the late 1970s, a commune in China was so broke, and the peasants who ran the commune were so hungry and poor that they decided to risk their lives and do the unthinkable: The peasants secretly privatized and divided up the land. Each farmer had his own plot with which to grow his own food, use it, and sell the extra, if any.

Within a year, that commune became one of the most prosperous in China and, not surprisingly, caught the eyes of government officials. Yet rather than condemn what was a decidedly noncommunist idea, the government gave private commune plots an official blessing. The rest, as they say, is history. This turn of China became the greatest antipoverty program in the history of the world, freeing millions of people from poverty in a few short decades.

That the government policy can have a huge impact on the growth and promotion of small business is a vast understatement. In a world beset by too much hunger and needy, small business is one thing with a proven capacity not only to ease suffering, but also to create a solid middle class, generate a secure tax base, and foster social stability. All in all, small business is good business.

Thus raises the question: For those countries wishing to promote small business, what policies can be adopted to encourage its growth? I suggest that there are five main areas where appropriate government policies can have a huge impact on small-business growth.

Make capital easily available

When I was a young boy, my father owned several carpet stores. One day, I was given the assignment in school to write an essay about what he did for a living. Because "retail carpet store owner" was hard for me to describe, I asked him what he did. "Well," he said, "I'm an entrepreneur." A bit confused, I asked him what that was, and he replied, "An entrepreneur is a person who takes a risk with money to make money."

That remains as good a description as I have ever heard, although since then I have learned that entrepreneurs actually like to take small, calculated risks. Therefore, if a government wants to promote small business, it must advance policies that reduce the risk inherent in entrepreneurship. That way, people will be more willing to leave the comforts of their jobs and start new businesses.

So the first policy necessary to promote small-business development is one that assists would-be entrepreneurs find the money they need to get started.

In the United States, we have a government agency called the Small Business Administration (SBA), whose duties include helping entrepreneurs get the money they need to take the risks necessary to start small businesses. Interestingly, the SBA does not actually make these loans, but it does guarantee them. Banks are more likely to loan money to risky new businesses when they know that the SBA and the U.S. government will guarantee repayment, even if the borrower defaults. The result is a vibrant U.S. economy in which 99 percent of all businesses are small businesses.

So the first thing any government seeking to promote small business should do is to establish a pool of federally guaranteed loans. Easy access to capital creates the foundation for a lively small-business sector.

Teach entrepreneurship

There are many things that go into creating a successful small-business economy, but surely a significant one is a collection of entrepreneurs willing to start new businesses. For that to occur, citizens must be able to learn business skills. There are several ways in which governments can assist them in doing this:

• Create "business incubators." A business incubator is a facility that offers start-up businesses a place to grow. Typically, business incubators are associated with universities, and professors and other experts that donate their time and expertise teaching new entrepreneurs everything from sales and marketing to laws and taxes. Once the would-be small-business owners conclude this crash course in business, they move on and start their businesses, and new entrepreneurs come into take their place. Governments can offer universities financial incentives for creating on-campus business incubators.

• Use the Internet. The SBA has online tutorials that teach business skills and ideas to anyone with Internet access. Any government that wishes to promote small and medium-sized enterprises should consider doing something similar.

• Hire experts. Likewise, private-sector small-business experts can be hired to teach business skills online.

Celebrate and foster small business

Not only must new entrepreneurs be taught the skills necessary to succeed, but existing entrepreneurs should be promoted so as to encourage more people to start small businesses. In Costa Rica and Uruguay, small-business fairs and expos recognize small business and entrepreneurship. Uruguay also has awards for small businesses that contribute to society. Indeed, there is plenty a government could do to promote small business. For example:

- Sponsor an "Entrepreneur of the Year" award. A yearly award, on both the local and national levels, if well publicized, could do much to create an entrepreneurial mind-set.

- Tap the expertise of business leaders. A country that wants to promote small business must work to have its population look up to entrepreneurs. One way to do this is for the government to tap business leaders to help solve various issues and problems. Blue-ribbon government panels should take advantage of the expertise of entrepreneurs.

Create the proper tax and regulatory environment

A country's tax code is one of the best tools it has for promoting small-business growth. In the United States, for instance, the tax code is changed often with the idea that certain tax credits, deductions, or reductions can be used to foster growth in one segment or another.

Here is another example: Nearly 98 percent of all Canadian businesses are small businesses. The Certified Management Accountants of Canada recently recommended to the Canadian Parliament that the best way to foster even more small-business growth is through changes in Canada's tax policies, such as:

- reducing the corporate tax rate;
- offering tax credits for investments in training and education;
- increasing the deductions for investments.

Aside from lowering taxes to encourage business formation, it is important to reduce and eventually eliminate those government regulations that stymie business growth. The simpler and more expedited the regulatory process, the greater the likelihood of small-business expansion.

Protect intellectual property

Any government that wants to encourage small business needs to produce laws that protect the innovations of entrepreneurs. Innovation is at the very heart of small-business growth, but if innovations are not legally protected, entrepreneurs will be unlikely to engage in the risks necessary to invent new solutions to societal problems. Accordingly, policies that protect patents, copyrights, and trademarks are critical if small business is to flourish.

In the end, any government wanting to promote small business needs to implement policies that help entrepreneurs take less risk and make more money. Do that, and small business success is yours.

Reading Comprehension
Choose the best answers to the following questions.
1. In a world with too much hunger and need, small business is one thing with a proven capacity not only to ease suffering, but also to _____.
   A. create a solid middle class
   B. generate a secure tax base
   C. foster social stability
   D. all of the above
2. According to this passage, the first government policy necessary to promote small-business development is one that _____.
   A. assists would-be entrepreneurs find the money they need to get started
   B. requires the commercial banks to give interest-free loan to would-be entrepreneurs
   C. approves tax reduction and exemption to would-be entrepreneurs
   D. helps would-be entrepreneurs identify new business opportunities
3. The following are several ways in which governments can help citizens learn business skills except _____.
   A. create "business incubators"
   B. establish schools to teach business skills
   C. teach business skills and ideas online
   D. hire experts to teach business skills
4. According to this passage, a country that wants to promote small business must work to have its population _____.
   A. look up to entrepreneurs
   B. like doing business
   C. be willing to take risks

D. know the economic policy

5. _____ the regulatory process, the greater the likelihood of small-business expansion.

   A. The more complex
   B. The slower
   C. The simpler and faster
   D. The staler

VI. Assignment

1. Interview some private-sector small-business. Ask them about how they got the ideas to do the present business. Write a report with about 200 words.
2. Please prepare a ten-minute presentation to introduce some business opportunities existing in your present situation.

Unit 4
Establishment of a Business

 Learning Objectives

After learning this unit, you should be able to:
1. Understand the right approach to making money.
2. Generate and evaluate ideas for your business.
3. Choose the right business organization.
4. Register a business name and get the license.
5. Know the significance and way of writing a business plan.

 Lead-in

The key to a strong economy is the creation of more small businesses. But statistics show that most startups are doomed to fail. However, the experts agree that with planning and hard work a new company can beat the odds. In this unit we will cover the basics of what you need to know to start your own small business. We will look into some tough questions about what it takes for businesses to successfully get off the ground.

Warm-up Questions/Discussion:
1. Is it good or not good for college students to start their own businesses?
2. Do you want to start a business? Tell us something about your plan.
3. What do we need to prepare when planning to start a new business?

How to Start Your Own Business[①]

Have you decided to start a business? Do you want to love what you do, be your own boss, make what you are worth, and make your own dreams come true instead of your boss's? There are millions of entrepreneurs who have made that jump and you can too. Now we are going to discuss how to start a business by taking a step-by-step approach to making those critical decisions that make the differences between success and failure of your business startup[②]. Here are the steps to teach you how to start a business. Take these steps in order and don't skip any to maximize your business startup success:

1. Taking the Right Approach to Make Real Money

You have probably asked yourself—how do I make money? There are basic principles which guide you on how to make real money. The most basic principle is to have the right approach. Business is not about tricks, win-lose deals, and dishonesty. It's about action, persistence, patience, honesty, faith and hard work. Business is about creating long-term relationships; it's about making those relationships win-win[③]. Business is about creating value in the world and being compensated because you have made people's lives better. Business is about getting what you want by giving people what they want or need.

You are suggested to use the READY, AIM, FIRE approach to starting a business. The READY steps include evaluating yourself to make sure you are ready for what is coming. These steps will also open the possibilities of different business types. Before you focus on one idea you should take the opportunity to look at all the possibilities. This is your chance to do that. Once you have taken into account all the relevant factors to make your choice, you are ready to focus on the business you want. These steps are the AIM part of the approach. Once you have a laser focus[④] on the business you want to start, the FIRE steps will take you through the process of preparing to start your business.

---

① The text is excerpted from www.how-to-start-a-business-guide.com with abridgment.
② startup （创业；启动）: The act of starting a new operation or practice.
③ win-win （双赢）: Of or being a situation in which the outcome benefits each of two often opposing groups.
④ laser focus （焦点；中心）: A center of interest or activity; close or narrow attention; concentration.

2. Generating Ideas for Your Business

What large need can you fill? What niche① can you occupy? Be a specialist, not a generalist. Consider what people will still want or need during a recession. In fact, think of what people need more during a recession. How about helping people create larger incomes or helping people save money?

Don't try to fight big companies unless you have a big competitive advantage. You will never be able to compete with the big companies on the issue of price. You will be able to win on the issue of service.

You can just consider the trends: Can you fill a growing need? Remember that business is about making people's lives better in some way. Think of solving a problem for people, filling a need, or satisfying a want. Determine your unique value proposition②.

Or you may establish repeatable business systems: <u>The more predictable, repeatable and reliable your business activities are, the more efficient you become. By studying, streamlining③ and then documenting a systemized approach to customer service, financial management, team communication, marketing, etc., you'll be able to free your mind of the procedural aspects of your business and focus more time on creative and innovative ways to be valuable to your customers.</u>

3. Determining Your Personal and Business Goals and Evaluate Your Business Ideas

Goals are your personal and business objectives—what you want out of your life and your career. What do you enjoy doing in life? What are your hobbies and interests? Do you enjoy dealing with people or are you happier working on your computer? What is important in your life? It is crucial to make sure you are setting and achieving goals. This is as true in business as it is in any endeavor. The most common and most costly mistake is choosing the wrong business. Choosing the wrong business most often comes from failing to set goals.

Goal setting is a powerful process for thinking about what you want out of life

---

① niche（缝隙市场；利基市场）: It means niche market. It is the subset of the market on which a specific product is focusing; therefore the niche market defines the specific product features aimed at satisfying specific market needs, as well as the price range, production quality and the demographics that it is intended to impact.

② value proposition（价值定位）: It summarizes why a consumer should buy a product or use a service. It is used to convince a potential consumer that a particular product or service will add more value or solve a problem better than other similar offerings will.

③ streamline（优化；改造）: To improve the appearance or efficiency.

Unit 4　Establishment of a Business

and transforming your dreams into reality. What follows is a goal setting form or goal setting worksheet, and it is a tool you can use for setting and achieving goals and for evaluating your business ideas.

Your goals	Your ideas
Set your own work-hours as you want (part or full time)	Yes/No
Flexible work schedule—work day or night, weekdays or weekends	
Work wherever you want to—home, RV, beach, golf course, lake, car, etc.	
No commute—no rush hour traffic to deal with	
Live wherever you want—small town, big city, different country, relocation, etc.	
No formal dress code—dress casually and comfortably	
Work for yourself-be your own boss—build equity in YOURSELF and not a boss	
Work with who you want—not whom your boss tells you to	
You cannot be downsized①	
Your business is willable to your children, loved ones or favorite charity	
Income is residual—you can continue to benefit from your initial efforts over and over	
None of the hassles, expenses or liabilities associated with having employees	
Potential tax benefits—especially on what you're already spending money on	
Low and attainable start up costs—little or no financial risk	
Free professional training & consultation available	
No traditional barriers—experience, education, gender, age, etc.	
Gain personal growth and development that improves all aspects of your life	
Work with positive, outgoing, professional people with similar goals	
You determine how much you earn	
Control of your own future	
Excellent timing—large and growing market for your product or service	
Perfect family business	
Minimal overhead—no office, warehouse, expensive equipment, etc.	
Ability to capitalize on a global market place—not just your local area or market	
Pay no royalties② or franchise fees③ to anyone	
Success through working as a team instead of cut-throat competition	
Ability to leverage④ your time with the efforts of others	

---

① downsize（裁员）：To dismiss or lay off from work.

② royalties（技术使用费）：The payment made to the owner of a copyright, patent, trademark or know-how for its use.

③ franchise fee（特许经销权使用费）：It is a fee that a person pays to operate a franchise branch of a larger company and enjoy the profits therefrom.

④ leverage（通过杠杆作用放大）：It is a general term for any technique to multiply gains and losses in finance.

4. Choosing the Right Business Organization

There are two decisions every entrepreneur must make fairly early in the life of a startup business. Will you go into business alone or with a partner? What type of legal business organization will you use?

The business organization you choose is one of the most important decisions you make. Your decision affects your level of risk, the taxes you pay, and how much accounting help you will need.

The choices for your business organization are:

- Sole proprietorship①—a sole proprietorship has no separate legal existence from its owner. Liabilities for business debts are not limited to assets of the business. The owner of the business is responsible for all debts incurred by the business. The owner can have the business under his/her name. The business, since it is not a separate legal entity, does not file a separate tax return. Accounting for a sole proprietorship is the most simple of legal forms.

- Partnership②—a partnership consists of two or more individuals who co-own a business. Although the business is not taxed separately, it must prepare a return which indicates the distribution of partnership profits and losses to the co-owners. The amount of money and time invested by each partner should be written down in a partnership agreement. In a partnership, any partner can be held liable for the entirety of the business' debts.

- Limited partnership③—a limited partnership is similar to a partnership except that there are one or more general partners in addition to one or more limited partners. The general partners are in the same position as partners above, having authority to act as agents of the partnership, having management control over the business, and being liable for the debts of the business. The limited partners, on the other hand, have limited liability, meaning they are only liable to the extent of their investments. Limited partners do not have authority over the management of the business. They invest in the business and receive a share of profits and losses as stated in the partnership agreement.

- Corporation④—a corporation is a legal entity⑤ separating from the persons

---

① sole proprietorship（个体工商户）: An unincorporated business owned by a single person who is responsible for its liabilities and entitled to its profits.

② partnership（合伙企业）: An association of two or more persons for carrying on business.

③ limited partnership（有限责任合伙企业）: A partnership in which some of the partners have a limited liability to the firm's creditors.

④ corporation（股份有限公司）: A group of people anthorized by law to act as a legal personality and having its own powers, duties, and liabilities.

⑤ legal entity（法人实体）: It is an organization that is identified through registration with a legal authority.

that formed it. Owners of a corporation are known as shareholders. The shareholders elect a Board of Directors who hires managers to manage the corporation. In a small corporation the owners, directors and employees may be the same people. Accounting for a corporation can be more complicated than for other forms of organization. The corporation is taxed on its profits and owners may receive dividends which are taxed again.

5. Registering a Business Name and Getting Your Licenses as Appropriate

Your next step is to register a new business name. Do some brainstorming[①] and write down different possibilities that might be suitable given your products or services.

If you think you may do business online, check if your business names are available as domain names. Choose a domain name ending with .com or .net. Resist the temptation to choose a domain name ending with any other suffixes. They don't connote business seriousness except for .org and .gov which are usually used by non-profits and governmental organizations.

If you use a business name different from your own name you are using a fictitious name. That name has to be registered in your country so that each name is only used once. Check with the local Administration of Industry and Commerce (AIC)[②] for a list of fictitious names to make sure your name is not already taken. If it is not taken, you can register it.

To obtain registration certification, the company must file a completed application form along with the following documents:

—Notice of approval of company name.
—Lease or other proof of company office.
—Capital verification certificate or appraisal report.
—Articles of association, executed by each shareholder.
—Representation authorization.
—Identity cards of shareholders and identification documents of officers.
—Appointment documents and identification documents (certifying name and address) of the directors, supervisors, and officers.

---

① brainstorming（头脑风暴;自由讨论）: It is a group creativity technique by which a group tries to find a solution for a specific problem by gathering a list of ideas spontaneously contributed by its members.

② Administration of Industry and Commerce (AIC)（工商行政管理局）: An organization under municipality with the responsibility of market supervision and administrative law enforcement.

—Appointment documents and identification documents of the company's legal representative①.

—If the initial contribution is in non-monetary assets, the document certifying transfer of the property title of such assets.

—Other documents as required by the authorities.

6. Writing a Business Plan

Writing business plans is like creating the crucial road map you draw when starting a business. An unknown author said: "When you fail to plan you plan to fail." The biggest reason for failing to plan is the perception that one doesn't have enough time. Unfortunately for those who think that way, they will pay many times later on in terms of time spent for their failure to find time to write business plans.

The best way to show bankers, venture capitalists, and angel investors② that you are worthy of financial support is to show them that you have written a great business plan. Make sure that your business plan is clear, focused and realistic. Then show them that you have the tools, talent and team to make it happen. Your written business plan is like your calling card; it will get you in the door where you'll have to convince investors and loan officers that you can put your plan into action.

Once you have raised the money to start or expand your business, your plan will serve as a road map for your business. It is not a static document that you write once and put away. You will reference it often, making sure you stay focused and on track, and meet milestones. It will change and develop as your business evolves.

There is no one fixed way to write a business plan. The nature of the business, its state of development, the need for outside capital and other factors will determine the exact outline of the plan and will also determine how specific the plan must be.

However, there are elements of a plan that are universal:

• Your business concept.

• Supply and demand for your product or service. What is the niche you are filling? How large is it? How will your customers find you? What about

---

① legal representative(法定代理人): A personal representative with legal standing (as by power of attorney or the executor of a will).

② angel investors (天使投资者性): An angel investor is an affluent individual who provides capital for a business start-up, usually in exchange for convertible debt or ownership equity.

Unit 4 Establishment of a Business

competition, today and in the future? What is your competitive advantage?

● The management structure you anticipate. Who are the key players? What is their experience in business? What is their experience in the industry? Will you have employees who complement your strengths and make up for your weaknesses?

● The financing for your startup. What is your overhead[①]? What are your fixed costs and your variable costs? Where is your break-even point? What will be your cash burn rate[②]? If these concepts are foreign to you now, you should be an expert by the time the business plan is written.

As you write your business plan, you will rework your plan again and again. Give yourself several weeks to formulate your business plan.

 Exercises

I. Reviewing Questions

Answer the following questions according to the text.

1. What is the most basic principle of making real money?
2. What approach is suggested to use when starting a business?
3. How can we generate ideas for our businesses?
4. How should we deal with the big companies?
5. What should be considered when setting personal and business goals?
6. Why is it so important to choose the right business organization?
7. What are the major choices for business organizations?
8. What documents should we prepare when applying for a license of business?
9. What is the significance of writing a business plan?
10. How can we write a good business plan?

II. Cloze

Read the following passage and fill in the blanks with the words given below. Change the form where necessary.

| encourage | traction | refine | launching | survive |
| commit | identified | viability | rush | potential |

---

① overhead（运营开支；经常性费用）: It is the ongoing operating costs of running a business.

② cash burn rate（烧钱率；现金消耗率）: It is a synonymous term for negative cash flow. It is a measure for how fast a company will use up its shareholder capital. The term came into common use during the dot-com era when many start-up companies went through several stages of funding before emerging into profitability.

Confidence in pursuing a small business sometimes comes from the incremental feedback people have received and the "chemistry" that has consistently improved in their team. The confidence was garnered in specific stages as they started and grew the business. If we try to "map out" the path people often take to gain confidence in the early days of ___1___ a business, we should focus on five distinct stages: (1) Gathering the panel: When you get a small group of like-minded individuals together to consider a new idea, one of two things happens: You either get more excited about the idea and decide to continue the discussion again, or you leave and lose interest. Sometimes the original "seed" ideas germinate and are developed by people that share an interest to "organize the creative world." Some ideas ___2___ while others die. There is something nice about the Darwinian approach to start a new business. (2) Put your money (or time) where your mouth is: When an idea starts gaining ___3___ in your mind, it is time to "invest" something in it. Whether it is a period of time that you ___4___ every week to research or an amount of money that you allocate for initial development—you need to invest something. Some companies start with a part-time employee who is being paid by the founder to "mock-up" a preliminary design, website, or concept. This is a great investment in the ___5___ of the business. (3) The controlled test: When the time is right, you will feel a ___6___ of motivation to "test" your concept. Often this is a controlled microcosm of the business you have in mind. Once you can "market" and gauge initial interest from ___7___ customers, you can become more confident in your concept. Your business doesn't need to be perfect or revenue-producing to generate confidence—it just needs to gain some traction. (4) Listen, listen, listen: The first realization you must have is that your business plan is likely wrong, and that the "needs" you first ___8___ may differ from the actual needs and frustrations you must address among your potential customers. To identify the true market opportunity, you must listen. Gathering a small focus group of potential customers and asking questions is the best way to ___9___ your marketing and product. (5) Debate toward shared conviction: As you incorporate the feedback you are getting and prepare to launch a real business, ___10___ debate among your team and advisors about the decisions you are making. As debate ensues, try to reach some level of shared conviction in your team. Remember that conviction does not necessarily mean consensus…just a mutual agreement to try a particular strategy. Of course, things will change—and if you continue to listen to the feedback—you can continue to tweak your strategy. Confidence ultimately comes from data (feedback), honest communication, and a team with a shared commitment.

III. Translation

1. Business is not about tricks, win-lose deals, and dishonesty. It's about action, persistence, patience, honesty, faith and hard work. Business is about creating long-term relationships; it's about making those relationships win-win. Business is about creating value in the world and being compensated because you have made people's lives better. Business is about getting what you want by giving people what they want or need.

2. The more predictable, repeatable and reliable your business activities are, the more efficient you become. By studying, streamlining and then documenting a systemized approach to customer service, financial management, team communication, marketing, etc., you'll be able to free your mind of the procedural aspects of your business and focus more time on creative and innovative ways to be valuable to your customers.

3. The limited partners, on the other hand, have limited liability, meaning they are only liable to the extent of their investments. Limited partners do not have authority over the management of the business. They invest in the business and receive a share of profits and losses as stated in the partnership agreement.

4. If you think you may do business online, check if your business names are available as domain names. Choose a domain name ending with.com or.net. Resist the temptation to choose a domain name ending with any other suffixes. They don't connote business seriousness except for.org and.gov which are usually used by non-profits and governmental organizations.

5. Writing business plans is like creating the crucial road map you draw when starting a business. An unknown author said: "When you fail to plan you plan to fail." The biggest reason for failing to plan is the perception that one doesn't have enough time. Unfortunately for those who think that way, they will pay many times later on in terms of time spent for their failure to find time to write business plans.

IV. Case Study

Chinese Grads Abuzz with Ideas

by Zhao Yanrong

While protests rage on about government accountability and low employment rates, Chinese students in the United States are trying to create jobs through business ideas.

The diversified education system in the U.S. helps college students create businesses before graduation, Kai-Fu Lee, former Google China president and current CEO of Innovation Works, said at a Chinese college students' innovation summit in April. Chinese students who have been studying in U.S. for a few years said they have more advantages in creating innovative ideas compared to their peers back in China. "I have never been so close to the idea of having my own company. I thought about it before I enrolled in Harvard, but it was just a thought," said Liu Zhonghua, a doctoral student at the Harvard School of Public Health (HSPH). He is studying molecular and genetic epidemiology and specializing in statistical genetics.

Liu and his roommates, Ke Weixiong and Weng Jia, who recently graduated from HSPH, plan to open an e-commerce company in Boston in a few months. Their idea is to provide information such as medical devices and products for pharmaceutical and biotech companies in the U.S. He would not reveal any specific details about his startup except to say their investor is a Chinese-Canadian who is an acquaintance. "Our target market right now is America, but we will likely expand our business to China after our company is listed in the U.S.," Liu said. The 26-year-old Chinese native said his company will have two major competitors in the market but he is confident that his company will surpass his American counterparts within one year. "Working with a Chinese student organization helped me realize my business idea," said Liu, who is the president of the HSPH Chinese Students and Scholars Association (CSSA).

Liu met many students who have their own business ideas as well as young business owners at social events hosted by the Chinese student organization. "Our ideas about this company became much clearer after talking with those people and attending events, such as startup competitions," he said.

An entrepreneurship club at HSPH CSSA was created to encourage more

Chinese students to start their own businesses. The student organization teaches Chinese students how to open a company in the U.S., how to make a profit and how to register a company in the U.S. as an international student.

"On the one hand, many Chinese students and graduates work for companies to legally remain in the country, while on the other hand, they are also creating their own businesses and companies," Liu said. "It's very common in the U.S. now."

In fact, more venture capital companies from China are holding innovation competitions among Chinese student communities at American colleges. In November, the Massachusetts Institute of Technology will announce the winner of the first Chinese student innovation competition called "Pitch to China." Six teams, culled from 98 total proposals, will divide $18,000 in cash prizes.

Many entrepreneurship competitions are held among American universities, but the participation from Chinese students has been low, said Cui Yuanyuan, an MIT student who is on the Pitch to China competition committee. "We are encouraging Chinese students and Chinese enterprisers to stand out and say what they want. We hope this will be a good opportunity for all Chinese," said Cui, a doctoral candidate in computational and biology systems.

Before finding their investor, Liu tried a few Chinese venture capital companies who prefer to invest in students' ideas overseas. But he never received any feedback after proposing his business plan. "A personal relationship makes it easier to build trust and cooperation with the investor. And we can make more public financing once our business expands," Liu said.

(The text is excerpted from www.chinadaily.com.cn)

Questions for discussion:
1. Do you think Chinese students who have been studying in U.S. for a few years have more advantages in creating innovative ideas compared to their peers back in China?
2. What kind of business does Liu Zhonghua want to set up? Is he confident of his future business? Why?
3. What business organization do you suggest Liu Zhonghua choose? Why?

V. Supplementary Reading

Michael Dell's Success Story

Here is a very inspiring success story about a billionaire who became a very successful entrepreneur at a very young age. Just like every other success people, he started with almost nothing but the ideas in his head.

Despite Mr. and Mrs. Dell's hopes that their son would become a doctor, by the time Michael Dell was in grade seven, the boy's only area of interest was computer. While his classmates started playing around under the hoods of classic cars, Dell spent all of his time with his Apple II.

Dell showed an aptitude for business from an early age. He was making thousands of dollars in mail-order sales to stamp collectors at the age of 12, and—through careful planning—earned an astonishing $18,000 by selling newspaper subscriptions for the Houston Post in his final year of high school. By 18, Dell began planning to build a company that could rival IBM.

Succumbing to his parents' wishes, Dell began a pre-med course at the University of Texas in 1983. However, all of his time outside the classroom was spent buying remaindered, out-of-date computers, upgrading them, and then selling them for a profit. His room became so cluttered with hardware that, out of consideration for his roommate, he finally decided to move his operation off campus. His parents were extremely disappointed at the news that Dell would be dropping out of university, but he promised to return if his venture failed to be profitable by the end of the summer. At the end of one month of operation, Dell had made $180,000 in PC sales. Needless to say, Dell did not go back to school.

As Dell planned out the future of his business, he identified price and delivery as the most important aspects of the growing computer business. By buying parts and putting the PC together on his own, Dell was able to put the machines together cheaply. He then decided to sell his computers over the phone to established brand name companies at a 15% discount, getting rid of the middleman and establishing a name for himself. "The direct model of selling," as it has come to be known, completely changed the way computers would be sold.

Dell called his company PCs Ltd., and at nineteen years old, his company had become one of the fastest growing in the U.S. The secret of Dell's success was the emphasis that was placed on creating customized computers to meet the specific demands of his clients.

Michael Dell is a very committed guy, when he created a plan, he'll pursue it with full strength. And this explains that how he made his $1,000 by just selling stamps at the age of 12! Can you imagine that? Selling stamps at such a young age and making $1,000 from that. Many of us can't even save $1,000 from our salary. But he made his first $1,000 by just selling stamps.

He later sold the newspaper subscription for Houston Post, which developed his confidence making even more money. It is told that he made enough money to buy a BMW by the age of 16. Most people can't earn enough money to buy a BMW even with their entire life saving. But this guy, Michael Dell, made enough money to purchase a BMW at the age of 16.

Michael then planned his life well at the age of 19. He knew exactly what he wanted to achieve in his life and eventually, he achieved it. Knowing what you want in your life is one of the most important success strategies that you must adopt. If you don't know what you want to achieve in your life, you'll never achieve it. First set your target, then keep on pursuing it. Just like what Michael Dell did at the age of 19, he planned his life and set his goals to achieve higher success.

Michael later went to college to study biology as his parents wanted him to be a doctor. However, a year later, he quit his studies and continued to pursue his dreams. He wanted to be a successful entrepreneur. This is what you have to do as well if you know exactly what you want. You need to have the courage to pursue your dreams.

Michael developed his intense passion in computers when he was 15. When his parents got him an Apple computer when he was 15, instead of using it, he dissembled the computer into parts to find out how it worked. After that, he bought an IBM computer and studied more about assembling computers. He finally mastered the technique that made him a billionaire at a very young age.

In 1984, Michael started his dream venture with $1,000. He followed through his business plan and kept on working on it. In his room in the university, he assembled computers for customers according to their requirements and sold them directly to his customers.

His business idea was new because he assembled all the computers according to his customers' preferences and sold directly at a low price. He was the first to introduce the direct sales method in the IT industry. The direct sales clicked and there was huge demand for computers. Dell knew that he could beat computer dealers by selling a lower price with good technical service.

Just like every other successful people, Dell started small. Most of his orders were placed through friends and acquaintances who spread the word around. And by steadily developing his business, he moved to a small office and hired a few people to take orders and upgrade machines. Avoiding a third party to sell computers turned out to be profitable and the company grew at a seriously fast clip.

Later in May 1983, Dell incorporated the company as Dell Computer Corporation. In 1985, Dell started to design and make computers with components sourced from outside. His focus, right from the beginning, was on customers and good service. He kept his vision and moved toward his dreams step-by-step.

All his hard work paid off handsomely. By 1992, Dell Computer Corporation entered the Fortune 500 list of the largest companies in the world. At the age of 27, he became the youngest CEO of a Fortune 500 company. And the rest is history.

Another one of the success strategies that Dell used is that the company was one of the very first to sell computers on the Internet. This too became a huge hit. In 1999, Dell launched Gigabuys.com, an online store featuring computer-related products.

Not only that, his business kept on growing and became the No. 1 player in the American market. Can you see it now? How Michael Dell started from $1,000 and built his giant IT business worth more than $100 billion. It has been a very successful journey for Dell.

In 1999, with his wife, he formed the Michael and Susan Dell Foundation, which has an endowment of more than $1 billion and focuses on children's issues. This shows that Dell knows the miracle of tithing. If you want to be successful in your life, you must first make other people successful. If you want to be a millionaire, donate and help more people to become richer. This is the law of the universe.

Reading Comprehension
Choose the best answers to the following questions.
1. Michael Dell's goal was _____ when he was 18 years old and began planning his own business.
   A. to build a company that could rival IBM
   B. to make enough money to purchase a BMW
   C. to make $1,000 by selling stamps
   D. to be a millionaire

Unit 4　Establishment of a Business

2. As Michael Dell planned out the future of his business, he identified _____ as the most important aspects of the growing computer business.
   A. product and service
   B. promotion and advertising
   C. price and delivery
   D. production and packaging
3. The secret of Michael Dell's success was _____.
   A. the emphasis on continual technological advancement
   B. the emphasis on customers relationship management
   C. the emphasis on new product development
   D. the emphasis on creating customized products to meet the specific demands
4. Michael Dell was the first to introduce _____ in the IT industry.
   A. the outsourcing method
   B. the direct sales method
   C. the customization method
   D. the low price method
5. All of the following are correct descriptions of Michael Dell's character except _____.
   A. that he has an aptitude for business from an early age
   B. that he is a good planner of his life
   C. that he is a very committed guy
   D. that he is an obedient child

VI. Assignment

1. Interview some people who have just started a new business. Ask them about the process of establishing a new business, the problems they met in this process and how they overcame the difficulties. Write a report with about 200 words.
2. Please prepare a ten-minute presentation to introduce how the governments encourage people to start their own businesses in different countries or areas.

Unit 5

Organizational Structure

 Learning Objectives

After learning this unit, you should be able to:
1. Describe the concept of organizational structure.
2. Know about different kinds of organizational structures.
3. Establish an effective organizational structure.
4. Understand the difference between formal and informal organizations.

 Lead-in

An organizational structure is the pattern or arrangement of jobs and groups of jobs within an organization. This pattern pertains to both reporting and operational relationships, provided they have some degree of permanence. Ideally, organizational structures should be shaped and implemented for the primary purpose of facilitating the achievement of organizational goals in an efficient manner.

Warm-up Questions/Discussion:
1. What kind of organizational structure have you heard about?
2. If you are going to set up your own enterprise, what kind of organizational structure do you want to apply? Why?
3. What are the elements for an effective organizational structure?

Organizational Structure and Design

An organizational structure consists of activities such as task allocation, coordination and supervision, which are directed towards the achievement of organizational aims. It can also be considered as the viewing glass or perspective through which individuals see their organization and its environment.

1. Significance of Organizational Structure

An organization can be structured in many different ways, depending on their objectives. The structure of an organization will determine the modes in which it operates and performs. Organizational structure allows the expressed allocation of responsibilities for different functions and processes to different entities such as the branch, department, work group and individual.

Organizational structure affects organizational action in two big ways. First, it provides the foundation on which standard operating procedures and routines rest. Second, it determines which individuals get to participate in which decision-making processes, and thus to what extent their views shape the organization's actions.

The set organizational structure may not coincide with facts, evolving in operational action. Such divergence decreases performance, when growing. E.g., a wrong organizational structure may hamper cooperation and thus hinder the completion of orders in due time and within limits of resources and budgets. Organizational structures shall be adaptive to process requirements, aiming to optimize① the ratio② of effort and input to output.

2. Types of Organizational Structure

There are mainly 7 kinds of common organizational structures, and they are: pre-bureaucratic, bureaucratic structures, post-bureaucratic, functional structure, divisional structure, matrix structure and flat structure. Now, let's learn about them one by one.

(1) Pre-bureaucratic structures

Pre-bureaucratic (entrepreneurial) structures lack standardization③ of tasks.

---

① optimize（优化）：To plan or carry out (an economic activity) with maximum efficiency.

② ratio（比率）：A relationship between two quantities, normally expressed as the quotient of one divided by the other.

③ standardization（标准化）：The imposition of standards or regulations.

This structure is most common in smaller organizations and is best used to solve simple tasks. The structure is totally centralized. The strategic leader makes all key decisions and most communication is done by one to one conversations. It is particularly useful for new (entrepreneurial) business as it enables the founder to control growth and development.

(2) Bureaucratic structures

The fully developed bureaucratic mechanism compares with other organizations exactly as does the machine compare with the non-mechanical modes of production. Precision, speed, unambiguity, strict subordination[①], reduction of friction and of material and personal costs are raised to the optimum point in the strictly bureaucratic administration. Bureaucratic structures have a certain degree of standardization. They are better suited for more complex or larger scale organizations, usually adopting a tall structure.

(3) Post-bureaucratic

Some theorists have developed the post-bureaucratic organization, in which decisions are based on dialogue and consensus[②] rather than authority and command, the organization is a network rather than a hierarchy, open at the boundaries (in direct contrast to culture management); there is an emphasis on meta-decision making rules rather than decision making rules. This sort of horizontal decision making by consensus model is often used when running a non-profit or community organization. It is used in order to encourage participation and help to empower[③] people who normally experience oppression in groups.

(4) Functional structure

Employees within the functional divisions of an organization tend to perform a specialized set of tasks, for instance, the engineering department would be staffed only with software engineers. This leads to operational efficiencies within that group. However it could also lead to a lack of communication between the functional groups within an organization, making the organization slow and inflexible.

As a whole, a functional organization is best suited as a producer of standardized goods and services at large volume and low cost. Coordination and specialization of tasks are centralized in a functional structure, which makes

---

① subordination（从属）: Subject to the authority or control of another.
② consensus（共识）: An opinion or position reached by a group as a whole.
③ empower（授权）: To give or delegate power or authority to; authorize.

producing a limited amount of products or services efficient and predictable. Moreover, efficiencies can further be realized as functional organizations integrate their activities vertically so that products are sold and distributed quickly and at low cost. For instance, a small business could make components used in production of its products instead of buying them. This benefits the organization and employees faiths.

(5) Divisional structure

Divisional structure is also called "product structure"; the divisional structure groups each organizational function into a division. Each division within a divisional structure contains all the necessary resources and functions within it. Divisions can be categorized from different points of view. One might make distinctions on a geographical basis (a U.S. division and an EU division, for example) or on product or service basis (different products for different customers: households or companies). In another example, an automobile company with a divisional structure might have one division for SUVs, another division for subcompact cars, and another division① for sedans. Each division may have its own sales, engineering and marketing departments.

(6) Matrix structure

The matrix structure groups employees by both function and product. This structure can combine the best of both separate structures. A matrix organization frequently uses teams of employees to accomplish work, in order to take advantage of the strengths, as well as make up for the weaknesses, of functional and decentralized forms. An example would be a company that produces two products, "product a" and "product b." Using the matrix structure, this company would organize functions within the company as follows: "product a" sales department, "product a" customer service department, "product a" accounting, "product b" sales department, "product b" customer service department, "product b" accounting department. Matrix structure is amongst the purest of organizational structures, a simple lattice② emulating order and regularity demonstrated in nature.

Starbucks is one of the numerous large organizations that successfully developed the matrix structure supporting their focused strategy. Its design combines functional and product based divisions, with employees reporting to two

---

① division（部门）: One of the parts, sections, or groups into which something is divided.

② lattice（格子）: An open framework made of strips of metal, wood, or similar material overlapped or overlaid in a regular, usually crisscross pattern.

heads. Creating a team spirit, the company empowers employees to make their own decisions and train them to develop both hard and soft skills[①]. That makes Starbucks one of the best at customer service.

Some experts also mention the multinational design, common in global companies, such as Procter & Gamble, Toyota and Unilever. This structure can be seen as a complex form of the matrix, as it maintains coordination among products, functions and geographic areas.

(7) Flat organizational structure

A flat organization structure is also known as a horizontal organization. It is a level wherein there is no level between the staff and managers. In such an organization the most trained employees are involved in the decision making process. This structure mostly takes place in smaller organizations or also on a small scale within large organization. However, when these organizations begin to grow and expand, the company turns into a hierarchical organization structure. In fact most of the organizations worldwide start with a flat organization structure.

With the help of flat organization structure the decision making process mostly involves most of the employees. Every employee's feedback as well as opinion is taken into consideration. Due to this kind of structure employees and the top management interact on regular basis and there is a very understanding bonding that takes place in the organization.

① Trend of development.

The flat structure is common in small companies (entrepreneurial start-ups[②], university spin offs[③]). As the company grows it becomes more complex and hierarchical, which leads to an expanded structure, with more levels and departments. Often, it would result in bureaucracy, and it's the most prevalent structure in the past.

In general, over the last decade, it has become increasingly clear that through the forces of globalization, competition and more demanding customers, the structure of many companies has become flatter, less hierarchical, more fluid and even virtual.

---

① soft skills（软技能）：Desirable qualities for certain forms of employment that do not depend on acquired knowledge: they include common sense, the ability to deal with people, and a positive and flexible attitude.

② start-ups（新成立的企业）：A business or an undertaking that has recently begun operation.

③ spin offs（分拆上市的公司）：A divestiture by a corporation of a division or subsidiary by issuing to stockholders shares in a new company set up to continue the operations of the division or subsidiary.

② Modern organizational structures.

With the development of the society, new categories of organizational structures like team and network and virtual organizational structures are also emerging now.

③ Team.

One of the newest organizational structures developed in the 20th century is team. In small businesses, the team structure can define the entire organization. Teams can be both horizontal and vertical. While an organization is constituted as a set of people who synergize① individual competencies to achieve newer dimensions, the quality of organizational structure revolves around the competencies of teams in totality. For example, every one of the Whole Foods Marketstores, the largest natural-foods grocery in the U.S. developing a focused strategy, is an autonomous profit centrecomposed of an average of 10 self-managed teams, while team leaders in each store and each region are also a team. Larger bureaucratic organizations can benefit from the flexibility of teams as well. Xerox, Motorola, and Daimler Chrysler are all among the companies that actively use teams to perform tasks.

④ Network.

Another modern structure is network. While business giants risk becoming too clumsy to act and react efficiently, the new network organizations contract out② any business functions that can be done better or more cheaply. In essence, managers in network structures spend most of their time coordinating and controlling external relations, usually by electronic means. H&M is outsourcing③ its clothing to a network of 700 suppliers, more than two-thirds of which are based in low-cost Asian countries. Not owning any factories, H&M can be more flexible than many other retailers in lowering its costs, which aligns with its low-cost strategy. The potential management opportunities offered by recent advances in complex networks theory have been demonstrated including applications to product design and development, and innovation problem in markets and industries.

⑤ Virtual.

A special form of boundaryless organization is virtual structure. The virtual

---

① synergize（协同加强）：The interaction of two or more agents or forces so that their combined effect is greater than the sum of their individual effects.

② contract out（退出合同）：To agree not to participate in something, esp the state pension scheme.

③ outsourcing（外包）：The procuring of services or products, such as the parts used in manufacturing a motor vehicle, from an outside supplier or manufacturer in order to cut costs.

organization does not physically exist as such, but enabled by software to exist. The virtual organization exists within a network of alliances, using the Internet. This means while the core of the organization can be small but still the company can operate globally and be a market leader in its niche. Because of the unlimited shelf space of the Web, the cost of reaching niche goods is falling dramatically. Although none sell in huge numbers, there are so many niche products that collectively they make a significant profit, and that is what made highly innovative Amazon.com so successful.

3. Keys to Erecting an Effective Organizational Structure

All sorts of different organizational structures have been proven effective in contributing to business success. Some firms choose highly centralized, rigidly maintained structures, while others—perhaps even in the same industry sector—develop decentralized, loose arrangements. Both of these organizational types can survive and even thrive. There is no one best way to design an organization. Organizational research has shown that the more we know about particular types of organizations, the less we can generalize about the optimal design for an effective organization. Generally, organizational theorists believe that no one structure, set of systems, or method of staffing is appropriate for every organization. Organizations operate in different environments with different products, strategies, constraints, and opportunities.

But despite the wide variety of organizational structures that can be found in the business world, the successful ones tend to share certain characteristics. <u>Indeed, business experts cite a number of characteristics that separate effective organizational structures from ineffective designs. Recognition of these factors is especially important for entrepreneurs and established business owners, since these individuals play such a pivotal role in determining the final organizational structure of their enterprises.</u>

As business owners weigh their various options in this realm, they should make sure that the following factors are taken into consideration:

- Relative strengths and weaknesses of various organizational forms.
- Legal advantages and disadvantages of organizational structure options.
- Advantages and drawbacks of departmentalization options.
- Likely growth patterns of the company.
- Reporting relationships that are currently in place.
- Reporting and authority relationships that you hope will be implemented in

the future.

- Optimum ratios of supervisors/managers to subordinates.
- Suitable level of autonomy/empowerment to be granted to employees at various levels of the organization (while still recognizing individual capacities for independent work).
- Structures that will produce greatest worker satisfaction.
- Structures that will produce optimum operational efficiency.

Once all these factors have been objectively examined and blended into an effective organizational structure, the small business owner will then be in a position to pursue his/her business goals with a far greater likelihood of success.

4. Formal and Informal Organizations

The formal organizations can be seen and represented in chart form. An organization chart displays the organizational structure and shows job titles, lines of authority, and relationships between departments. The informal organization is the network, unrelated to the firm's formal authority structure, of social interactions among its employees. It is the personal and social relationships that arise spontaneously as people associate with one another in the work environment.

The informal organizations can pressure group members to conform to the expectations of the informal group that conflict with those of the formal organization. The supervisor should recognize the existence of informal groups, identify the roles members play within these groups, and use knowledge of the groups to work effectively with them. The informal organization can make the formal organization more effective by providing support to management, stability to the environment, and useful communication channels.

Exercises

I. Reviewing Questions
Answer the following questions according to the text.
1. What's the primary purpose of organizational structures?
2. Why are organizational structures very important?
3. How can organizational structures affect organizational actions?
4. What kind of organizations should adopt the bureaucratic structure?
5. In what situations should we use a post-bureaucratic structure?
6. Could you give us an example of functional structure?

7. What are the defects of the flat organizational structure?
8. Could you define "virtual structure"?
9. Is there a best way to design an organization, why or why not?
10. In your opinion, what factors are the most important when designing an organizational structure?

II. Cloze

Read the following passage and fill in the blanks with the words given below. Change the form where necessary.

scene	demands	inefficiency	maximize	coordinate
evolve	achieve	staffing	flaws	criticisms

A myriad of new organizational structures have seemed on the ___1___ within the last couple of decades nonetheless they still lack many of the desirable qualities in the standard methods. Ultimately, project direction directors seek organizational solutions that facilitate teamwork, can ___2___ the use of limited resources, efficiency and quality in the way a project is finalized and how goals and objectives are ___3___. Now we will examine a few main traditional organizational structures for project management. The three kinds of structure are functional organization, project organization and matrix organization.

Functional organization is definitely the oldest of the organizational structures but remains one of the most successful. This method performs best when raised for routine work functions and the upholding of quality together with work standards. Functional Organization structures determine projects in two different ways. One way involves this project being assigned for a specific functional manager who then ___4___ with the other departments to enable them to each contribute. Alternatively, projects can be shuffled around to several departments where each department manager makes sure that their parts of the effort have been completed. This method can not work very effectively when used in facilitating complex projects. One of many major ___5___ of this organizational structure is the lack of built-in employee recognition, dimension and reward for project performance. Similarly, there is very little individual accountability for almost any project management tasks that need to be performed.

Project Organization is a structure that is produced for executing projects. It's specifically tailored to meet the ___6___ of complex assignments by isolating unique work and maintaining a strong focus on completing this project. Once the undertaking is completed, this composition disbands. This structure is most effective in maintaining dedicated resources in the life of the project. The major criticism from this structure is it's inefficient in transferring technology and the utilization of resources. Also, by plenty of time the members actually begin acting as a cohesive team, the project is passed and the organization dissolves. Considering this project has dedicated resources throughout its lifetime, major ___7___ ensues when you can find underutilized employees during certain portions of the project.

Matrix Organization is a project management structure that ___8___ in the recognition of inherent flaws inside Functional Organization and project Organization structures. Created in the 1970s, this structure combined the best components of these a few structures. This model functions very well when there are several projects being coordinated at once. The functional managers manage the ___9___, training, job assignment and evaluation in the project's personnel. The functional specialists are assigned one or more projects and oversee that these individualized projects achieve their own objectives and are completed through maximum resource efficiency. Despite its recognition and avoidance in the ___10___ involved in many other structures, Matrix Organization still does have some problems of its very own. That individual employees report to at the least two managers may lead to ambiguity and conflict. These problems may be avoided through good connection and solid leadership concerning managers.

III. Translation

1. The set organizational structure may not coincide with facts, evolving in operational action. Such divergence decreases performance, when growing. E.g., a wrong organizational structure may hamper cooperation and thus hinder the completion of orders in due time and within limits of resources and budgets.

2. Some theorists have developed the post-bureaucratic organization, in which decisions are based on dialogue and consensus rather than authority and command, the organization is a network rather than a hierarchy, open at the boundaries (in direct contrast to culture management); there is an emphasis on meta-decision making rules rather than decision making rules.

3. Coordination and specialization of tasks are centralized in a functional structure, which makes producing a limited amount of products or services efficient and predictable. Moreover, efficiencies can further be realized as functional organizations integrate their activities vertically so that products are sold and distributed quickly and at low cost.

4. Another modern structure is network. While business giants risk becoming too clumsy to act and react efficiently, the new network organizations contract out any business functions that can be done better or more cheaply. In essence, managers in network structures spend most of their time coordinating and controlling external relations, usually by electronic means.

5. Indeed, business experts cite a number of characteristics that separate effective organizational structures from ineffective designs. Recognition of these factors is especially important for entrepreneurs and established business owners, since these individuals play such a pivotal role in determining the final organizational structure of their enterprises.

IV. Case Study

The Story of Syngenta

Syngenta is a world-leading plant science business. It is committed to promoting sustainable agriculture through innovative research and technology. Its purpose is "bringing plant potential to life." Syngenta currently employs more than 24,000 people in over 90 countries. Its customers range from farmers to governments.

Well-qualified innovative scientists are core strength of the business. However, the company also needs people in other supporting roles to ensure the products that its scientists develop can reach their chosen markets and customers. A strong focus on recruiting and developing its employees helps Syngenta remain a major player in a highly competitive market. The business prides itself on attracting motivated, talented and involved employees. Once people are recruited, it fully utilizes the breadth and depth of their available talent.

Throughout the world, farmers and growers are looking to increase the yield from their land. Syngenta's research teams are devoted to researching and developing products to meet worldwide demand. This involves staff from different departments working together in teams on specific projects and tasks. This approach helps to make the most of all employees' talents and abilities and enables functions to work together more effectively.

Syngenta is committed to empowering its staff and a hierarchical structure is not suited to its innovative style. Like many large businesses working in both national and international markets, Syngenta has adopted a matrix structure.

A matrix structure is often referred to as the project team structure. In this approach, team leaders manage specific tasks and projects. Each team will consist of members from different departments, each with their own specialisms and expertise related to the project. It takes employees out of their usual functional areas to work with other employees with different expertise and specialisms. This ensures the project has all the skills it needs to achieve its target. It also means the employees may benefit from each other's abilities.

Some teams are only formed for a short period of time. They disband when their projects have been completed and the team members are redeployed on other projects. Other teams have a longer or sometimes permanent remit. The matrix structure is not an alternative to functional management but works alongside it. Syngenta's project teams all support one or more of its business strategies.

Syngenta uses the skills and competencies of its people to bridge its functional areas. By using people with specific scientific knowledge or experience to lead teams in areas like marketing and production, communication is better within the team. Team members know that the leader understands the issues they face. This can also help to ensure that problems are understood and resolved quickly. These profiles help to demonstrate how Syngenta uses this "cross-over" of talent.

Syngenta has a culture of empowering its workers. This enables them to be in control of their work. To fulfil Syngenta's aims and objectives, employees must also demonstrate specific skills and competencies. Dr Kathryn Brocklehurst explains what this means for her: "As a manager and scientist, time management, planning and communication are key skills. I manage a research team and it is vital that our work meets deadlines in order to get products developed for our customers."

Kathryn's planning skills are essential as delays could mean that competitors bring out new products first. As a result, Syngenta could lose business. Investment costs are high in the research area. Large research projects can run for 10 years, costing up to £100 million per project. Clear leadership is essential to make this product development work as efficiently as possible.

Questions for discussion:

1. According to this passage and your own understanding, why does Syngenta choose the matrix structure?
2. In your opinion, besides matrix structure, what structure can be adopted by Syngenta? Why?
3. Try to summarize what factors can contribute to Syngenta's success and briefly state the reasons.

V. Supplementary Reading

General Electric: A Boundaryless Company

"Boundarylessness" was developed at General Electric in the late 1980s and early 1990s, and it is one of the cultural elements General Electric credits for its phenomenal success over the last fifteen years. Proponents of boundarylessness believe traditional boundaries between layers of management (vertical boundaries) and divisions between functional areas (horizontal boundaries) have stifled the flow of information and ideas among employees. A boundaryless culture seeks to overcome the limitations imposed by these and other internal corporate divisions.

1. Development of Boundarylessness at General Electric

Jack Welch certainly propelled it into the world's corporate consciousness with his Work-Out program at General Electric in the early 1990s.

In 1992, he described boundarylessness this way: GE's diversity creates a huge laboratory of innovation and ideas that reside in each of the businesses, and mining them is both our challenge and an awesome opportunity. Boundaryless behavior is what integrates us and turns this opportunity into reality, creating the real value of a multi-business company—the big competitive advantage we call Integrated Diversity.

Jack Welch believed that rigid, hierarchical organizations were poorly structured to compete in the fast-moving, information-centric, customer-focused competitive environment of the 1990s and beyond. He also recognized that General Electric's people, and especially their diversity of knowledge, talents, and ideas could become a tremendous competitive weapon for the company in the new business environment.

2. The Boundaryless Organization, Breaking the Chains of Organizational Structure

Boundarylessness (or boundaryfullness) can be seen along four dimensions: vertical, horizontal, external, and geographic. Vertical boundaries divide management from employees and divide layers of management from each other. Do the different layers communicate effectively? Horizontal boundaries divide divisions and departments within a corporation from each other. Do different functional areas cooperate with or compete against each other? External boundaries divide a company from others in its value chain. Geographic boundaries are a special form of horizontal boundary. How well does a company cross the national and cultural boundaries that divide its international operations from each other and itself from foreign markets?

Although all four dimensions are important in the boundaryless literature, the horizontal and vertical dimensions are most important for this evolutionary evaluation of boundarylessness at General Electric because those are the two dimensions concerned with day-to-day interactions among coworkers.

It is important to point out that "boundarylessness" should not be taken literally. It does not imply a completely amorphous organization. Rather, a boundaryless organization has learned to permeate the four boundary types listed above to better serve its customers and capitalize on good ideas. According to proponents of boundarylessness, for most of the 20th century, size, role clarity, specialization, and control are among the crucial dimensions against which companies measure themselves to become successful. Economies of scale are the crucial driver here, and to take advantage of them, companies become as large and as specialized as possible.

(1) Vertical boundaries

This de-emphasis of hierarchical status is problematic where Organizational Evolution is concerned. On the one hand, since shared information and improved communication among employees at different levels is a goal of a healthy hierarchy, one can imagine that healthy hierarchies would allow for more recombination than rigid hierarchies. On the other hand, however, the corporate hierarchy is one of a company's most powerful pointing and pushing mechanisms. One would therefore expect to see boundaryless organizations employing other pointing and pushing mechanisms to compensate.

Reward systems are the drivers of employee behavior, so it is crucial to ensure congruence between corporate reward systems and desired performance. Healthy hierarchies have flexible reward systems, allowing managers to assign compensation at all levels based on results, not position. Pointing and pushing is critical here, and it is interesting that the boundaryless literature does employ pointing and pushing based rewards when it discusses creating boundarylessness, but then does not consider pointing and pushing when rewarding other performance criteria. Boundaryless organization literature stresses that managers should always publicly recognize good boundaryless behavior in employees to establish and maintain a boundaryless culture.

(2) Horizontal boundaries

In *The Wealth of Nations*, Adam Smith described the efficiencies gained in a pin factory when each worker concentrated on a portion of the process and passed the in-process work off to other workers. In addition to dividing the various specialties (marketing, engineering, finance, etc.) from each other, horizontal boundaries can also separate employees along other dimensions: union vs. non-union, exempt vs. non-exempt, full-time vs. part-time, etc.

Product development is a frequent example here. Research & Development designs a product, passes it to engineering, which redoes the design, builds a prototype and passes it to manufacturing. Manufacturing alters the design to make the product easier to build, and then passes the whole thing on to marketing, which only then figures out how to sell the product. In shielding people from each other, horizontal boundaries can inhibit collaboration.

Viewing product design from a holistic perspective, R & D can no longer design new products without input from engineering, marketing, and manufacturing. Holistic processes are in and of themselves interdisciplinary, and the recombination that results from interdisciplinary work should improve the process, the product (or service), and those who develop it.

3. Implementing Boundarylessness at General Electric
(1) Adaptation vs. invention

"Boundaryless behavior has become the 'right' behavior at GE, and aligned with this behavior is a rewards system that recognizes the adapter or implementer of an idea as much as its originator. Creating this open, sharing climate magnifies the enormous and unique advantage of a multibusiness GE, as our wide diversity of service and industrial businesses exchange an endless stream of new ideas and best practices."

This quote ignited my interest in the link between organizational evolution and boundarylessness. Because of its unique position as a "multibusiness" company, General Electric recognized the importance of idea adaptation, or in organizational evolution terms, recombination. By creating an atmosphere where adapting and implementing a good idea from another area of GE or from outside is valued as much as or more than generating the good idea, Jack Welch focused his company on getting the maximum benefit from its diverse and powerful intellectual capital.

(2) Town meetings and other "recombination labs"

"Town meetings," developed at GE as it embraced boundarylessness, are an important tool in creating boundaryless organizations. In the organizational evolution reading of boundarylessness, town meetings are recombination workshops. Groups work for a few days before town meetings to generate and refine new ideas, and the ideas are presented, discussed, and either killed or implemented at the meetings. The town meeting format provides "safe ways" for anyone's ideas to be challenged by anyone else, without regard to position or authority. Town meetings have two purposes. First, of course, is to generate and implement change ideas. Second however, is to educate people on their "real degrees of freedom," to let employees know what decisions they can make on their own and to encourage them to do so. This creates an atmosphere where change, i.e. recombination, is not only encouraged at town meetings; it is encouraged throughout the organization whenever and wherever it is necessary.

Reading Comprehension
Choose the best answers to the following questions.
1. Boundaryless behavior can do the following except _____.
   A. creating the real value of a multi-business company
   B. having the advantage we call Integrated Diversity
   C. creating a huge laboratory of innovations and ideas
   D. attracting numerous of customers
2. Jack Welch recognized that General Electric's people, and especially their _____ could become a tremendous competitive weapon for the company in the new business environment.
   A. hard-working spirit
   B. brilliant learning ability
   C. innovational ideas

D. diversity of knowledge, talents, and ideas
3. Which of the following divide management from employees and divide layers of management from each other?
   A. Horizontal boundaries
   B. Vertical boundaries
   C. External boundaries
   D. Geographic boundaries
4. Which of the following statement is true according to this passage?
   A. Boundarylessness implies a completely amorphous organization.
   B. External boundaries are most important for this evolutionary evaluation of boundarylessness at General Electric.
   C. Viewing product design from a holistic perspective, R & D can no longer design new products without input from engineering, marketing, and manufacturing.
   D. The town meeting format provides "safe ways" for anyone's ideas to be challenged by anyone else, with regarding to position or authority.
5. We can infer from the passage that _____.
   A. Traditional boundaries between layers of management don't have a big influence on the exchanges between employees
   B. Rigid, hierarchical organizations don't fit the present economic environment
   C. Geographic boundaries view cooperation and collaboration among members of its value chain as a way to improve everyone's bottom line
   D. Companies became as large and as specialized as possible because of the development of technology

VI. Assignment

1. Visit at least six companies or organizations and find out what kind of organizational structure they are using. Ask their managers about the advantages and disadvantages of their organizational structure.
2. Teamwork is very important in this age, please prepare a short presentation to introduce this modern organizational structure.

Unit 6
Recruiting and Training Employees

 Learning Objectives

After learning this unit, you should be able to:
1. Know the significance of recruiting and training employees.
2. Understand the function of human resource department.
3. Know the recruiting process and different methods.
4. Know how to recruit the best employees for an enterprise.
5. Know the different methods of training employees.

 Lead-in

The recruitment as well as training of new employees has a bearing on the very success of a business. As the world becomes a global village, businesses are increasingly taking deliberate steps to ensure that they assemble a stellar cast of employees so as to remain relevant in the largely competitive marketplace. Training and development are used together to bring about the overall acclimation, improvement, and education of an organization's employees.

Warm-up Questions/Discussion:
1. Have you ever applied for a job? What kind of recruitment method do they use?
2. Do you think it's necessary to train employees? Why or why not?
3. Could you give us an example of successful campus recruitment?

Recruiting and Training Employees

1. Recruiting Employees

The first step of the hiring process is recruitment. This is an extremely important step for an organization as it is meant to attract only those individuals who are fully qualified and have the specific requirements the job demands. Recruitment precedes all the other steps of the hiring process including selection and training and hence its relevance cannot be overstated. This is because once the organization is able to attract a given pool of talent; the selection process is made easier and the organization can zero in on the most qualified employees.

2. Recruitment Approaches

There are two broad categorizations of recruitment: internal recruitment and external recruitment. On one hand, internal recruitment concerns itself with filling an existing vacancy within the organization from amongst the current pool of employees. On the other hand, external recruitment concerns itself with filling existing vacancies within the organization from amongst a pool of applicants who do not comprise the existing workforce of the organization.

It is important to note that each category has its benefits and disadvantages and hence the best approach a company should adopt must be hinged on[①] its specific circumstances. When it comes to the recruitment of new employees, a number of approaches have been proven to be most appropriate. Below, some of the most effective employee recruitment approaches as well as strategies are discussed.

(1) Referrals from employees

The employee referral[②] program basically seeks to source new employees through consultation with existing employees where the current employees are asked to forward the names as well as contacts of those they know can fill a certain vacant position within an organization. In this case, employees may avail individuals from their personal contacts, friends as well as family. However, though the program has enormous benefits as far as cost savings are concerned, it should be noted that care must be taken not to over-rely on the approach. One of the risk factors of the employee referral program is misuse.

---

① be hinged on（依靠，依赖）: Depend on; be subject to.

② referral（参照）: The act of referring (as forwarding an applicant for employment or referring a matter to an appropriate agency).

For instance, some managers may see the program as a way to reward their business associates, cronies or family members without any insistence on professionalism① or qualifications. One of the most significant advantages of employee referral programs apart from cost savings is their inherent ability to increase the pool of potential employees for the organization. This is because the program tends to net② even those who are not actively scouting for③ new positions. Further, a company or organization that utilizes the employee referral program has a high chance of attracting the most qualified employees.

The premise here is that since the referring employee has a reputation to protect, he is most likely to refer only those individuals whose abilities to perform are not in doubt. This is essentially because a chain of wrong referrals on the part of the employee can negatively impact on the reputation as well as career development of this employee. However, as stated above, the company must not overly rely on employee referral programs and hence a balance of sorts must be found between the employee referral programs and other recruitment approaches.

(2) Recruitment exercises at universities as well as vocational facilities

This is another recruitment approach that has gained prominence in the recent past mainly due to the need for businesses to make cost savings. It essentially involves paying universities and other vocational centers a visit and seeking to introduce the organization and its various vacant positions to students. It is important to note that this recruitment approach has two main benefits for the organization. First and foremost, it can provide the organization with a pool of applicants on a need basis. And secondly, it can create awareness of the various positions available to the target group hence availing the organization a future pool of talent. This recruitment approach is most appropriate when the vacant positions are entry level i.e. trainee level, apprentice positions etc. Further, as already stated above, most employers prefer this approach as it is inherently cheap as compared to other recruitment methods like placing adverts in the classified sections of the dailies or paying professional recruitment firms.

However, it is equally important to note that this recruitment method has a number of cons④ in that it cannot be used as the primary recruitment approach for

---

① professionalism（专业水平）：Professional status, methods, characters, or standards.
② net（得到）：Bring in, yield.
③ scout for（搜索，寻找）：Search for.
④ cons（反对）：An argument or opinion against something.

the company. Hence just like the case of employee referral programs, a balance of sorts must be found. It should be noted that recruiting at universities as well as vocational schools tends to be limiting as it is inappropriate for more senior positions as most of those targeted at this level have no track record which might be utilized to gauge① their performance.

(3) Advertising

This is one of the most popular recruitment methods. Many companies in the global marketplace allocate a significant portion of their budget towards this important approach to external recruitment. One of the most significant advantages of placing paid job adverts for prospective candidates to respond to includes their abilities to reach a significant portion of the market depending on the media chosen.

However, it can be noted that the decision of a business to advertise or not to largely depends on a number of factors including but not limited to the needed coverage as well as the advertising costs involved. With that in mind, an employer may decide to place job adverts in a wide variety of mediums including but not in any way limited to the dailies② (local and international), journals (specialist or general), notice boards as well as job posters. This is a recruitment method that calls for much creativity if cost savings are to be made.

For instance, a hospital seeking to fill a vacancy for a nurse would rather place an advert at a medical journal other than a journal or publication whose target is the general market. Same applies for a blue-chip③ company seeking an executive for its international operations or otherwise where in such a case it might consider placing job adverts in a management journal. Today, as the popularity of the internet continues to increase, there is a growing need to utilize the online platform to fill existing positions in a firm.

(4) Employment agencies/executive recruiters

Employment agencies or executive recruiters are sometimes simply known as "head hunters④" and their main brief includes scouting for the right candidate to fill a vacant position existing in a firm. Also known as recruitment agencies, employment agencies are contracted by the recruiting firm and are usually paid a certain predetermined fee for their services. However, most employment agencies

---

① gauge（测量）: To measure precisely.
② dailies（日报）: A newspaper published every day or every weekday.
③ blue-chip（第一流的）: Extremely valuable.
④ head hunters（猎头）: A recruiter of personnel (especially for corporations).

specialize in a given area of recruitment i.e. engineering, financial analysis as well as nursing and hence this is one of the considerations that must be taken by the recruiting company before engaging such services.

Contracting the services of recruitment agencies remains one of the best ways to source for individual to fill the higher level or management positions within the organization. <u>Further, it can be seen as a way of reducing costs associated with recruitment as well as a time saving approach to the recruitment process as in most cases, only a few names are submitted to the recruiting company for consideration as opposed to the other recruitment methods or approaches where the recruiting company has to sort through voluminous applications and come up with the best candidates; an approach which might be time consuming as well as labor intensive</u>[①].

3. Training New Employees

After the recruitment process, an organization must ensure that the new employees are accustomed to the systems as well as the procedures of their new workplace. This is to say that regardless of the professionalism that informs the recruitment as well as selection process, employees cannot perform optimally in their new positions without the proper abilities, skills as well as knowledge required of them.

Hence to enhance the performance of employees in their new workplace, the importance of training cannot be overlooked. Employee training can be defined as all the actions undertaken by the employer in an effort to ensure that the employees execute the tasks allocated by the employer in a certain way. It is important to note that contrary to popular belief, training should not be limited to new employees only.

However, this text focuses on training for new employees only. To facilitate employee training, organizations should come up with an employee training plan which must include a number of things including but not in any way limited to a conductive[②] learning environment. To come up with a conductive as well as ideal learning situation, the organization must embrace the following approaches.

- Employee training should be made a continuous process
- The learning process must be guided and have a direction

---

① labor intensive (劳动密集型): Requiring a large expenditure of labor but not much capital.
② conductive (有助于的): Having the property of conduction, helpful.

- The learning process must be made sequential
- Employees must be given the opportunity as well as time to practice what they learn

It is important to note that the training of new employees can not stop on their supposed completion of the "training process" discussed below. It must be an ongoing process to ensure that such employees are responsive to① the various changes in job requirements.

(1) The training process of new employees

Below, a new employee training model is introduced, which includes all the vital steps in the training process.

① The identification of training needs.

No meaningful training of new employees can take place without the apparent identification of the training needs of the new employees in relation with the job description. The organization can identify the training needs of a new employee by integrating three human resource factors i.e. the needs of the whole organization, the specific job characteristics and lastly the specific individual needs. The identification of the key component areas in which the employee needs training in order to effectively perform his or her duties is hence of utmost importance as it helps in the development of training manuals② as well as a means of evaluation.

② The formulation of a training program as well as training goals.

It is important to note that the formulation of the training program should be hinged on the needs assessment as mentioned above. This program must identify the skills as well as behaviors which the training initiative should help the new employee to acquire. It hence follows that the training program should be founded on the need to take the new employee from where he or she is currently to where the company or organization would want him or her to be.

(2) Training methods

There are two primary training approaches which organizations may adopt in respect to new employees. This includes on-the-job training and off-the-job training. On-the-job training is essentially training availed③ to new employees in the course

---

① be responsive to（对……敏感）：Be sensitive to.

② training manuals（训练手册）：A training manual may form an important part of a formal training program. For example, it may help ensure consistency in presentation of content. It may also ensure that all training information on skills, processes, and other information necessary to perform tasks is together in one place.

③ availed（有用的，有利的）：Useful.

Unit 6 Recruiting and Training Employees

of performing their duties. This approach is preferred by those organizations which do not want to loose time as the new employee is trained. It is most common for senior positions of management.

When it comes to off-the-job training, the company can organize special seminars, lectures as well as conferences for new employees as they seek to equip them with necessary skills for the effective performance of their duties. However, most companies do not prefer to use this approach to train their employees as it may end up being a tad too expansive. Another approach synonymous with new employee training is orientation.

Research indicates that close to 60% of new employees who quit their jobs do so in the initial two weeks since their confirmation. Hence employee orientation which can be taken as an approach to employee training is extremely important and it should focus on a number of things including but not in any way limited to the various personnel regulations and rules, organization's key officers as well as members and last but not least, the mission, history and culture of the organization.

I. Reviewing Questions

Answer the following questions according to the text.

1. Why is recruitment important for a company?
2. What is internal recruitment? Try to give us an example.
3. What are the benefits and disadvantages of referral program?
4. What's the premise for the employee referral program?
5. Why do some employers prefer recruitment exercises at universities?
6. Give us the definition of employee training.
7. How to come up with a conductive training program?
8. How to identify the training needs of a new employee?
9. Generally speaking, what kind of situation is on-the-job-training appropriate for?
10. When conducting the employee orientation, what should be taken into consideration?

II. Cloze

Read the following passage and fill in the blanks with the words given below. Change the form where necessary.

concentrate	minimize	meet	link	prepare
organization	enable	apply	communications	goal

Companies can ___1___ different methods of training and development to any number of subjects to ensure the skills needed for various positions are instilled. Companies gear training and development programs towards both specific and general skills, including technical training, sales training, clerical training, computer training, communications training, organizational development, career development, supervisory development, and management development. The ___2___ of these programs is for trainees to acquire new knowledge or skills in fields such as sales or computers or to enhance their knowledge and skills in these areas. The following are some methods of training often used by companies:

Technical training seeking to impart technical knowledge and skills uses common training methods for instruction of technical concepts, factual information, and procedures, as well as technical processes and principles. Likewise, sales training ___3___ on the education and training of individuals to communicate with customers in a persuasive manner and inculcates other skills useful for sales positions.

___4___ training concentrates on the improvement of interpersonal communication skills, including writing, oral presentation, listening, and reading. In order to be successful, any form of communications training should be focused on the basic improvement of skills and not just on stylistic considerations. Furthermore, the training should serve to build on present skills rather than rebuilding from the ground up. Communications training can be taught separately or can be effectively integrated into other types of training, since it is fundamentally related to other disciplines.

Organizational development (OD) refers to the use of knowledge and techniques from the behavioral sciences to analyze existing organizational structure and implement changes in order to improve organizational effectiveness. OD is useful in such varied areas as the alignment of employee goals with those of the organization, communications, team functioning, and decision making. In short, it is a development process with an organizational focus to achieve the same goals as other training and development activities aimed at individuals. OD practitioners commonly practice what has been termed "action research" to effect an orderly change that has been carefully planned to ___5___ the occurrence of unpredicted or unforeseen events. Action research refers to a systematic analysis of an organization to acquire a better understanding of the nature of problems and forces within an organization.

Career development of employees covers the formal development of an employee's position within an organization by providing a long-term development strategy and training programs to implement this strategy and achieve individual goals. Career development represents a growing concern for employee welfare and the long-term needs of employees. For the individual, it involves stating and describing career goals, the assessment of necessary action, and the choice and implementation of necessary actions. For the ___6___, career development represents the systematic development and improvement of employees. To remain effective, career development programs must allow individuals to articulate their desires. At the same time, the organization strives to meet those stated needs as much as possible by consistently following through on commitments and ___7___ the expectations of the employees raised by the program.

Management and supervisory development involves the training of managers and supervisors in basic leadership skills enabling them to function effectively in their positions. For managers this typically involves the development of the ability to focus on the effective management of their employee resources, while striving to understand and achieve the strategies and goals of the organization. Management training typically involves individuals above the first two levels of supervision and below senior executive management. Managers learn to effectively develop their employees by helping employees learn and change, as well as by identifying and ___8___ them for future responsibilities. Management development may also include programs that teach decision-making skills, creating and managing successful work teams, allocating resources effectively, budgeting, communication skills, business planning, and goal setting.

Supervisory development addresses the unique situation of the supervisor as a ___9___ between the organization's management and workforce. It must focus on ___10___ supervisors to deal with their responsibilities to labor and management, as well as coworkers, and staff departments. Important considerations include the development of personal and interpersonal skills, understanding the management process, and productivity and quality improvement.

III. Translation

1. The employee referral program basically seeks to source new employees through consultation with existing employees where the current employees are asked to forward the names as well as contacts of those they know can fill a certain vacant

position within an organization.

2. It should be noted that recruiting at universities as well as vocational schools tends to be limiting as it is inappropriate for more senior positions as most of those targeted at this level have no track record which might be utilized to gauge their performance.

3. Further, they can be seen as a way of reducing costs associated with recruitment as well as a time saving approach to the recruitment process as in most cases, only a few names are submitted to the recruiting company for consideration as opposed to the other recruitment methods or approaches where the recruiting company has to sort through voluminous applications and come up with the best candidates; an approach which might be time consuming as well as labor intensive.

4. The organization can identify the training needs of a new employee by integrating three human resource factors i.e. the needs of the whole organization, the specific job characteristics and lastly the specific individual needs. The identification of the key component areas in which the employee needs training in order to effectively perform his or her duties is hence of utmost importance as it helps in the development of training manuals as well as a means of evaluation.

5. Hence employee orientation which can be taken as an approach to employee training is extremely important and it should focus on a number of things including but not in any way limited to the various personnel regulations and rules, organization's key officers as well as members and last but not least, the mission, history and culture of the organization.

IV. Case Study

McDonald's Recruitment

Under McDonald's recruitment policy, each individual restaurant is responsible for filling hourly-paid positions. For recruiting hourly-paid employees McDonald's use several avenues. Positions are generally advertised in the restaurant. McDonald's also uses local job centers, career fairs and other local facilities. It is vital to use effective hiring material with a clear message targeted at the right audience.

A well-run interview will identify an applicant's potential to be a successful McDonald's employee. To find people who will be committed to excel in delivering outstanding service, McDonald's scripts an interview guide that helps the company predict how an applicant's past behavior is likely to influence the future performance. It uses a fact-based decision-making process.

McDonald's future managers come from two main sources. More than half of all salaried management positions are taken up by hourly-paid employees who earn promotion. The remainders are predominately graduates. Wherever possible, McDonald's directs applicants towards applying on line at www.mcdonalds.co.uk. People who cannot access the web can call the Recruitment Hotline, or pick up a pre-paid Business Reply Card from a McDonald's restaurant.

The selection process includes an initial online psychometric test. This test produces an initial score. The applicant then attends a first stage interview and is offered "On Job Experience" (OJE). This is a 2-day assessment in a restaurant. Successful completion at OJE will lead to a final interview, after which the manager decides whether or not to hire the applicant.

After the final interview the manager will rate the applicant's responses. A successful applicant will have demonstrated skills and behaviors that have been identified as being the key to the position. McDonald's inducts all new employees into the business through a Welcome Meeting, which they must attend. The Welcome Meeting gives an overview of the Company, including job role; food, hygiene and safety training; policies and procedures; administration; benefits; training and development.

Questions for discussion:
1. Have you ever applied for a position in McDonalds? What kind of recruitment procedure or method do they use?
2. What are the main sources for McDonald's future managers?
3. Could you make some comments on McDonald's recruitment?

V. Supplementary Reading

Enterprise Rent-A-Car (Enterprise)'s Successful Story

Enterprise Rent-A-Car (Enterprise) was founded by Jack Taylor in 1957 in the basement of a car dealership in St Louis in the USA. The business began with only seven cars. Today, Enterprise is the largest car rental business in North America with more than 7,000 offices in the USA and more than 900 in Canada, Puerto Rico, the UK, Germany and Ireland. In 2007, Enterprise had 728,000 rental cars in use, employing over 65,000 people with an annual turnover of over £4.5 billion.

Maintaining high levels of customer satisfaction is a key driver of growth for Enterprise. Enterprise emphasizes delivering first-class customer service, regularly winning awards for its efforts in this area. Its small, local office structure and entrepreneurial team working means its employees are able to make decisions independently to achieve their goals.

This study explores how Enterprise ensures it has the right people and skills to achieve its business aims and objectives.

The Role of Human Resource Management

The purpose of Human Resource Management (HRM) is to hire, train and develop staff and where necessary to discipline or dismiss them. Through effective training and development, employees at Enterprise achieve promotion within the company and reach their full potential.

This reduces the need for external recruitment and makes maximum use of existing talent. This is a cost-effective way for a business to manage its people.

The HRM function not only manages existing staff, but it also plans for changes that will affect its future staffing needs. This is known as workforce planning. For example, the business may grow into new markets, such as Enterprise moving into truck rental; it may use new technology which requires new skills; staff may retire or be promoted, leaving gaps which need to be filled.

There may also be external changes in the labor market, meaning that there will be fewer skills available or too many in a particular area. HRM monitors all of these things in planning recruitment strategy. This places the HRM function in a central role in the business because all managers use this expertise to acquire staff.

Enterprise has a policy of promoting its managers from within its existing workforce. This means the business must recruit people with the potential to grow.

Attracting Applicants

In order to attract high quality candidates, Enterprise is raising the company profile within UK universities using Campus Brand Managers. These are students or interns who work for Enterprise and act as liaisons for potential applicants. Other activities in universities to attract interested applicants include presentations on the company, relationships with clubs and organizations, attending Careers Fairs, "drop-in" sessions, skills sessions and mentoring programs.

Students can also visit Enterprise and spend time learning about how it does business and what opportunities it offers.

Enterprise offers a good salary and training as part of its benefits. However, the real attraction is the chance of a career rather than just a job. Most employees start out as Management Trainees with the potential to progress to Vice President/General Manager.

Employees also have opportunities to specialize in specific areas such as finance, human resource management, vehicle acquisition, risk management and many others. This allows individuals to develop their career path as they progress within the company.

Enterprise makes every effort to ensure that its workforce is representative of the cultural and ethnic diversity in the wider population. Job advertisements state: "Enterprise Rent-A-Car seeks and values people of all backgrounds because every employee, customer and business partner is important. We are proud to be an equal opportunities employer."

Recruitment

Enterprise's online recruitment process is an important part of its strategy. This improves the speed and efficiency of the application for both the company and the applicant. The website provides a registration function and lists available jobs. It also provides a lot of information about the Management Trainee role and the company culture and values. This allows applicants to get a good idea of whether Enterprise would suit them.

New recruits can enter the business in different ways.

An "internship" scheme is available for first and second year university students. This gives students an opportunity to work with Enterprise. Students gain valuable experience and there is the possibility of becoming a full-time employee after graduation. Interns participate in an initial classroom-based training session.

After this, they work in a branch office where they begin on-the-job training.

Interns take on the same responsibilities as management trainees and learn about sales, marketing, customer service, business management and administration support.

Enterprise advertises its vacancies and opportunities across a wide range of media. This includes media such as newspapers, magazines and online.

To target graduate recruits, Enterprise has developed a dedicated recruitment brand and website—"Come Alive." The website shows potential employees the benefits of career opportunities with Enterprise and provides a medium through which students can submit their applications. It also presents profiles of Enterprise employees with their career stories.

Enterprise also uses specialist graduate recruitment websites at peak times throughout the year in order to attract the maximum audience. Approximately 50% of its total UK and Ireland workforce is recruited via the website strategy.

Selection

Enterprise seeks competencies in its recruits both for an immediate job role and also for development over the longer term to support the business growth. HR managers often use standard documentation in order to match job roles with personal qualities and skills. These include the job description, which summarizes a job role within an organization and lists the main tasks; a person specification, which highlights the characteristics a candidate needs for a post, as well as the desirable qualities the company is looking for.

Enterprise combines the person specification within the job description by using a skills and competencies framework.

The Enterprise selection process offers candidates several opportunities to show their best in different situations:

To screen candidates, Enterprise recruitment managers compare the online application forms (which reflect candidates' CVs) to the skills and competencies the role needs.

Candidates then have an initial face-to-face interview with an Enterprise recruitment manager.

This is followed by an interview with a branch manager.

From this, selected candidates are invited to an assessment day.

The assessment day is a standard part of the Enterprise recruitment process.

Candidates take part in practical exercises, including role-play, as well as individual and group activities. Role-play is a valuable way of testing core skills like communication and customer service. Enterprise can assess a candidate's performance by different methods and in different work related tasks. This makes the selection process fairer. Areas tested include customer service skills, flexibility, sales aptitude, work ethic, leadership and teamwork. The assessment day ends with another interview with a senior manager in order to make the final selection.

The different parts of the selection process help to identify the qualities the company is looking for. For example:

Laurent is an Area Manager. The selection process highlighted within him a keenness for sales and a real care for customers. This enabled him to take on the challenges of responding to changing customer needs whilst meeting business aims and objectives. His role includes leading managers of several rental branches to develop a culture of customer services and sales. Through coaching, mentoring and training, he motivates his team by recognizing them, and rewarding their achievements so that they can meet their business goals.

Reading Comprehension
Choose the best answers to the following questions.
1. What is the key driver of the growth for enterprise?
   A. Investing more money to the program
   B. Maintaining high level of customer satisfaction
   C. Recruiting high quality employees
   D. Finding niche market for the company
2. Workforce planning includes the following except _____.
   A. training the existing employees
   B. being prepared for the gaps left by employees
   C. attracting new employees even when there are fewer talents
   D. developing a new kind of product
3. The main reason for employees to choose Enterprise is _____.
   A. they can learn about their enterprise culture
   B. they could get a reasonable amount of money
   C. they can enjoy wonderful welfare
   D. they have opportunities to specialize in many specific areas
4. Online recruitment process has the following benefits except _____.

A. applicants can get a good idea of whether Enterprise suits them
B. it can improve the speed and efficiency for both the company and the applicants
C. it will help the company to get more information about its potential employees
D. it provides a lot of information about the Management Trainee role

5. All of the following is right except _____ according to this passage.
    A. Enterprise recruits people with the right skills and provides continuing development and training for them
    B. Enterprise has built special websites for its potential employees
    C. the "internship" scheme is available for all university students
    D. Enterprises advertises its vacancies and opportunities by using both traditional and modern media

VI. Assignment

1. Divide the class into several groups and simulate the recruitment process, in which some of you play the role of HR, while the rest play the role of applicant. Try to be as formal as possible and each group will be accessed by the whole class and the teacher who will make a comment on your performance in the end. Finally you should submit a report about what you've learnt in this activity.
2. Make a thorough research on the different ways of training employees, point out which one do you like best and give reasons for your choice.

Unit 7

Employee Motivation

 Learning Objectives

After learning this unit, you should be able to:
1. Understand the concept of employee motivation.
2. Know some basic theories of employee motivation.
3. Describe the difference of intrinsic and extrinsic motivation.
4. Know the tips of improving the employee motivation.
5. Choose appropriate tools to motivate different employees.

 Lead-in

Employee motivation is a process or program employers will initiate to motivate employees. Employers motivate employees to work harder or to increase attendance. Employees are the lifeblood of the company. Therefore, it is of great significance to use effective employee motivation techniques so they can stay happy and inspired with their work. This, in turn, will also make them more productive. If a manager knows how to motivate his employees, the company's overall status and profits will improve as a result.

Warm-up Questions/Discussion:
1. What methods are often used when the managers want to motivate the employees?
2. In your opinion, how can the employees be effectively motivated?
3. Do you know any theories about motivation ? What are they?

How to Motivate Your Employees

The word motivation is coined from the Latin word "movere," which means to move. Motivation has been defined as: the psychological process that gives behavior purpose and direction; a predisposition① to behave in a purposive manner to achieve specific, unmet needs; an internal drive to satisfy an unsatisfied need; and the will to achieve.

Why do we need motivated employees? The answer is survival. Motivated employees are needed in our rapidly changing workplaces. Motivated employees help organizations survive. Motivated employees are more productive. To be effective, managers need to understand what motivates employees within the context of the roles they perform. Of all the functions a manager performs, motivating employees is arguably the most complex. This is due, in part, to the fact that what motivates employees changes constantly. For example, research suggests that as employees' income increases, money becomes less of a motivator②.

Also, as employees get older, interesting work becomes more of a motivator. Workers in any organization need something to keep them working. Most of the time, the salary of the employee is enough to keep him or her working for an organization. An employee must be motivated to work for a company or an organization. If no motivation is present in an employee, then the quality of that employee's work or all work in general will deteriorate.

1. Intrinsic and Extrinsic Motivation

Intrinsic motivation refers to motivation that is driven by an interest or enjoyment in the task itself, and exists within the individual rather than relying on any external pressure. Intrinsic motivation is based on taking pleasure in an activity rather than working towards an external reward. Extrinsic motivation refers to the performance of an activity in order to attain an outcome, which then contradicts intrinsic motivation. Thus, motives can be divided into two types: external and internal. Internal motives are considered as the needs that every human being experiences, while external motives indicate the presence of specific situations where these needs arise. Social psychological research has indicated that extrinsic

---

① predisposition (倾向): Tendency, an attitude of mind, especially one that favors one alternative over others.
② motivator (动力,激励因素): Incentive, a positive motivational influence.

rewards can lead to overjustification① and a subsequent reduction in intrinsic motivation.

2. Theories of Employee Motivation

(1) Taylor and the "piece rate"

Frederick W. Taylor (1911) was the creator of "scientific management." He felt that every job was measurable and each element of a job could be timed. What all managers had to do was to pay for every item the workers produced and thus they would work harder to get more money. This led to a long established pay scheme called the "piece rate,②" where workers received a fixed amount for every unit of output. Schemes like this are usually associated with manufacturing industries and are not appropriate for a complex service-led organization.

(2) McGregor's theory X and theory Y

Theory X and Theory Y are theories of human motivation created and developed by Douglas McGregor at the MIT Sloan School of Management in the 1960s that have been used in human resource management.

In theory X, management assumes employees are inherently lazy and will avoid work if they can and that they inherently dislike work. As a result of this, management believes that workers need to be closely supervised and comprehensive systems of controls developed, and employees will show little ambition without an enticing③ incentive program and will avoid responsibility whenever they can. Theory X managers rely heavily on threat and coercion④ to gain their employees' compliance. Beliefs of this theory lead to mistrust, highly restrictive supervision, and a punitive atmosphere.

In theory Y, management assumes employees may be ambitious and self-motivated and exercise self-control. It is believed that employees enjoy their mental and physical work duties. They possess the ability for creative problem solving, but their talents are underused in most organizations. Given the proper conditions, theory Y managers believe that, most people will want to do well at

---

① overjustification（过度合理化）: The overjustification effect occurs when an external incentive such as money or prizes decreases a person's intrinsic motivation to perform a task.

② piece rate（计件工资，按劳计酬）: Piece work or piecework describes types of employment in which a worker is paid a fixed "piece rate" for each unit produced or action performed regardless of time. Piece work is also a form of performance-related pay.

③ enticing（迷人的，诱人的）: Highly attractive or appealing and able to arouse hope or desire.

④ coercion（强制，威压）: The act of compelling by force of authority.

work. They believe that the satisfaction of doing a good job is a strong motivation.

(3) Herzberg and "two-factor" theory

Another theorist, Frederick Herzberg (1959), carried out a large-scale survey into motivation in American industry. The results of his survey led him to develop a "two-factor" theory of motivation. Firstly, he established that if an employee's basic needs (such as a suitable working environment and a basic rate of pay) were not met, then this would create a source of dissatisfaction. Herzberg termed these "hygiene factors.[①]" On the other hand, the presence of less tangible factors, such as the provision of challenging work and recognition for doing well, can create or increase work motivation. Herzberg termed these "motivators."

A company can put in place some of Herzberg's "motivators" in the following ways: employees get recognition for good work; they have a collective sense of achievement when the whole business does well; they gain extra responsibility and advancement through regular performance reviews; when employees do well in their work, the company rewards them.

(4) Maslow's Hierarchy of Needs

The theory of Abraham H. Maslow (1943) on staff motivation is also very popular. Maslow referred to a "Hierarchy of Needs" which is usually drawn as a pyramid.

According to Maslow, the most basic needs on this hierarchy had to be satisfied before workers could look to the next level. Basic physical needs were things like shelter, food, warmth and bodily functions. Next, people had to feel safe in their environment. A company can provide these basic needs when it creates jobs.

Maslow's higher levels of need are less obvious and less easy to describe but of great importance. Social needs refer to the fact that we want to feel part of something we share in. A company can create the opportunity for its employees to share in its common goals and vision[②] for the group. It does this by rewarding the people who contribute to its success through their commitment[③] and hard work.

The next level "esteem" refers to people's need to feel valued, and what they do matters. The employees can make it happen themselves. A company can provide

---

① hygiene factors（保健因素）: Hygiene factors are job factors that can cause dissatisfaction if missing but do not necessarily motivate employees if increased, and they have mostly to do with the job environment. These factors are important or notable only when they are lacking.

② vision（愿景）: A euphemism for planning in commerce and in sport, a corporate long-term goal.

③ commitment（承诺，承担义务）: To show loyalty, duty or pledge to something or someone.

opportunities for all employees through promotion or training and then recognizes their achievements. Through this the employees can improve their self-esteem.

At the very top of Maslow's hierarchy is our human need for "self actualization." This means people will work hard in order to be as good as we possibly can be. A company can meet this by offering recognition, promotion opportunities and the chance to develop a lifelong career with the group.

3. Specific Actions to Increase Employee Motivation

The following are seven consequential ways in which a manager or supervisor can create a work environment that will foster and influence increases in employee motivation quickly.

(1) Communicate responsibly and effectively any information employees need to perform their jobs most effectively

Employees want to be members of the in-crowd, people who know what is happening at work as soon as other employees know. They want the information necessary to do their jobs. They need enough information so that they make good decisions about their work. The managers are suggested to:

• Meet with employees following management staff meetings to update them about any company information that may impact their work. Changing due dates, customer feedback, and product improvements, training opportunities, and updates on new departmental reporting or interaction structures are all important to employees.

• Stop by the work area of employees who are particularly affected by a change to communicate more. Make sure the employee is clear about what the change means for their job, goals, time allocation, and decisions.

• Communicate daily with every employee who reports to you. Even a pleasant "good morning" enables the employee to engage with you.

• Hold a weekly one-on-one meeting with each employee who reports to the manager. The employees like to know that they will have this time every week. Encourage employees to come prepared with questions, requests for support, troubleshooting[①] ideas for their work, and information that will keep you from

---

① troubleshooting（解决问题）：Troubleshooting is a form of problem solving, often applied to repair failed products or processes. It is a logical, systematic search for the source of a problem so that it can be solved, and so the product or process can be made operational again. Troubleshooting is needed to develop and maintain complex systems where the symptoms of a problem can have many possible causes.

being blindsided or disappointed by a failure to produce on schedule or as committed.

(2) Employees find interaction and communication with and attention from senior and executive managers motivational

Studies indicate that the role of senior managers in attracting employee discretionary[①] effort exceeded that of immediate supervisors. The managers are suggested to:

- Communicate openly, honestly and frequently. Hold whole staff meetings periodically, attend department meetings regularly, and communicate by wandering around work areas, engaging staff and demonstrating interest in their work.

- Implement an open door policy for staff members to talk, share ideas, and discuss concerns. Make sure that managers understand the problems that they can and should solve will be directed back to them, but it is the executive's job to listen.

- Congratulate staff on life events such as new babies, inquire about vacation trips, and ask about how both personal and company events turn out. Care enough to stay tuned into these kinds of employee life events and activities.

(3) Provide the opportunity for employees to develop their skills and abilities

Employees often want to continue to develop their knowledge and skills. They do not want jobs that they perceive as no-brain drudge[②] work. The managers are suggested to:

- Allow staff members to attend important meetings, meetings that cross functional areas, and that the supervisor normally attends.

- Bring staff to interesting, unusual events, activities, and meetings. It's quite a learning experience for a staff person to attend an executive meeting with managers or represent the department in the managers' absence.

- Make sure the employee has several goals that he or she wants to pursue as part of every quarter's performance development plan. Personal development goals belong to the same plan.

- Reassign responsibilities that the employee does not like or that are routine. Newer staff, interns, and contract employees may find the work challenging and rewarding. Or, at least, all employees have their turns.

---

① discretionary（自由决定的）：Having or using the ability to act or decide according to your own discretion or judgment.

② drudge（苦力活）：To do tedious, unpleasant, dull or menial work.

• Provide the opportunity for the employees to cross-train① in other roles and responsibilities. Assign backup responsibilities for tasks, functions, and projects.

(4) Employees gain a lot of motivation from the nature of the work itself

Employees seek autonomy and independence in decision making and in how they approach accomplishing their work and job. The managers are suggested to:

• <u>Provide more authority for the employees to self-manage and make decisions. Within the clear framework and ongoing effective communication, delegate decision making after defining limits, boundaries, and critical points at which the managers want to receive feedback.</u>

• Expand the job to include new, higher level responsibilities. Assign responsibilities to the employees that will help them grow their skills and knowledge.

• Provide the employee with a voice in higher level meetings; provide more access to important and desirable meetings and projects.

• Provide more information by including the employee on specific mailing lists, in company briefings, and in your confidence.

• Provide more opportunities for the employee to impact department or company goals, priorities, and measurements.

• Assign the employee to head up② projects or teams. Assign reporting staff members to their leadership on projects or teams or under their direct supervision.

• Enable the employee to spend more time with his or her boss. Most employees find this attention rewarding.

(5) Elicit and address employee concerns and complaints before they make an employee or workplace dysfunctional③

Listening to employee complaints and keeping the employee informed about how you are addressing the complaint are critical to producing a motivating work environment.

<u>Even if the complaint cannot be resolved to the employee's satisfaction, the fact that you addressed the complaint and provided feedback about the consideration and resolution of the complaint to the employee is appreciated. The importance of the feedback loop in addressing employee concerns cannot be</u>

---

① cross-train（对……进行交叉训练）：To undergo or provide training in different tasks or skills.

② head up（领导）：Be the first or leading member of (a group) and excel.

③ dysfunctional（不正常的，不良的）：Abnormal or impaired functioning, especially of a bodily system or social group. (Of a trait or condition) failing to serve an adjustive purpose.

overemphasized. The managers are suggested to:

- Keep the door open and encourage employees to come to the manager with legitimate concerns and questions.
- Always address and provide feedback to the employees about the status of their expressed concerns. The concern or complaint cannot disappear into a dark hole forever. Nothing causes more consternation① for an employee than feeling that their legitimate concern goes unaddressed.

(6) Recognition of employee performance is high on the list of employee needs for motivation

Many supervisors equate reward and recognition with monetary gifts. While employees appreciate money, they also appreciate praise, a verbal or written thank you, out-of-the-ordinary job content opportunities, and attention from their supervisors. The managers are suggested to:

- Write a thank-you note that praises and thanks an employee for a specific contribution in as much detail as possible to reinforce and communicate to the employee the behaviors you want to continue to see.
- Verbally praise and recognize an employee for a contribution. Visit the employee in his or her work space.
- Give the employee a small token of gratitude. A card, their favorite candy bars, a cutting from a plant in your office, fruit for the whole office, and more, based on the traditions and interaction in your office, will make an employee's day.

(7) Employees appreciate a responsive and involved relationship with their immediate supervisors

The managers are suggested to:

- Avoid canceling regular meetings, and if it's a must, stop by the employee's work area to apologize, offer the reason, and immediately reschedule. Regularly missing an employee meeting send a powerful message of disrespect.
- Talk daily with each employee who reports to you. The daily interaction builds the relationship and will stand for a lot when times are troubled, disappointments occur, or you need to address employee performance improvement.

The interaction of an employee with his or her immediate supervisor is the most significant factor in an employee's satisfaction with work. Practise just

---

① consternation（惊愕）: A feeling of anxiety, dismay, dread, or confusion.

Unit 7 Employee Motivation   107

listening. Encourage the employee who brings you an idea or improvement.

Remember that the supervisor's nonverbal communication communicates more expressively than the words to convey their honest response to the employees' thoughts, concerns, and suggestions. Pay attention, ask questions to further elicit information, and focus on understanding the employee's communication.

The supervisor's relationship to reporting staff is the single most important factor in employee retention. Stay on top of what your staff needs and wants to provide a work environment for employee motivation.

 Exercises

I. Reviewing Questions
Answer the following questions according to the text.
1. What are the benefits of that motivating employees?
2. Is money the only factor that can be used in motivating employees? Why or why not?
3. What's the difference between intrinsic motivation and extrinsic motivation?
4. Try to differentiate "hygiene factors" and "motivators" by giving specific examples.
5. In your opinion, which one of McGregor's theory X and theory Y is more close to the reality or more correct?
6. What are the main "motivators" according to Herzberg?
7. Why is Malslow's theory more hierarchical rather than flat?
8. In what ways can interactions and communication between managers and employees be guaranteed?
9. How should we handle employees' concerns and complaints?
10. What's the most important factor in employee retention? Why?

II. Cloze
Read the following passage and fill in the blanks with the words given below. Change the form where necessary.

accuse	revolve	impact	assume	exhibit
foster	success	squelch	deliver	fulfill

Every employee is motivated about something in his or her life. Motivating employees about work is the combination of ___1___ the employee's needs and expectations from work and workplace factors that enable employee motivation—or not.

Too many workplaces still act as if the employee should be grateful to have a job. Managers are on power trips and employee policies and procedures are formulated based on the ___2___ that you can't trust employees to do the right thing. Communication is never transparent and there is always a secret message or a hidden agenda. Motivating employees in this work environment is tough, if not impossible.

Fortunately, most work environments are not this extreme. They each have their own set of problems, but managers appreciate that motivating employees will bring positive results for the organization. The following ten tips about motivating employees provide a basic understanding of employee motivation. They also target key areas for ___3___ in motivating employees.

(1) Every person is motivated. Whether that motivation ___4___ around work, a hobby, the family, the spiritual side of life, or food, each person has some items or issues about which he or she feels motivated to take action in his or her life.

(2) Your actions in the workplace either encourage motivated behavior or they discourage employee motivation. In some workplaces, company policies and management behavior actually ___5___ motivation.

(3) Actions and activities in the workplace that provide an environment supportive of motivating employees don't have to be expensive. Activities and recognition that cost money are welcomed by employees as part of the motivation mix, but their ___6___ on motivating employees is short term and will not over-ride the consequences of how people feel treated everyday in the workplace.

(4) Much of the workplace environment that encourages employee motivation involves management time and commitment: genuine interest and caring, employee-oriented policies and procedures, and attention from both senior managers and line managers are all appreciated and valued.

(5) Motivation is prevalent in workplaces where people are treated as valued human beings. Trust, respect, civil conversation, and listening prevail in a workplace that ___7___ employee motivation.

(6) Clear direction plays a serious role in motivating employees. Employees want to know exactly what you expect from them. When they have the reassurance of clear direction, motivating employees become easier because you and they have

created a framework for their expected performance.

(7) Supervisors can create an environment for motivating employees. You just do not consistently, in a disciplined manner, adhere to what you already know about motivating employees. To be perfectly honest, since I am often ___8___ of viewing the world through rose-colored glasses, some supervisors just don't care. They work to collect a paycheck and all of this stuff about motivating employees is just gabbled gook.

(8) Employee motivation is a constant challenge. What motivates one employee is not motivating for another. After all, a workplace of happy employees is great, but it doesn't guarantee quality products ___9___ on time, delighted customers, or profitability – all essential to providing those happy employees with jobs.

(9) Actively solicit information from the employees about what motivates them. Responding to employee needs and complaints is key for motivating employees. People expect to see something changed as a result of their responses. If it doesn't change, and you don't tell them why, you risk wasting all of your efforts in motivating employees.

(10) Motivation at work is a choice employees make. Employees choose to ___10___ motivated behavior at work. You can know and do everything discussed here, but employees are ultimately in charge of motivating themselves.

III. Translation

1. The word motivation is coined from the Latin word "movere," which means to move. Motivation has been defined as: the psychological process that gives behavior purpose and direction; a predisposition to behave in a purposive manner to achieve specific, unmet needs; an internal drive to satisfy an unsatisfied need; and the will to achieve.

2. As a result of this, management believes that workers need to be closely supervised and comprehensive systems of controls developed, and employees will show little ambition without an enticing incentive program and will avoid responsibility whenever they can. Theory X managers rely heavily on threat and coercion to gain their employees' compliance. Beliefs of this theory lead to mistrust, highly restrictive supervision, and a punitive atmosphere.

3. Maslow's higher levels of need are less obvious and less easy to describe but of

great importance. Social needs refer to the fact that we want to feel part of something we share in. A company can create the opportunity for its employees to share in its common goals and vision for the group. It does this by rewarding the people who contribute to its success through their commitment and hard work.

4. Provide more authority for the employees to self-manage and make decisions. Within the clear framework and ongoing effective communication, delegate decision making after defining limits, boundaries, and critical points at which the managers want to receive feedback.

5. Even if the complaint cannot be resolved to the employee's satisfaction, the fact that you addressed the complaint and provided feedback about the consideration and resolution of the complaint to the employee is appreciated. The importance of the feedback loop in addressing employee concerns cannot be overemphasized.

IV. Case Study

Motivating Through Total Reward

The Royal Bank of Scotland Group (RBS) is one of the largest financial institutions in the world. It is a global business with a range of operations in Europe, North America and Asia Pacific. RBS has centers in thirteen European countries, sixteen North American states and eight major Asia Pacific cities. RBS provides a range of retail and corporate banking, financial markets, consumer finance, insurance, and wealth management services.

Performance Management

At RBS almost every role can be described in terms of specific job targets. This method of performance management allows managers to measure each individual's performance in a specific way and reward them accordingly. RBS employees will agree job objectives and targets with their line manager at the beginning of the year. Their performance is then measured and reported on during the year. At the end of the year they will have a performance review. Payments for results are an effective motivator for high performance.

Some jobs are paid according to the achievement of targeted results. This means that a bonus is paid if the employee achieves agreed targets for the job. Particularly challenging or difficult to achieve targets are known as "stretch targets" and the reward for achieving these will be greater.

Motivation at RBS—Total Reward

RBS offers benefits for each member of staff that include not just money, but also personal choice in working hours and security.

The RBS Total Reward package also offers flexible pension funding, health and medical benefits, paid holidays, and a confidential advice service. Employees have a generous holiday allowance (between 25 and 30 days for full-time staff), with the option of buying or even selling days. Employees may also choose from a wide range of lifestyle benefits, including discounted shopping vouchers, childcare facilities and RBS financial products, such as mortgages, currency exchange, personal loans and banking at special staff discounted rates.

Non-Financial Rewards

Whilst money may be an incentive to go to work; at work, pay cannot motivate people to give more. Theorists have long understood that staff needs a combination of motivators. This is why RBS offers so many non-financial rewards which can improve personal lifestyle.

One of the most important motivators for RBS employees is the recognition of good performance by graded progression. Development can involve more training, attending courses or gaining new understanding and skills. This can improve the prospects of promotion and allow employees to move up the organization and increase their Total Reward.

RBS also believes in giving its people the chance to help put something back into their own communities. Wherever RBS operates, the Group supports community involvement in projects that matter to its people. For every pound raised for charity by a member of staff, RBS will double-match the donation, making every pound raised count three times.

Flexible Working

RBS gives all employees the "right to work flexibly." This can be through a range of flexible working practices covering job sharing, part-time working, home working, variable working hours, compressed hours and term-time working. These are adapted to suit the local needs of each RBS centre. The policies and procedures for applying are easily available on the RBS website. RBS provides a free advice service called "Help Direct." Employees can call for advice on making the most of their time at and away from work. It also offers counseling on a range of life issues.

The Benefits of Flexible Working Practices

The policies of RBS in relation to work-life balance help to create a working atmosphere that relieves stress. They also help to create greater equality of opportunity for everyone. For example, this flexibility enables employees to choose working patterns that fit with their childcare arrangements or their personal lives.

Following these flexible practices allows RBS to attract more talented people. Theoretical work on motivation by Elton Mayo in the 1920s showed that contented people, who are satisfied with their working environment, were likely to be more productive. The distractions of home or community pressures can be handled far more comfortably with the support of an employer such as RBS. In return, RBS gains staff loyalty and commitment, which in turn drives higher performance.

Questions for discussion:
1. Do you think RBS's management is effective enough? Why? Which method do you appreciate most? Why?
2. If you are going to apply for a position in RBS, which position will you apply for and what factors attract you most?
3. Can flexible working pattern bring a win-win result for both the staff and the company? Why or why not?

V. Supplementary Reading

Motivation Within an Innovative Work Environment

For many people, their careers are on-going learning experiences. This is known as intrinsic motivation. When individuals are intrinsically motivated, they are interested in their work. Put simply, it creates enjoyment whilst enabling them to achieve and contribute to desired goals. However, individuals also need extrinsic motivation. This is motivation arising from factors outside the immediate work that an individual undertakes. For example, this might include pay, conditions, grades and promotional opportunities.

ARM is the world's leading semiconductor intellectual property supplier. The ARM business model involves the design and licensing of intellectual property in the field of semiconductor chips. ARM was founded in 1990 and now has offices around the world. ARM's main technology is its microprocessor which is at the "brain" of most modern gadgets. With more than 15 billion chips manufactured, this has enabled ARM to grow dramatically and become a global player in the semiconductor industry.

Technology and Innovation

ARM has a diverse global workforce. Its 2,050 employees work across 30 sites in 15 countries. Employees come from a wide range of backgrounds from over 50 nationalities. ARM is a knowledge intensive business focused on innovation. This innovation comes from the whole business and not just its research and development team.

ARM therefore relies on its people to achieve this innovation. Its HR strategy is focused on global learning and development, talent management and appropriate reward systems in order to develop and retain the skills and expertise its people need to create innovative solutions. This will enable the business to achieve its business strategy of providing sustained returns for shareholders and employees.

Engaging Employees

Due to the technical nature of the business, the organization is constantly changing as technologies advance. Managing change effectively requires employee engagement. ARM describes engagement as "commitment to the job, manager, team and organization which drives effort and intent to stay, resulting in improved performance and retention."

Motivation

Research has indicated that around 75% of an organization's employees are neither "engaged" nor "disengaged." Considering ARM's description of how engagement can drive performance, this means that, if more of these employees were engaged, the organizations could expect to improve performance.

Benefits of Motivating People

Motivating people benefits not just the individual. It also provides significant benefits for the business. A series of values help to underpin ARM's approach to motivation. These include respecting and involving others, being proactive and adopting a "can-do" approach to solving problems. For example, ARM employees work in teams within which they are encouraged to communicate openly and honestly and act on behalf of the business. They are also encouraged to produce solutions to problems. This all helps not just the business but also their personal development.

Motivation within HR Strategy

ARM demonstrates how it gains employee engagement through the various elements of its HR strategy of global team working: Buying into and sharing common values supports a collaborative approach to innovation. Sharing knowledge helps to develop relationships and networks within the business and leads to the creation of new ideas. Developing talent through training to acquire or improve expertise benefits individuals but also helps to ensure ARM will have key skills despite global shortages in some areas. Providing opportunities for individuals to grow into new roles also supports succession planning for future leadership. Various reward systems, including equity in the company, recognize individual and team effort.

Maslow (hierarchy of needs)

ARM provides employees with opportunities to fulfill higher order needs such as those of esteem and self-actualization through challenging and interesting work. Engaging employees in changing programmes and providing solutions enables them to contribute to the direction of the business. For example, recently more than 120 ARM employees were involved in developing ideas to improve how the company is run. Their ideas led to a wide variety of initiatives including "innovation days" and an increased use of social networking, such as "ARM TV"—an internal YouTube. The responsibilities associated with this help individuals to fulfill their potential in a creative way, providing them with the opportunity for developing self esteem.

Taylor and Scientific Management

Taylor's view has limited relevance at ARM. His approach was narrow and simply related pay to output. ARM is not about more pay bringing more output. Creating innovative products in teams needs people to genuinely want to do whatever it takes to make a product work. This is not just a product of time but of how people feel, how they communicate and how they work together to achieve a common vision.

ARM employees are intrinsically motivated. They are expected to understand a range of different fields. They are also expected to be flexible and creative using advancements in technology to deliver changes to the complex environment in which the business operates in.

Herzberg and 2-factor Theory

Henry Herzberg's theory of motivation is of more relevance to ARM employees. His theory is sometimes called the two-factor theory. He looked at motivators and hygiene factors. Hygiene factors, often referred to as "dissatisfiers," are elements in the work environment that could make employees unhappy. For example, if an organization has an autocratic management style, this may have a negative impact on motivation. Motivators, often referred to as "satisfiers," are aspects of the work environment that provide employees with job satisfaction, for example, recognition for effort and performance. Satisfied employees then become more productive.

ARM uses employee engagement as a key tool in motivation. This is a satisfier as employees develop a genuine attachment to the teams in which they work. A variety of other satisfiers are used at ARM, such as employees receiving shares in the company as well as bonuses based on how well the business as a whole is doing. The aim is for employees to act and feel like owners of the business. These also help them to be recognized for their contributions.

Mayo (human relations approach)

Elton Mayo founded the Human Relations Movement. Experiments undertaken by Mayo took place at the Hawthorne plant in the USA during the 1930s. His work illustrated that if the company or managers took an interest in employees and cared for them, it had a positive effect on their motivations. When managers took a greater interest in employees they felt more valued and empowered. His work also showed that employees often work best in teams. He also showed that they were more motivated if they managed and were consulted more.

Developing People

The Mayo principles are very much in line with ARM's focus on developing its people as part of its business strategy. Employees at ARM work within learning and development teams. Information is shared and employees are viewed both as partners in the business and as internal customers.

Managers have responsibility for motivating individuals and their teams, providing appropriate training and induction for new employees as well as coaching for all in order to develop skills, confidence and self-reliance.

Personal development is a key HR strategy at ARM. Regular reviews encourage individuals to reflect upon the contributions that they make whilst providing feedback and support enables them to develop their professional capability.

Reading Comprehension

Choose the best answers to the following questions.

1. All of the following are extrinsic motivations except _____.
   A. a considerate amount of salary
   B. nice and warm working environment
   C. the pleasure the job itself generates
   D. an opportunity to be the group leader

2. Which sentence of the following is not true about ARM?_____
   A. It manufactures chips and is a global player in the semiconductor industry.
   B. ARM's main technology is its microprocessor and it is widely used all over the world.
   C. Its HR strategy is focused on global learning and development, talent management and appropriate reward systems.
   D. It is a labor-intensive enterprise. Therefore, talents are of great importance to them.

3. _____ can help employees of ARM to develop self-esteem.
   A. Buying into and sharing common values
   B. Holding a Christmas party for staff
   C. Providing suggestions for the policy of the company
   D. Buying health insurance for staff

4. The theory put forward by _____ is not so relevant at ARM.
   A. Taylor
   B. Mayo
   C. Maslow

D. Herzberg

5. _____ is not the satisfier that used by ARM.

   A. Mployee engagement

   B. Utocratic management style

   C. Mployee receiving shares of the company

   D. Onus based on how well the company as a whole is doing

VI. Assignment

1. Create a large Hierarchy of Needs diagram. To each level add the methods that are adopted by an organization of your choice to motivate its workers. A possible organization you could use to complete this is your school or college, as it should be easier to find out the relevant methods used.

2. Either individually or in small groups, write a song, poem or rap to explain your learning points from the session about Maslow's Hierarchy of Needs. Keep it relatively short so it is easier to remember in future.

Unit 8

Corporate Culture

 Learning Objectives

After learning this unit, you should be able to:
1. Define corporate culture.
2. Understand the formation of corporate culture.
3. Know the differences between strong culture and weak culture.
4. Know the relationship between national culture and corporate culture.
5. Understand the importance of corporate culture.

 Lead-in

Corporate culture is the total sum of the values, customs, traditions, and meanings that make a company unique. Corporate culture is often called "the character of an organization," since it embodies the vision of the company's founders. The values of a corporate culture influence the ethical standards within a corporation, as well as managerial behavior.

Warm-up Questions/Discussion:
1. What kind of colleagues do you want to work with, an easy-going one or a competitive one?
2. How will you accomplish a task, all alone or with your workmates?
3. Talk about some kinds of corporate culture in China and abroad.

Corporate Culture[1]

Corporate culture is the collective behaviors of people that are part of an organization, it is also formed by the organization values, visions, norms, working language, systems, and symbols, and it includes beliefs and habits. It is also the pattern of such collective behaviors and assumptions that are taught to new organizational members as a way of perceiving, and even thinking and feeling. Corporate culture affects the way people and groups interact with each other, with clients, and with stakeholders[2].

1. Formation of Corporate Culture

Corporate culture is shaped by corporate vision, shared value, beliefs, past experiences, learning, leadership and communication.

(1) Corporate vision

Corporate vision may contain commitment to:
- Creating an extraordinary customer value
- Developing a great new product or service
- Serving customers through the defined service portfolio
- Ensuring quality and responsiveness of customer services
- Providing an enjoyable work environment for employees
- Ensuring financial strength and sustainable growth of the company for the benefit of its stakeholders

(2) Shared value

Values are about how we have learnt to think things ought to be or people ought to behave, especially in terms of qualities such as honesty, integrity and openness. Shared values are what engender[3] trust and link an organization together. Shared values are also the identity by which the organization is known throughout its business areas. These values must be stated as both corporate objectives and individual values. Every organization and every leader will have a different set of values that are appropriate to its business situation.

Ensuring employees' understanding of organization's values and visions requires the organization to have clearly defined values. Without this, the

---

[1] The text is excerpted from www.1000ventures.com with abridgment.
[2] stakeholder (股东): A person or group owning a significant percentage of a company's shares.
[3] engender (产生，引起): To bring about or give rise to; produce or cause.

organization can get itself into real trouble. Defining shared values is more than putting words on paper. Most organizations have values statements or mission statements; yet many do not follow them. Winning organizations create successful cultures in a systematic way using various approaches that may include visual representations, training seminars, and/or socializing events.

(3) Beliefs

Beliefs are the assumptions we make about ourselves, about others in the world and about how we expect things to be. <u>Beliefs are about how we think things really are, what we think is really true and what we therefore expect as likely consequences that will follow from our behavior. The clearer you are about what you value and believe in, the happier and more effective you will be.</u>

Members of the same organization often share the similar beliefs. For example, if a manager and his or her employee have similar beliefs, then the manager will be more comfortable to let the employee(who may have more time or better local information) make the decision and will feel less of a need to monitor the employee. In the same way, when performance depends on correct decisions, people in an organization prefer to work with others who have beliefs that are similar to their own because such others "will do the right thing" from their perspectives.

(4) Past experiences

In handling a business, one should be as knowledgeable enough to know the day to day processes of their business, particularly with a distribution type of business such as a wholesale clothing business. According to many business experts, one should not endeavor on a business that they have no idea of what goes on and what are the usual risks they would likely encounter in their business.

Lack of experience is also the reason why many business start ups fail at their first year. Although most of them would come back and try another go, many of them would normally drop the idea of handling a business such as a wholesale clothing business.

(5) Learning

Learning is the key competency required by any organization that wants to survive and thrive in the new knowledge economy. Market champions keep asking learning questions, keep learning how to do things better, and keep spreading that knowledge throughout their organization. Learning provides the catalyst[①] and the

---

[①] catalyst (促进因素；催化剂): A substance that modifies and increases the rate of a reaction without being consumed in the process.

intellectual resource to create a sustainable competitive advantage.

Knowledge organizations obtain competitive advantage from continuous learning, both individual and collective. In organizations with a well established knowledge management system, learning by the people within an organization becomes learning by the organization itself. The changes in people's attitudes are reflected in changes in the formal and informal rules that govern the organization's behavior.

(6) Leadership

Leadership is the process of directing the behavior of others toward the accomplishment of some common objectives. The role of leadership in business is indisputable①. Great leaders create great businesses. Mediocre② leaders create mediocre businesses.

Leadership is a requirement to any successful business because the nature of good leadership is that it provides important direction to an organization. But one thing that leaders need in order to be leaders is: followers. Forcing people to be the followers will never work, but there are things that you can learn, and practice and do that will make people willing to follow you.

(7) Communication

Communication is extremely important within a business and is what every good business should be built upon, giving a business the power to send a message to employees, prospective customers and the general public that they are one of the best at what they do. Communication makes a business grow and develop, and it gives a company the chance to inform, educate or instruct employees. Both bilateral and downward communication is important within business. Bilateral communication allows businesses to send messages between people on the same level or position within a company, while downward communication sees messages sent from superiors to subordinates. Both of these communication types have a large role in the workplace.

Effective communication will keep employees well informed and give a business a higher productivity rate. Many companies that carry out staff satisfaction surveys find that employees who are kept up to date with effective communication are more satisfied in their roles. Employees tend to have higher levels of job

---

① indisputable（无可争辩的，无可置疑的）: Beyond dispute or doubt; undeniable.
② mediocre（平庸的，平凡的）: Moderate to inferior in quality; ordinary.

performance when there is a congruence① of individual needs and job characteristics that exists and is communicated well. In turn, a happy and hard working team of employees helps give a business a corporate image that the public will find impressive and appealing.

2. Strong Culture and Weak Culture

Strong culture is said to exist where staff respond to stimulus because of their alignment② to organizational values. In such environments, strong cultures help firms operate like well-oiled machines, cruising along with outstanding execution and perhaps minor tweaking of existing procedures here and there. Conversely, there is weak culture where there is little alignment with organizational values and control must be exercised through extensive procedures and bureaucracy.

Research shows that organizations that foster strong cultures have clear values that give employees a reason to embrace the culture. A "strong" culture may be especially beneficial to firms operating in the service sector since members of these organizations are responsible for delivering the service and for evaluations of important constituents about firms. Research indicates that organizations may derive the following benefits from developing strong and productive cultures:

● Better aligning the company towards achieving its vision, mission, and goals

● High employee's motivation and loyalty

● Increased team cohesiveness among the company's various departments and divisions

● Promoting consistency and encouraging coordination and control within the company

● Shaping employee behavior at work, enabling the organization to be more efficient

3. National Culture and Corporate Culture

National culture is the values and attitudes shared by individuals from a specific country. It shapes behaviors and beliefs. And getting information about a country's cultural differences is difficult. Corporate culture is used to control, coordinate, and integrate company subsidiaries. However, differences in national cultures exist contributing to differences in the views on the management.

---

① congruence（适合，相合性，一致）：Agreement, harmony, conformity, or correspondence.

② alignment（符合，保持一致）：Identification with or matching of the behavior, thoughts, etc. of another person.

Differences between national cultures are deep rooted values of the respective cultures, and these cultural values can shape how people expect companies to be run, and how relationships between leaders and followers should be resulting in differences between the employer and the employee on expectations. The national culture determines the corporate culture, and influences the company's structure and marketing behavior, and its views on the international business partners and contracts.

A question many people have asked is how national and organizational cultures related and which of them is stronger. The answer is "It depends." There is no doubt that the two kinds of culture both exert powerful influences on people. It is anything but rare for employees, especially those of foreign companies, to be facing conflicts between them. A company's culture may be informal while a country's culture could be rather formal. A company may be encouraging and rewarding risk-taking in a country where people are generally risk-averse①, or vice versa.

4. The Importance of Corporate Culture

Research suggests that numerous outcomes have been associated either directly or indirectly with corporate culture. A healthy and robust corporate culture may provide various benefits, including the following:

- Competitive edge derived from innovation and customer service
- Consistent, efficient employee performance
- Team cohesiveness②
- High employee morale
- Strong company alignment towards goal achievement

Although little empirical research exists to support the link between corporate culture and organizational performance, there is little doubt among experts that this relationship exists. Corporate culture can be a factor in the survival or failure of an organization, although this is difficult to prove considering the necessary longitudinal③ analyses are hardly feasible. The sustained superior performance of firms like IBM, Hewlett-Packard, Procter & Gamble, and McDonald's may be, at least partly, a reflection of their organizational cultures.

Corporate culture is reflected in the way people perform tasks, set objectives,

---

① risk-averse （规避风险）: A strong disinclination to take risks.
② cohesiveness （团结，结合在一起）: The state of being connected.
③ longitudinal （纵向的）: Of or relating to lines of longitude.

and administer the necessary resources to achieve objectives. Culture affects the way individuals make decisions, feel, and act in response to the opportunities and threats affecting the organization.

Experts found that job satisfaction was positively associated with the degree to which employees fit into both the overall culture and subculture in which they worked. <u>A perceived mismatch of the organization's culture and what employees felt the culture should be is related to a number of negative consequences including lower job satisfaction, higher job strain, general stress, and turnover intent.</u>

It has been proposed that corporate culture may impact the level of employee's creativity, the strength of employee motivation, and the reporting of unethical behavior, but more research is needed to support these conclusions.

Corporate culture also has an impact on recruitment and retention. Individuals tend to be attracted to and remain engaged in organizations that they perceive to be compatible. Additionally, high turnover① may be a mediating factor in the relationship between culture and organizational performance. Deteriorating company performance and an unhealthy work environment are signs of an overdue cultural assessment.

Exercises

I. Reviewing Questions

Answer the following questions according to the text.

1. What is corporate culture?
2. What are the commitments contained in corporate vision?
3. Give an example of that people in the same organization often share the similar beliefs.
4. Why do many business start ups fail at their first year?
5. How important is learning in the new knowledge economy?
6. What are the two types of communication, and why are they important?
7. What benefits can firms derive from developing strong and productive cultures?
8. How are national and organizational cultures related and which of them is stronger, why?
9. Why is corporate culture important?

---

① turnover(人员流动性): The ratio of the number of workers that have to be replaced in a given time period to the average number of workers.

10. How does corporate culture influence recruitment and retention?

II. Cloze
Read the following passage and fill in the blanks with the words given below. Change the form where necessary.

| loyalty | interest | speeches | adaptive | sort |
| succession | colleagues | cost | elements | capacity |

We can learn a great deal from organizations whose strong and __1__ ownership cultures give them a powerful competitive edge. Here are our top ten lessons: 1. Leadership is critical in codifying and maintaining an organizational purpose, values, and vision. Leaders must set the example by living the __2__ of culture: values, behaviors, measures, and actions. Values are meaningless without the other elements. 2. Like anything worthwhile, culture is something in which you invest. An organization's norms and values aren't formed through __3__ but through actions and team learning. Strong cultures have teeth. They are much more than slogans and empty promises. Some organizations choose to part ways with those who do not manage according to the values and behaviors that other employees embrace. Others accomplish the same objective more positively. 3. Employees at all levels in an organization notice and validate the elements of culture. As owners, they judge every management decision to hire, reward, promote, and fire __4__. Their reactions often come through in comments about subjects such as the "fairness of my boss." The underlying theme in such conversations, though, is the strength and appropriateness of the organization's culture. 4. Organizations with clearly codified cultures enjoy labor __5__ advantages for the following reasons: They often become better places to work. They become well known among prospective employees. The level of ownership—referral rates and ideas for improving the business of existing employees—is often high. The screening process is simplified, because employees tend to refer acquaintances who behave like them. The pool of prospective employees grows. The cost of selecting among many applicants is offset by cost savings as prospective employees __6__ themselves into and out of consideration for jobs. This self-selection process reduces the number of mismatches among new hires. 5. Organizations with clearly codified and enforced cultures enjoy great employee and customer __7__, in large part because they are effective in either altering ineffective behaviors or disengaging from values-challenged employees in a timely manner. 6. An operating strategy based on a strong, effective culture is selective of prospective customers. It also requires the periodic "firing" of customers, as pointed out in our examples of companies like ING Direct, where thousands are fired every month. This strategy is especially important when customers "abuse" employees or make unreasonable demands on them. 7. The result of all this is "the best serving the best," or as Ritz-Carlton's mission states, "Ladies and gentlemen serving ladies and gentlemen." 8. This self-reinforcing source of operating leverage must be managed carefully to make sure that it does not result in the development of dogmatic cults with little ___8___ for change. High-performing organizations periodically revisit and reaffirm their core values and associated behaviors. Further, they often subscribe to some kind of initiative that requires constant benchmarking and searching for best practices both inside and outside the organization. 9. Organizations with strong and adaptive cultures foster effective ___9___ in the leadership ranks. In large part, the culture both prepares successors and eases the transition. 10. Cultures can sour. Among the reasons for this are success itself, the loss of curiosity and ___10___ in change, the triumph of culture over performance, the failure of leaders to reinforce desired behaviors, the breakdown of consistent communication, and leaders who are overcome by their own sense of importance.

III. Translation

1. Beliefs are about how we think things really are, what we think is really true and what we therefore expect as likely consequences that will follow from our behavior. The clearer you are about what you value and believe in, the happier and more effective you will be.

2. Knowledge organizations obtain competitive advantage from continuous learning, both individual and collective. In organizations with a well established knowledge management system, learning by the people within an organization becomes learning by the organization itself. The changes in people's attitudes are reflected in changes in the formal and informal rules that govern the organization's behavior.

3. Communication makes a business grow and develop, and it gives a company the

chance to inform, educate or instruct employees. Both bilateral and downward communication is important within business. Bilateral communication allows businesses to send messages between people on the same level or position within a company, while downward communication sees messages sent from superiors to subordinates. Both of these communication types have a large role in the workplace.

4. However, differences in national cultures exist contributing to differences in the views on the management. Differences between national cultures are deep rooted values of the respective cultures, and these cultural values can shape how people expect companies to be run, and how relationships between leaders and followers should be resulting in differences between the employer and the employee on expectations.

5. A perceived mismatch of the organization's culture and what employees felt the culture should be is related to a number of negative consequences including lower job satisfaction, higher job strain, general stress, and turnover intent.

IV. Case Study

Business Is People

Although he is no longer with us in body, the spirit of Panasonic's founder Konosuke Matsushita（松下幸之助）lives on in his principles, which are widely respected within the company and around the world. Born November 27, 1894, in a small village near Osaka, Japan, Matsushita was the youngest of eight children and enjoyed a comfortable early childhood. His fortunes changed when his father lost property, and at the age of nine he was forced to venture alone to take a job in the big city. A few years later when Matsushita was considering leaving an apprenticeship at a bicycle shop to pursue an education, his father gave him the advice that would shape the course of his future: "The skills you are learning will ensure your future. Succeed as an entrepreneur, and you can hire people who have an education."

In the belief that electricity would become the wave of the future, Matsushita followed his instincts and applied for a job at the Osaka Electric Light Company. Remembering his father's advice about the advantages of being an entrepreneur, he left the security of his well-paid job in 1917 to set up his own small manufacturing company. Producing an improved electrical socket he had designed and built in his spare time, he quickly earned the company a reputation for high quality at low prices.

During a visit to a popular Shinto shrine, Matsushita was struck by the complementary roles religion and business can play in life. Shortly after his return he made an announcement that was to guide the company for decades to come, "Our mission as a manufacturer is to create material abundance by providing goods as plentifully and inexpensively as tap water. This is how we can banish poverty, bring happiness to people's lives, and make this world a better place."

"Business is people," was one of his favorite sayings. Matsushita's work embodied this ideology and he quickly won the support of his employees by making it clear that he placed a high priority on their interests. During a presentation on his management philosophy at an international management conference in New York, his emphasis on management concepts, fair competition, coexistence and mutual prosperity received a warm response from everyone in attendance.

Today Panasonic still embraces the principles from Matsushita and is turning their focusd toward bettering life for people with disabilities by addressing accessibility issues in many of their product lines. "One of the unique aspects of our copiers is that Panasonic was the first and remains one of the few companies to offer copiers that are accessible to wheelchair users," notes Paul Wharton, National Marketing Manager for Panasonic Document Imaging Company.

Eugene Seagriff, Product Accessibility Manager, Panasonic Technologies, Inc. adds, "This year we have two phones featuring our new Voice Enhancer technology. The phone line only transmits frequencies from about 300 to 3000 Hz. Actual speech has a much wider frequency range. Voice Enhancer artificially recreates the full speech frequency range from the incoming signal, making the incoming caller's speech easier to understand. Next year Voice Enhancer will be on a wide variety of Panasonic phones."

(The text is excerpted from www. abilitymagazine.com)

Questions for discussion:
1. How could Matsushita receive respect from people all over the world?
2. Compared with the corporate culture "business is people," what do you think of the corporate culture in our country?
3. If you were the CEO of Panasonic, how would you develop the corporate

culture? Describe your leadership style.

V. Supplementary Reading

Apple's Corporate Culture: 10 Lessons for Staying in Steve Jobs' Good Graces

The announcement that Apple Senior Vice President Mark Papermaster left Apple sent shockwaves through the tech industry. Papermaster came to Apple from IBM after the companies waged a short-lived battle over exactly when he could start working at the hardware company.

After that, he took over the iPhone and iPod Touch and, at least to outsiders, did a fine job of delivering products that consumers wanted. His departure from Apple was very much a surprise.

But it didn't take long for some details and speculation about the reasons for Papermaster's departure from anonymous sources to make their way into news reports. One claim made by the Wall Street Journal stood out. The publication said that its sources claimed Papermaster didn't match well with Apple's corporate culture. As those problems persisted, Steve Jobs started losing faith in his ability to lead the mobile devices division.

Admittedly, the report has not been confirmed by Apple or Papermaster, so it's impossible to say why he really left. But the source's claim of cultural incompatibility seems to be something that some employees suffer from at Apple. And that's unfortunate because Jobs has created one of the most distinct corporate cultures in the business. Here is what makes Apple's corporate culture so unique.

1. Focus on Design

The first thing that every employee must remember about Apple is that the company cares more about the design of products than any other firm in the market. Unlike Microsoft, which has historically done a poor job of creating aesthetically pleasing products, Apple really gets design. It understands what consumers want, it knows how to meet those desires, and it sets out to beat any and all expectations. It's not always easy, but Apple seems to get it right every time.

2. Believe in Jobs

Apple is an interesting firm. Its corporate culture extends beyond its employees to its consumers. So, what it expects from its employees, it also expects from its customers. One of the most important things it expects is for both stakeholders to believe in Steve Jobs. Over the past decade, Jobs has been Apple's savior. He has helped the company revive its aging business model, innovate beyond all expectations and deliver some of the better products on the market. Sometimes, that belief in Jobs can go too far, as evidenced by the most recent iPhone antenna debacle, but for the most part, believing in Steve Jobs has been good for Apple and good for both employees and consumers.

3. Forget Everything That Came Before It

When employees come to Apple, they're expected to immediately do one thing: forget everything they ever knew about the technology world. Apple does everything differently. Whether it's the design of products, how it goes about devising ideas for new products or simply the way it carries itself, everything is different at Apple. To pretend like something is similar to a past is a mistake that could cause more trouble than it's worth. Apple is different.

4. Believe Apple Is Better Than All Others

Apple has an ego unlike any other company in the space. Whereas Microsoft always believes that the other shoe is about to drop, Apple believes that it can stop the shoe from ever falling. Part of that is due to Steve Jobs' ego. He believes that his company is the best in the world and it should carry itself that way. Apple haters can't stand that, but it has become a call to arms for all of the company's lovers and employees.

5. Take Flaws to Heart

Because of its ego, Apple takes it to heart when it hears people criticize its products. In true Apple fashion, it responds with a level of venom that most other companies in the industry can't muster. After all, what other firm in the space could have taken an antenna issue as bad as the iPhone 4s and turned it on the competition without thinking twice? Apple doesn't like being told that it's wrong. And both its employees and its fans are expected to dislike it, as well.

6. Never Admit Defeat

Part of Apple's allure is its desire to never admit defeat. No matter how badly its products are getting beaten, the company seems to find a way to pull itself out of the fire with one last shot to save the day. Nowhere is that more evident than in the computing market. With the right strategies, Steve Jobs turned things around after making more than a few controversial (and risky) decisions that paid off. Today, Apple is setting record profits. There is nothing that Steve Jobs hates more than to see a competitor beat his company.

7. Remember Attention to Detail

If Apple understands anything, it's that attention to detail pays off in the long run. Google's Android operating system, for example, might be selling well, but after using the software for a while and comparing it to iOS, most consumers will find that it lacks some of the flashiness of iOS. That doesn't make it any less useful—in fact, it's arguably just as useful as iOS—but it does leave some consumers wondering why Google didn't go the extra mile. In most cases, Apple goes that extra mile. It has become a staple of the company's vision. And it's something that it expects from its employees.

8. Only Steve Jobs Is Indispensable

If Papermaster's departure is any indication of how Apple is run, it's clear that only Steve Jobs is indispensable. What other company, cultural differences or not, would be willing to see the person who has helped the world's most recognizable smartphone succeed beyond most expectations leave without any remorse? It goes back to Steve Jobs' ego. He ostensibly believes that he is the key to Apple's success. Apple lovers and some employees might agree, but Papermaster was also integral to the success of the iPhone. Who Apple will get to run the iPhone team as effectively as Papermaster did is anyone's guess. But perhaps it doesn't matter. Apple has proved once again that only Steve Jobs' job is safe at the company.

9. Secrecy Reigns Supreme

A discussion on Apple's corporate culture isn't complete without mentioning its penchant for secrecy. Unlike so many other tech firms in the space, Apple's upcoming updates rarely get leaked. In fact, it took a mistake by one employee for the world to find out about the iPhone 4 before it was announced. Perhaps that's why Apple has had a long-standing rule that secrecy will govern success at the company. People who leak the firm's secrets, even accidentally, will almost certainly find themselves being escorted out the front door by security.

10. Domination Is Everything

Steve Jobs has one goal in mind when it comes to technology: domination. He doesn't simply want to beat the competition in all the market his company competes in, he wants to destroy them. He wants to make it clear to the world that his company can best them all. Steve Jobs has something to prove to the competition, customers and just about everyone else. And he expects his staff to help him achieve that. If they don't, they will find themselves working at Microsoft in no time.

Reading Comprehension

Choose the best answers to the following questions.

1. After Papermaster came to Apple from IBM, he took over _____.
   A. the iPhone, iPod Touch and iPad
   B. the iPhone and iPod Touch
   C. the iPhone and iPad
   D. the iPod Touch and iPad

2. The corporate culture most expects from _____.
   A. the researchers
   B. the employees and the customers
   C. the customers and stakeholders
   D. Steve Jobs

3. When employees come to Apple, what are they expected to do immediately?
   A. Get themselves trained in a different way
   B. Know the design of Apple products and how it goes about devising ideas for new products
   C. Forget everything they ever knew about the technology world
   D. Believe Apple is better than all others

4. When comparing Google's Android operating system to iOS, _____.
   A. most people will find that it more useful with better functions
   B. most people will find that it lacks some of the flashiness of iOS
   C. most people will argue that it is as useful as iOS
   D. most people tend to use it because it's cheaper

5. Which one below is not the reason for the unique Apple's corporate culture?

Unit 8 Corporate Culture 133

A. Believe Apple is better than all others
B. Never admit defeat
C. Focus on design
D. Advanced technology

VI. Assignment

1. Suppose you are the manager of a large transnational company whose corporate culture is very different from the local culture. And most of your employees are local people. How would you deal with the conflict of the corporate culture and national culture?
2. Interview several employees in different firms and ask about their corporate cultures, then make a 5-minute presentation in your class.

Unit 9

Production and Product

 Learning Objectives

After learning this unit, you should be able to:
1. Define production and product.
2. Know the factors of production.
3. Understand the types of products.
4. List the steps in the new product development process.
5. Describe the product life cycle.

 Lead-in

In economics, production means the creation or manufacture for sale of goods and services with exchange value. For a manufacturing company, production is obviously one of the four key functions, along with human resources, marketing and finance. Products are the result of the production process. The production of the right kind of products and good design of the products are crucial for the success of an organization.

Warm-up Questions/Discussion:
1. What kinds of product do we use everyday? Give some examples.
2. What kinds of factor do you think are necessary in the production process?
3. Why did many products become less popular and at last withdraw from the market?

Production and Product[①]

Production is the act of creating output, a good or service which has value and contributes to the utility[②] of individuals. The act may or may not include factors of production other than labor. Any effort directed toward the realization of a desired product or service is a "productive" effort and the performance of such act is production.

In general, the product is defined as "a thing produced by labor or effort" or the "result of an act or a process." In economics and commerce, products belong to a broader category of goods. In marketing, a product is anything that can be offered to a market and might satisfy a want or need. In retailing, products are called merchandise. In manufacturing, products are purchased as raw materials and sold as finished goods. Commodities[③] are usually raw materials such as metals and agricultural products, but a commodity can also be anything widely available in the open market. In project management, products are the formal definition of the project deliverables that make up or contribute to delivering the objectives of the project. In insurance, the policies are considered products offered for sale by the insurance company that created the contract.

1. Factors of Production

Choices concerning what goods and services to produce are choices about an economy's use of its factors of production, the resources available to it for the production of goods and services. The value, or satisfaction, that people derive from the goods and services they consume and the activities they pursue are called utility. Ultimately, then, an economy's factors of production create utility; they serve the interests of people.

The factors of production in an economy are its labor, capital, and natural resources. Labor is the human effort that can be applied to the production of goods and services. People who are employed or would like to be are considered part of the labor available to the economy. Capital is a factor of production that has been produced for use in the production of other goods and services. Office buildings,

---

① The text is excerpted from www.web-books.com, www.morebusiness.com and www.altiusdirectory.com.
② utility (效用): The quality or condition of being useful; usefulness.
③ commodity (商品，货物): An article of trade or commerce, especially an agricultural or mining product that can be processed and resold.

machinery, and tools are examples of capital. Natural resources are the resources of nature that can be used for the production of goods and services.

In this section, we will take a closer look at the factors of production we use to produce the goods and services we consume. The three basic building blocks of labor, capital, and natural resources may be used in different ways to produce different goods and services, but they still lie at the core of production. We will also look at the roles played by technology and entrepreneurs in putting these factors of production to work. As economists began to grapple with the problems of scarcity①, choice, and opportunity cost two centuries ago, they focused on these concepts, just as they are likely to do two centuries hence.

(1) Labor

Labor is human effort that can be applied to production. People who work to repair tires, pilot airplanes, teach children, or enforce laws are all part of the economy's labor. People who would like to work but have not found employment—who are unemployed—are also considered part of the labor available to the economy.

In some contexts, it is useful to distinguish two forms of labor. The first is the human equivalent of a natural resource. It is the natural ability an untrained, uneducated person brings to a particular production process. But most workers bring far more. The skills a worker has as a result of education, training, or experience that can be used in production are called human capital. Students who are attending a college or university are acquiring human capital. Workers who are gaining skills through experience or through training are acquiring human capital. Children who are learning to read are acquiring human capital.

The amount of labor available to an economy can be increased in two ways. One is to increase the total quantity of labor, either by increasing the number of people available to work or by increasing the average number of hours of work per week. The other is to increase the amount of human capital possessed by workers.

(2) Capital

Long ago, when the first human beings walked the earth, they produced food by picking leaves or fruit off a plant or by catching an animal and eating it. We know that very early on, however, they began shaping stones into tools, apparently for use in butchering② animals. Those tools were the first capital because they were produced for use in producing other goods—food and clothing.

---

① scarcity（缺乏，不足）：Insufficiency of amount or supply; shortage.
② butcher（屠宰牲口）：To slaughter or prepare (animals) for market.

Modern versions of the first stone tools include saws, meat cleavers, hooks, and grinders; all are used in butchering animals. Tools such as hammers, screwdrivers, and wrenches are also used as capital. Transportation equipment, such as cars and trucks, is capital. Facilities such as roads, bridges, ports, and airports are capital. Buildings, too, are capital; they help us to produce goods and services.

Capital does not consist solely of physical objects. The score for a new symphony① is capital because it will be used to produce concerts. Computer software used by business firms or government agencies to produce goods and services is capital. Capital may thus include physical goods and intellectual discoveries. Any resource is capital if it satisfies two criteria: Firstly, the resource must have been produced. Secondly, the resource can be used to produce other goods and services.

One thing that is not considered capital is money. A firm cannot use money directly to produce other goods, so money does not satisfy the second criterion for capital. Firms can, however, use money to acquire capital. Money is a form of financial capital. Financial capital includes money and other "paper" assets (such as stocks and bonds②) that represent claims on future payments. These financial assets are not capital, but they can be used directly or indirectly to purchase factors of production or goods and services.

(3) Natural resources

There are two essential characteristics of natural resources. The first is that they are found in nature—that no human effort has been used to make or alter them. The second is that they can be used for the production of goods and services. That requires knowledge; we must know how to use the things we find in nature before they become resources.

For example, oil in the ground is a natural resource because it is found (not manufactured) and can be used to produce goods and services. However, 250 years ago oil was a nuisance③, not a natural resource. In the eighteenth century Pennsylvania farmers who found oil oozing up through their soil were dismayed, not delighted. No one knew what could be done with the oil. It was not until the mid-nineteenth century that a method was found for refining oil into kerosene④ that

---

① symphony（交响乐）: An extended piece in three or more movements for symphony orchestra.
② bond（债券）: A certificate of debt issued in order to raise funds.
③ nuisance（公害）: A person or thing that causes annoyance or bother.
④ kerosene（煤油）: A thin oil distilled from petroleum or shale oil, used as a fuel for heating and cooking, in lamps, and as a denaturant for alcohol. Also called coal oil, lamp oil.

could be used to generate energy, transforming oil into a natural resource. Oil is now used to make all sorts of things, including clothing, drugs, gasoline, and plastic. It became a natural resource because people discovered and implemented a way to use it.

Defining something as a natural resource only if it can be used to produce goods and services does not mean that a tree has value only for its wood or that a mountain has value only for its minerals. If people gain utility from the existence of a beautiful wilderness area, then that wilderness provides a service. The wilderness is thus a natural resource.

The natural resources available to us can be expanded in three ways. One is the discovery of new natural resources, such as the discovery of a deposit of ore containing titanium[①]. The second is the discovery of new uses for resources, as happened when new techniques allowed oil to be put to productive use or sand to be used in manufacturing computer chips. The third is the discovery of new ways to extract natural resources in order to use them. New methods of discovering and mapping oil deposits have increased the world's supply of this important natural resource.

(4) Technology and the entrepreneur

Goods and services are produced using the factors of production available to the economy. Two things play a crucial role in putting these factors of production to work. The first is technology, the knowledge that can be applied to the production of goods and services. The second is an individual who plays a key role in a market economy: the entrepreneur. An entrepreneur is a person who, operating within the context of a market economy, seeks to earn profits by finding new ways to organize factors of production. In non-market economies the role of the entrepreneur is played by bureaucrats[②] and other decision makers who respond to incentives other than profit to guide their choices about resource allocation decisions.

2. Types of Products

Products generally fall into two categories: consumer products and industrial products.

---

① titanium（钛）: A strong, low-density, highly corrosion-resistant, lustrous white metallic element that occurs widely in igneous rocks and is used to alloy aircraft metals for low weight, strength, and high-temperature stability.

② bureaucrat（官僚）: An official who is rigidly devoted to the details of administrative procedure.

(1) Consumer products

A consumer product is generally any tangible personal property for sale and is used for personal, family, household or non-business purposes. It can be further classified into three subcategories: convenience goods, shopping goods, specialty goods.

Convenience goods are easily available to consumer, without any extra effort. Mostly, convenience goods come in the category of nondurable goods such as fast foods, confectionaries①, and cigarettes, with low value. The goods are mostly sold by wholesalers to make them available to the consumers in good volume.

When buying shopping goods, consumers often do a lot of selection and comparison based on various parameters such as cost, brand, style, comfort etc., before buying an item. Shopping goods are costlier than convenience goods and are durable nature. Companies usually set up their shops and show rooms in active shopping area to attract customer's attention to shopping goods.

Goods which are very unique, unusual, and luxurious in nature are called specialty goods. Specialty goods are mostly purchased by upper-class of society as they are expensive in nature. The goods don't come under the category of necessity rather they are purchased on the basis of personal preference or desire. Brand name and unique and special features of an item are major attributes which attract customer in buying them.

(2) Industrial products

Sometimes referred to as intermediate or intermediary goods, industrial goods are any types of products that are used in the production of other goods. This can include a wide range of raw materials, as well as various components that are eventually assembled to produce a finished product. Machinery used in the production process is also often classified as an industrial good.

One of the more common types of industrial goods is the raw materials used in the creation of various products. These raw materials undergo some type of fashioning or transformation in preparation for use in the manufacturing of different kinds of goods and services. At times, these raw materials are leftovers② from the creation of other products, as with the remnants of oil sludge that are used to create various types of artificial fibers. Those fibers are eventually used to manufacture upholstery for furnishings, car seats, and various other textile products.

---

① confectionary (糕点糖果总称): Candies and other confections considered as a group.
② leftover (残余物): A remnant or an unused portion.

In addition to raw materials, industrial goods also include the resources used in the actual production process. For example, hammers, drills, screwdrivers, and other types of tools would be considered industrial goods, since they are used in the process of assembling parts for the creation of different products. In like manner, machinery and equipment that are used in the manufacturing process would also be considered industrial goods. This would include heavy equipment such as molds for plastics and metals, heating and cooling chambers, and even machines used to automate the packing process for the finished goods.

3. New Product Development Process

Today's businesses offer customers many choices. If you sell **widgets**① and so do 1,000 other people, it's hard to get your name out there. Price can be a business killer to compete on, because someone is always able to do it cheaper than you. So what's the solution? Develop new products is the solution. The following are the steps businesses often take in new product development:

(1) Idea generation

Use creative idea starters like **brainstorming**② to help you find the ideas you're looking for. Try to combine two products you have into a single package or perhaps a product and a service, something to set your offering apart from others. If you can't think of anything, try considering a partnership or joint venture with another company.

(2) Screening

Analyze the potential success by asking some of your customers what they think. You don't need to do anything formal, just do some informal polling with the people who come in the door or through your opt in newsletter. Give them a couple of different options and ask them which one they'd buy if they were in the market for whatever you are selling.

(3) Development

If you're packaging products or services together that already exist, the job is mostly done for you. However, you will still want to consider branding them as your own items. A simple example is the combination of 3 simple products (a burger, fries, and soft drink) into another product that is separately branded (a McDonald's Happy Meal).

---

① widget（作附件用的小机械）：A small mechanical device or control.
② brainstorming（集体研讨，头脑风暴法）：A method of shared problem solving in which all members of a group spontaneously contribute ideas.

(4) Testing

Although you did take a poll, polls are not always accurate. After all, you're not asking people to actually pony up with any money! This is where the rubber meets the road and you need to find out if people are actually willing to buy your new and improved product. Be ready to make instant changes, if necessary, including raising or lowering the price or offering other incentives to move the product.

(5) Marketing

After the testing stage has helped you refine your product a little more, you can move on to actively marketing your new product on a full scale, hopefully with noticeable improvements in sales.

4. Product Life Cycle

The product life cycle explains the product evolution stages. There are generally four stages in product life cycle (see graphic 1): market introduction, market growth, market maturity, and market decline.

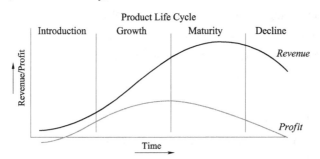

Graphic 1　Product Life Cycle

(1) Market introduction

During this stage the product has been introduced for a first time by using above average advertising and promotional investments by the company to introduce the new product to the target market. The demand for the new product has to be created and target customers are attracted to try the new product. Generally during the market introduction stage the revenues are very low and the investments are very high. Most businesses do not generate any profits during this stage but use marketing and sales strategies and tactics to successfully position the new product or service in the marketplace and hopefully generate profits in the next product life cycle stages.

(2) Market growth

During this stage revenues and profit increase. The target market is already familiar with the product and customers already purchase the product. More competitors try to enter this business as they see the positive market trend development and increased profits generated by the companies. Due to economies of scale the overall cost of doing business is decreasing and the product profitability increases.

(3) Market maturity

During this stage market is already saturated① with the product and competition is very strong. <u>The growth in revenues starts to decline and profitability decreases as competitors start to compete more on price and less through product differentiation since most of the competitors can offer the same product. At the same time strong competition requires more marketing and sales investments to keep the market share which increases the overall cost of doing business.</u>

The set of business metrics should be simplified as much as possible. The bottom-line is to improve visibility and save time for decision makers who will use the report continuously.

(4) Market decline

During this stage both revenues and profits decline. New products are introduced in the marketplace and replace the old products. Many competitors will not be profitable and they will withdraw from the market.

Exercises

I. Reviewing Questions

Answer the following questions according to the text.

1. What is production and product?
2. What are the two forms of labor?
3. Is money considered capital? Why?
4. What are the essential characteristics of natural resources?
5. Who will play the role of the entrepreneur in non-market economies?
6. What are the three subcategories of consumer products?
7. What are industrial products?
8. How many steps should be taken in the new product process? What are they?
9. Could any business generate profits during the market introduction stage? Why?
10. What do most competitors do when both revenues and profits decline?

---

① saturate（使饱和）: To cause (a substance) to unite with the greatest possible amount of another substance.

II. Cloze
Read the following passage and fill in the blanks with the words given below. Change the form where necessary.

share	abandon	fluctuations	responding	maturity
specifics	release	saturated	design	distinct

Product life cycle (PLC) is the theory that recognizes four separate developmental stages in the life span of a product, with each stage characterized by its own ___1___ marketing opportunities and restraints. The theory of a product life cycle was first introduced in the 1950s to explain the expected life cycle of a typical product from ___2___ to obsolescence. The advantage of the product life cycle concept is that it provides a basic structure that allows you to see where you are, and what lies ahead. There are four components to the cycle: introduction, growth, ___3___ and decline.

The first component is fairly self-explanatory; when a new product is introduced, market gain tends to be very slight, and it is almost impossible to spot any kind of emerging patterns in demand. Depending on how you launch the product, marketing costs may be high, and it is unlikely that there are any profits as such. After the creation and subsequent ___4___ of your product, this often boils down to gritting your teeth and waiting. If this stage doesn't lead into the next, then it may be time to jump ship.

The growth stage exhibits a rapid increase in both sales and profits, and this is the time to try and increase your product's market ___5___. By now you should be seeing where your demand is coming from, and which of your efforts are worth spending time and energy on. With a little bit of luck, you might even have knocked some of the competition out of the way too!

As more and more competitors come into the market, the product enters into the third stage in which the product becomes "mature" and the market gets ___6___. Price wars often break out. The total sales volume begins to fall, and the profits start to shrink.

The final stage in the life cycle is the decline. This doesn't necessarily mean that it's time to ___7___ your product altogether, but rather that the introduction of new strategies might be in order. These could include new versions, new distribution methods, price reductions, in short anything that will inject a little life into the cycle.

Each of the four stages has their own characteristics, and each is open to different strategies being implemented. However, for much this stage will prove to be the critical one; many wait until this period before acting, and it is the only stage where some sort of action is critical. Theoretically the product life-cycle is a smooth and elegant curve; in reality there are constant short-term ___8___ due to external factors.

The advantages of the product life cycle concept speak for themselves. Once you've applied this model to your product, there are an unlimited number of options and strategies that may be implemented, according to the ___9___ of your product and its current stage in the life cycle. For example, you may wish to consider product life cycle acceleration strategies, or at the very least recognize where you are, and what lies ahead. Before ___10___ to any of the stage characteristics, don't forget to consider the external factors, particularly in response to the decline phase.

III. Translation

1. The skills a worker has as a result of education, training, or experience that can be used in production are called human capital. Students who are attending a college or university are acquiring human capital. Workers who are gaining skills through experience or through training are acquiring human capital. Children who are learning to read are acquiring human capital.

2. In the eighteenth century Pennsylvania farmers who found oil oozing up through their soil were dismayed, not delighted. No one knew what could be done with the oil. It was not until the mid-nineteenth century that a method was found for refining oil into kerosene that could be used to generate energy, transforming oil into a natural resource.

3. Specialty goods are mostly purchased by upper-class of society as they are expensive in nature. The goods don't come under the category of necessity rather they are purchased on the basis of personal preference or desire. Brand name and unique and special features of an item are major attributes which attract customer in buying them.

4. In like manner, machinery and equipment that are used in the manufacturing

process would also be considered industrial goods. This would include heavy equipment such as molds for plastics and metals, heating and cooling chambers, and even machines used to automate the packing process for the finished goods.

5. The growth in revenues starts to decline and profitability decreases as competitors start to compete more on price and less through product differentiation since most of the competitors can offer the same product. At the same time strong competition requires more marketing and sales investments to keep the market share which increases the overall cost of doing business.

IV. Case Study

Technology Cuts Costs, Boosts Productivity and Profits

Technology can be considered as an abstract force in the economy. It is not invisible to the 130 people who work on a Shell Oil Company oil rig called Mars, located in the deep waters of the Gulf of Mexico, about 160 miles southwest of Pensacola, Florida. The name Mars reflects its otherworld appearance—it extends 300 feet above the water's surface and has steel tendons that reach 3,000 feet to the floor of the gulf. This facility would not exist if it were not for the development of better oil discovery methods that include three-dimensional seismic mapping techniques, satellites that locate oil from space, and drills that can make turns as drilling foremen steer them by monitoring them on computer screens from the comfort of Mars. "We don't hit as many dry holes," commented Shell manager Miles Barrett. As a result of these new technologies, over the past two decades, the cost of discovering a barrel of oil dropped from $20 to under $5. And the technologies continue to improve. Three-dimensional surveys are being replaced with four-dimensional ones that allow geologists to see how the oil fields change over time.

The Mars project was destroyed by Hurricane Katrina in 2005. Royal Dutch Shell completed repairs in 2006—at a cost of $200 million. But, the facility is again pumping 130,000 barrels of oil per day and 150 million cubic feet of natural gas—the energy equivalent of an additional 26,000 barrels of oil.

Technology is doing more than helping energy companies track oil deposits. It is changing the way soft drinks and other grocery items are delivered to retail stores. For example, when a PepsiCo delivery driver arrives at a Seven-Eleven, the driver keys into a handheld computer the inventory of soft drinks, chips, and other PepsiCo products. The information is transmitted to a main computer at the warehouse that begins processing the next order for that store. The result is that the driver can visit more stores in a day and PepsiCo can cover a given territory with fewer drivers and trucks.

New technology is even helping to produce more milk from cows. Ed Larsen, who owns a 1,200-cow dairy farm in Wisconsin, never gets up before dawn to milk the cows, the way he did as a boy. Rather, the cows are hooked up to electronic milkers. Computers measure each cow's output, and cows producing little milk are sent to a "hospital wing" for treatment. With the help of such technology, as well as better feed, today's dairy cows produce 50% more milk than did cows 20 years ago. Even though the number of dairy cows in the United States in the last 20 years has fallen 17%, milk output has increased 25%.

Who benefits from technological progress? Consumers gain from lower prices and better service. Workers gain: Their greater abilities to produce goods and services translates into higher wages. And firms gain: Lower production costs mean higher profits. Of course, some people lose as technology advances. Some jobs are eliminated, and some firms find their services are no longer needed. One can argue about whether particular technological changes have improved our lives, but they have clearly made—and will continue to make—them far different.

(The text is excerpted from www.web-books.com/eLibrary)

Questions for discussion:
1. According to the text, how did technology help develop the project Mars?
2. Thanks to the technology, cows can produce more milk than they did before. Please give another example like this.
3. In your opinion, who benefits most from technological progress? Why?

V. Supplementary Reading

This Is how Apple's Top Secret Product Development Process Works

Many aspects of Apple's product development process have long been shrouded in mystery. The process is discussed in a new book *Inside Apple: How America's Most Admired–and Secretive–Company Really Works*, by Adam Lashinsky, which is out now. The book talks about a variety of different aspects of Apple as a company; its philosophy, its hiring process and its legendary secrecy.

But Apple's product process has held a strong fascination for many over the years as it defies long-held conventions about how it should work for companies as large as it is. While some of these points have been revealed before, there is much here that is new to me. Lashinsky's compact tome, which is fantastic, goes into detail on every aspect of the process and is well worth a read.

This is the framework on which every Apple product development is hung:

Every Product at Apple Starts with Design

Designers are treated like royalty at Apple, where the entire product conforms to their visions. This is polar opposite of the way it works at other companies. Instead of the design being beholden to the manufacturing, finance or manufacturing departments, these all conform to the will of the design department headed by Jony Ive.

Designers at Apple have literally no contact with the finance departments at all and are considered to be unlimited in terms of the costs or manufacturing practicality of the materials used. The Industrial Design studio is the womb of all Apple products. It is where they are first generated and it is only accessible to a small number of Apple employees including Jonathan Ive.

A Start-up Is Formed

Once a new product has been decided on, a team is organized and segregated from the rest of the company by secrecy agreements and sometimes physical barriers. Sections of the building may be locked or cordoned off to make room for the teams working on a sensitive new project. This effectively creates a "start-up" inside the company that is only responsible to the executive team, freeing them from the reporting structure of a big company.

Apple New Product Process (ANPP)

Once the design of the product has begun, the ANPP is put into action. This is a document that sets out every step in the development process of a product in detail. It's not an original Apple concept but was first applied at the company during the development of the Macintosh. It maps out the stages of the creation, which is responsible for completion, who will work on each stage and when they will be completed.

Products Are Reviewed Every Monday

The ET (Executive Team) meets every Monday to go over every product that the company has in process. It is able to accomplish this because Apple has so few products in production at any given time. Any that do not get a review are rolled over to the next review Monday. This means that no product is ever more than two-weeks away from a key decision being made.

The EPM Mafia

Once a product begins production, two responsible people are enlisted to bring it to fruition. The engineering program manager (EPM) and the global supply manager (GSM), the former has absolute control of the product process and is so powerful that it is referred to as the "EPM mafia." Both of these positions are held by executives that spend most of their time in China overseeing the production process. The supply manager and program manager collaborate, but not without tension, always making decisions based on "what is best for the product."

Once a Product Is Done, It Is Designed, Built and Tested Again

At times there are leaks that display versions of a product like the iPhone that we never see released. Many times these leaks come from China, where a factory worker has been paid to hand off a prototype to a blogger or journalist. It turns out that once Apple is done building a product, it redesigns the product and sends it through the manufacturing process again, explaining the various versions we may see leaked. This is a 4-6 week process that ends with a gathering of responsible Apple employees at the factory.

The EPM then takes the beta device back to Cupertino for examination and comments, hopping right back on a plane to China to oversee the next iteration of the product. This means that many versions of any given device have been completed, not just partially prototyped. This is an insanely expensive way of building a new product, but it is the standard at Apple.

The Packaging Room

A room in the Marketing building is completely dedicated to device packaging. The security here is matched only by the sections of the building dedicated to new products and design. At one point before a new iPod was launched there was an employee who spent hours every day for months simply opening the hundreds of box prototypes within in order to experience and refine the unboxing process.

The Launch Is Controlled by The Rules of The Road

An action plan for the product launch is generated, called the Rules of the Road. It's a top secret document that lists every significant milestone of a product's development up until launch. Each milestone is annotated with a DRI (directly responsible individual) that is in charge of making that item happen. Losing or revealing this document to the wrong people results in an immediate firing, as noted in the document itself.

As you can see from the breakdown, Apple often makes decisions that make the process more expensive and less efficient in order to produce a seriously better product. These are things that shouldn't pay nearly the dividends they do, but consistently fail to disappoint. Many companies are too complex, or too hidebound in the traditional way of doing things, to take on many, if any, aspects of Apple's process. Still, there is an alluring simplicity to Apple's accountability schemes and its devotion to "good products first." And there is, of course, the massive financial success of the company over the past 10 years.

This product development process is just a fraction of the information revealed in Lashinsky's book, which is available today in a variety of formats. If you're a student of Apple or of electronics manufacturing at large then it should be added to your reading list post-haste.

(The text is excerpted from thenextweb.com)

Reading Comprehension
Choose the best answers to the following questions.
1. The book *How America's Most Admired–and Secretive–Company Really Works*, written by Adam Lashinsky, talks about a variety of different aspects except _____.
   A. Apple's legendary secrecy
   B. Apple's marketing strategies
   C. Apple's philosophy
   D. Apple as a company
2. Designers at Apple _____.
   A. don't have to work with colleagues in the finance departments
   B. sometimes are limited in terms of the costs or manufacturing practicality of the materials used
   C. don't have to care about the money used in design
   D. have lots of contact with the finance departments
3. Which is true about products in Apple?
   A. The ANPP is put into action right after the design of the product is finished.
   B. No product is ever more than two-weeks away from a key decision being made.

C. Products are reviewed every other Monday.

D. Once a product is done, it is designed, built and tested again.

4. The room in the Marketing building is _____.

   A. completely dedicated to device packaging

   B. controlled by the sales manager

   C. sometimes used as resting room for the staff

   D. mostly used to device packaging.

5. Which one below is not mentioned in the framework of Apple product development?

   A. Apple often makes decisions that make the process more expensive and less efficient in order to produce a seriously better product.

   B. Apple is done building a product, it redesigns the product and sends it through the manufacturing process again, explaining the various versions we may see leaked.

   C. The ET (Executive Team) meets everyday to go over every product that the company has in process.

   D. Once a new product has been decided on, a team is organized and segregated from the rest of the company by secrecy agreements and sometimes physical barriers.

VI. Assignment

1. You are a product manager in a firm that manufactures toys. The branded toy line is five years old and the profit is less and less. Propose some strategies based on the brand's current product life-cycle position.

2. Form small groups and generate ideas for a new consumer product that satisfies an existing need but does not currently exist. Choose the one idea that you think is best.

Unit 10

Marketing

Learning Objectives

After learning this unit, you should be able to:
1. Define marketing correctly.
2. Understand the functions of marketing.
3. List the Seven Ps of the marketing mix.
4. Know the three key elements to the marketing environment.
5. Describe the process of market segmentation, targeting and positioning.

Lead-in

Marketing is the wide range of activities involved in making sure that you're continuing to meet the needs of your customers and are getting appropriate value in return. Marketing mix generally falls into the seven controllable categories (Seven Ps): product, price, promotion, place, people, process, and physical evidence. Marketing strategy decisions include market segmentation, targeting and positioning.

Warm-up Questions/Discussion:
1. What do you know about marketing? Could you give some examples of successful marketing?
2. In your opinion, how can a product become famous in the fierce competition?
3. If you were a manager of a small company, what strategies would you take to expand your market share?

Marketing[1]

1. Definition of Marketing

Marketing involves selling products and services, but that doesn't mean marketing is limited to sales activities. The American Marketing Association defines marketing as "the activity, set of institutions, and processes for creating, communicating, delivering, and exchanging offerings that have value for customers, clients, partners, and society at large."

In some ways marketing is as old as civilization itself. You may have seen films based in ancient Greece or Rome with images of bustling[2] market stalls and traders actively engaged in persuasive communications. Of course these traders would not have called their activities marketing and their activities may seem far removed from someone ordering airline tickets via a website.

The concept of marketing that we now see has more to do with developments during the industrial revolution of the 18th and 19th centuries. This was a period of rapid social change driven by technological and scientific innovation. One result was that for the first time the production of goods was separated from their consumption. Mass production, developing transport infrastructure and growing mass media meant that producers needed to, and could develop more sophisticated[3] ways of managing the distribution of goods.

(1) The production orientation era

For much of the industrial revolution, goods were generally scarce and producers could sell pretty much all that they could produce, as long as people could afford to buy them. Their focus was therefore on production and distribution at the lowest possible cost and issues considered by marketing management (for example, reducing distribution costs, opening new markets).

(2) The sales orientation era

From the start of the twentieth century to the period following the Second World War (although the development was interrupted by the wars) competition grew and the focus of marketing turned to selling. Communications, advertising and branding started to become more important as companies needed to sell the increasing outputs of production in an increasingly crowded market. Marketing was

---

[1] The text is excerpted from www.johnmossmarketing.com, www.gb3group.com and www.quickmba.com.
[2] bustling (熙熙攘攘的，忙碌的): Being full of energetic and noisy activity.
[3] sophisticated (精细的，复杂的): (of machines, methods, etc.) Being complex and refined.

therefore still a "slave" to production, but focused on distribution, communication and persuading customers that one manufacturer's goods were better than another's.

(3) The marketing orientation era

From the 1960s onwards, most markets have become saturated① (the size of the market remains the same). This means that there is now intense competition for customers. The sophistication of marketing management has therefore developed into what we now see in a modern marketing department. Marketers are involved at a strategic level within the organization and therefore inform an organization about what should be produced, where it should be sold, how much should be charged for it and how it should be communicated to consumers. Modern marketers research markets and consumers. They attempt to understand consumer needs (and potential needs) and allocate organizational resources appropriately to meet these needs. Modern marketers are particularly interested in brands. They are also increasingly interested in ensuring that employees understand marketing, i.e. that everyone within the organization involves themselves with marketing activities.

2. The Functions of Marketing

The functions of marketing are embodied in the aggregate of economic activities related to the transfer of property right, selling and buying, the transport and storage of goods, distribution, packaging, financing and procurement. All these areas involve numerous marketing actions that are distinguished between general and specific functions.

The general functions of marketing are:

(1) Market and consumer research

This is the main function of all marketing activities. This function implies obtaining the information about the current market situation and future perspectives. This is the foundation of all decisions: formulating the strategy, designing a new product or service, extension to a new market, targeting a specific market.

(2) Permanent adaptation to the requirements of social and economic environment

This implies the employment of all resources in order to operatively accommodate to the market demands. A company's adaptability can be measured by comparing the dynamics of the supply it is providing to the dimension②, structure and

---

① saturated (饱和的): Unable to hold or contain more; full.
② dimension (规模): Extent or magnitude; scope.

level of demand. It depends on the capacity of the management to use the resources effectively.

(3) Full satisfaction of demand

This is the objective of any company that aims for a rewarding economic activity. As a company manages to accomplish better the market requirements, its chances to gain profit, increase its turnover[①] and surpass its competitors, rise.

(4) Maximizing of economic efficiency

It assumes the optimization of all economic processes (production, transportation, storage, distribution) so that the profitability is increasing.

3. Marketing Mix

Marketing mix is often crucial when determining a product or brand's unique selling point (the unique quality that differentiates a product from its competitors), and is often synonymous[②] with the four Ps: "product" "price" "promotion" and "place." However, in recent times, the "four Ps" have been expanded to the "seven Ps" with the addition of "people" "process" and "physical evidence."

(1) Product

Product means the goods-and-services combination the company offers to the target market. Products generally fall into two categories: consumer products and industrial products. The Product Life Cycle (PLC) is based upon the biological life cycle. For example, a seed is planted (introduction); it begins to sprout (growth); it shoots out leaves and puts down roots as it becomes an adult (maturity); after a long period as an adult, the plant begins to shrink and die out (decline).

(2) Price

Of all the aspects of the marketing mix, price is the one that creates sales revenue—all the others are costs. <u>The price of an item is clearly an important determinant of the value of sales made. In theory, price is really determined by the discovery of what customers perceive is the value of the item on sale. Researching consumers' opinions about pricing is important as it indicates how they value what they are looking for as well as what they want to pay. An organization's pricing policy will vary according to time and circumstances.</u> Crudely speaking, the value

---

① turnover（营业额，销售量）: The amount of business transacted during a given period of time; the number of shares of stock sold on the market during a given period of time.

② synonymous （同义的）: Having the same or a similar meaning.

of water in the Lake District① will be considerably different from the value of water in the desert.

(3) Promotion

Promotion is the business of communicating with customers. It will provide information that will assist them in making a decision to purchase a product or service. The razzmatazz②, pace and creativity of some promotional activities are almost alien to normal business activities.

<u>The cost associated with promotion or advertising goods and services often represents a sizeable proportion of the overall cost of producing an item. However, successful promotion increases sales so that advertising and other costs are spread over a larger output. Though increased promotional activity is often a sign of a response to a problem such as competitive activity, it enables an organization to develop and build up a succession of messages and can be extremely cost-effective</u>③.

(4) Place

Although figures vary widely from product to product, roughly a fifth of the cost of a product goes on getting it to the customer. "Place" is concerned with various methods of transporting and storing goods, and then making them available for the customer. Getting the right product to the right place at the right time involves the distribution system. The choice of distribution method will depend on a variety of circumstances. It will be more convenient for some manufacturers to sell to wholesalers④ who then sell to retailers⑤, while others will prefer to sell directly to retailers or customers.

(5) People

An essential ingredient to any service provision is the use of appropriate staff and people. Recruiting the right staff and training them appropriately in the delivery of their service is essential if the organization wants to obtain a form of competitive advantage. Consumers make judgments and deliver perceptions of the service based on the employees they interact with. Staff should have the appropriate interpersonal

---

① Lake District (英格兰西北部风景地，湖区): A scenic area of northwest England including the Cumbrian Mountains and some 15 lakes.

② razzmatazz (噱头): A flashy action or display intended to bewilder, confuse, or deceive.

③ cost-effective (划算的): Economical in terms of the goods or services received for the money spent.

④ wholesaler (批发商): Someone who buys large quantities of goods and resells to merchants rather than to the ultimate customers.

⑤ retailer (零售商): A merchant who sells goods at retail.

skills, attitude, and service knowledge to provide the service that consumers are paying for.

(6) Process

Refers to the systems used to assist the organization in delivering the service. Imagine you walk into Burger King① and you order a Whopper Meal and you get it delivered within two minutes. What was the process that allowed you to obtain an efficient service delivery? Banks that send out credit cards automatically when their customer's old one has expired again require an efficient process to identify expiry dates and renewal. An efficient service that replaces old credit cards will foster consumer loyalty and confidence in the company.

(7) Physical Evidence

Where is the service being delivered? Physical Evidence is the element of the service mix which allows the consumer again to make judgments on the organization. If you walk into a restaurant your expectations are of a clean, friendly environment. On an aircraft if you travel first class you expect enough room to be able to lie down!

Physical evidence is an essential ingredient of the service mix; consumers will make perceptions based on their sight of the service provision which will have an impact on the organization's perceptual plan of the service.

4. Marketing Environment

The marketing environment surrounds and impacts upon the organization. There are three key elements to the marketing environment which are the internal environment, the microenvironment and the macroenvironment. Why are they important? Well marketers build both internal and external relationships. Marketers aim to deliver value to satisfied customers, so we need to assess and evaluate our internal business/corporate environment and our external environment which is subdivided into micro and macro.

5. Three Key Marketing Strategy Decisions: Market Segmentation, Targeting and Positioning

(1) Market segmentation

Market segmentation is a strategy that involves dividing a larger market into

---

① Burger King（汉堡王）：Burger King, often abbreviated as BK, is a global chain of hamburger fast food restaurants headquartered in unincorporated Miami-Dade County, Florida, United States.

subsets of consumers who have common needs and applications for the goods and services offered in the market. These subgroups of consumers can be identified by a number of different demographics①, depending on the purposes behind identifying the groups. Marketing campaigns are often designed and implemented based on this type of customer segmentation.

Three main categories generally define a market segment. The first, homogeneity, is the degree to which a common need for a product or service exists within a group. The second, distinction, is what makes this targeted group different and unique from other groups. The third, reaction, is how similar this group's response and decision-making would be to an event or situation that occurs in the market.

(2) Market targeting

Market targeting is a broad term that is used to describe the process of identifying groups of consumers who are highly likely to purchase a specific good or service. There are several different approaches to this process, with some of them allowing for a broad cultivation of a market, while others are focused more on identifying markets that are small but somewhat lucrative②. Businesses of all sizes adopt some form of this marketing essential as part of their efforts to secure and maintain customers.

One approach to market targeting is known as broad or undifferentiated marketing. Instead of attempting to tailor marketing and sales strategies to cultivate sales within one or two groups of consumers, the approach will be a marketing campaign that is aimed at gathering customers from all walks of life. Market targeting may also take on a form that is known as selective or differentiated marketing. With this approach, the business will identify two or more specific consumer groups that are highly likely to become loyal customers. A third approach to market targeting is known as focused or concentrated marketing. With this strategy, the business will identify a specific group of consumers that is highly likely to generate enough revenue to allow the company to enjoy a profit.

(3) Market positioning

Market positioning is the manipulation③ of a brand or family of brands to

---

① demographics（人口统计资料，如年龄、性别、收入等）: Demographics or demographic data are the characteristics of a human population, which are used widely in sociology, public policy, and marketing. Commonly used demographics include gender, race, age, income, etc.

② lucrative（赚钱的，有利可图的）: To gain in terms of money or wealth.

③ manipulation（处理，操作，操纵）: The act or practice of manipulating.

create a positive perception in the eyes of the public. If a product is well positioned, it will have strong sales, and it may become the go-to brand for people who need that particular product. Poor positioning, on the other hand, can lead to bad sales and a dubious① reputation.

Market positioning is a tricky process. Companies need to see how consumers perceive their products, and how differences in presentation can impact perception. Periodically, companies may reposition, trying to adjust their perception among the public.

<u>Companies also engage in depositioning, in which they attempt to alter the perception of other brands. While outright attacks on rival brands are frowned upon and may be illegal unless they are framed very carefully, companies can use language like "compared to the leading brand" or "we're not like those other brands."</u>

Developing a market positioning strategy is an important part of the research and development process. The marketing department may provide notes during product development which are designed to enhance the product's position, and which also determine the price, where the product should be sold, and how it should be advertised. Every aspect of the product's presentation will be carefully calculated to maximize its position, with the goal of market positioning being domination.

Exercises

I. Reviewing Questions

Answer the following questions according to the text.

1. Could you give a definition of marketing?
2. How did marketing develop in the history?
3. What are the functions of marketing?
4. List the seven Ps of marketing mix.
5. What are the two subcategories of products?
6. What's the importance of recruiting the right staff and training them appropriately?
7. What are the three key elements to the marketing environment?
8. What is a market segment?
9. What are the approaches to market targeting?
10. Describe the process of marketing positioning.

---

① dubious（可疑的；不确定的）: Fraught with uncertainty or doubt; undecided.

II. Cloze

Read the following passage and fill in the blanks with the words given below. Change the form where necessary.

inferior	reduction	promotions	increase	established
purchases	live	benefit	targeting	marketing

While all marketers do not agree on a common definition of marketing strategy, the term generally refers to a company plan that allocates resources in ways to generate profits by positioning products or services and __1__ specific consumer groups. Marketing strategy focuses on the long-term company objectives and involves planning marketing programs so that they help a company realize its goals. Companies rely on marketing strategies for __2__ product lines or services as well as for new products and services.

While marketing practices no doubt have existed as long as commerce has, marketing did not become a formal discipline until the 1950s. At this point, businesses began to investigate how to better serve and satisfy their customers and deal with competition. Consequently, marketing became the process of focusing business on the customer in order to continue providing goods or services valued by consumers. Marketing includes a plethora of decisions that affect consumers interest in a company: advertising, pricing, location, product line, promotions, and so forth. The majors concerns of marketing are usually referred to as the "four Ps" or the "__3__ mix": product, price, place, and promotion.

Hence, marketing involves establishing a company vision and definition and implementing policies that will enable a company to __4__ up to its vision or maintain its vision. Marketing strategy is the process of planning and implementing company policies towards realizing company goals in accordance with the company vision. Marketing strategies include general ones such as price __5__ for market share growth, product differentiation, and market segmentation, as well as numerous specific strategies for specific areas of marketing.

Competition is the primary motivation for adopting a marketing strategy. In industries monopolized by one company, marketing needs only be minimal to spur on increased consumption. Utilities long enjoyed monopolized markets, allowing them to rely on general mass marketing programs to maintain and __6__ their sales levels. Utility companies had rather fixed market positions and steady demand, which rendered advanced concern for marketing unnecessary. Now, however, most companies face some form of competition, no matter what the industry, because of deregulation and the globalization of many industries. Consequently, marketing strategy has become all the more important for companies to continue being profitable.

Contemporary approaches to marketing often fall into two general but not mutually exclusive categories: customer-oriented marketing strategies and competitor-oriented marketing strategies. Since many marketers believe that striving to satisfy customers can ___7___ both consumers and businesses, they contend that marketing strategy should focus on customers. This strategy assumes that customers tend to make more ___8___ and remain loyal to specific brands when they are satisfied, rather than dissatisfied, with a company. Hence, customer-oriented marketing strategies try to help establish long-term relationships between customers and businesses.

Competitor-oriented marketing strategies, on the other hand, focuses on outdoing competitors by strategically manipulating the marketing mix: product, price, place, and promotion. Competitor-oriented strategies will lead companies to imitate competitor products, match prices, and offer similar ___9___. This kind of marketing strategy parallels military strategy. For example, this approach to marketing strategy leads to price wars among competitors. Successful marketing strategies, however, usually incorporate elements from both of these orientations, because focusing on customer satisfaction alone will not help a company if its competitors already have high levels of customer satisfaction and because trying to outdo a competitor will not help a company if it provides ___10___ products and customer service.

III. Translation

1. This was a period of rapid social change driven by technological and scientific innovation. One result was that for the first time the production of goods was separated from their consumption. Mass production, developing transport infrastructure and growing mass media meant that producers needed to, and could develop more sophisticated ways of managing the distribution of goods.

2. The price of an item is clearly an important determinant of the value of sales made. In theory, price is really determined by the discovery of what customers

perceive is the value of the item on sale. Researching consumers' opinions about pricing is important as it indicates how they value what they are looking for as well as what they want to pay. An organization's pricing policy will vary according to time and circumstances.

3. The cost associated with promotion or advertising goods and services often represents a sizeable proportion of the overall cost of producing an item. However, successful promotion increases sales, so that advertising and other costs are spread over a larger output. Though increased promotional activity is often a sign of a response to a problem such as competitive activity, it enables an organization to develop and build up a succession of messages and can be extremely cost-effective.

4. Market segmentation is a strategy that involves dividing a larger market into subsets of consumers who have common needs and applications for the goods and services offered in the market. These subgroups of consumers can be identified by a number of different demographics, depending on the purposes behind identifying the groups.

5. Companies also engage in depositioning, in which they attempt to alter the perception of other brands. While outright attacks on rival brands are frowned upon and may be illegal unless they are framed very carefully, companies can use language like "compared to the leading brand" or "we're not like those other brands."

IV. Case Study

As Middle Class Shrinks, P&G Aims High and Low

by Ellen Byron

For generations, Procter & Gamble Co.'s growth strategy was focused on developing household staples for the vast American middle class.

Now, P&G executives say many of its former middle-market shoppers are trading down to lower-priced goods—widening the pools of have and have-not consumers at the expense of the middle.

That forced P&G, which is estimated to have at least one product in 98% of American households, to fundamentally change the way it develops and sells its goods. For the first time in 38 years, for example, the company launched new dish soap in the U.S. at a bargain price.

P&G's roll out of Gain dish soap says a lot about the health of the American middle class: The world's largest maker of consumer products is now betting that the squeeze on Middle America will be long lasting.

"It required us to think differently about our product portfolio and how to please the high-end and lower-end markets," says Melanie Healey, group president of P&G's North America business. "That's frankly where a lot of the growth is happening."

In the wake of the worst recession in 50 years, there's little doubt that the American middle class—the 40% of households with annual incomes between $50,000 and $140,000 a year—is in distress. Even before the recession, incomes of American middle-class families weren't keeping up with inflation, especially with the rising costs of what are considered the essential ingredients of middle-class life—college education, health care and housing. In 2009, the income of the median family, the one smack in the middle of the middle, was lower, adjusted for inflation, than in 1998, the Census Bureau says.

The slumping stock market and collapse in housing prices have also hit middle-class Americans. At the end of March, Americans had $6.1 trillion in equity in their houses—the value of the house minus mortgages—half the 2006 level, according to the Federal Reserve. Economist Edward Wolff of New York University estimates that the net worth—household assets minus debts—of the middle American households grew by 2.4% a year between 2001 and 2007 and plunged by 26.2% in the following two years.

P&G isn't the only company adjusting its business. A wide swath of American companies are convinced that the consumer market is bifurcating into high and low ends and eroding in the middle. They have begun to alter the way they research, develop and market their products.

Food giant H.J. Heinz Co., for example, is developing more products at lower price ranges. Luxury retailer Saks Inc. is bolstering its high-end apparel and accessories because its wealthiest customers—not those drawn to entry-level items—are driving the chain's growth.

Questions for discussion:
1. According to the text, why didn't P&G's growth strategy target at the vast American middle class any more?
2. How did P&G adjust its business?
3. What do you think of P&G's changes of strategy?

V. Supplementary Reading

The Marketing Practices in China

by Anthony CL

The concept of marketing has only recently been introduced to China as a university course, not as a tool in supporting sales efforts. Since China's entry into the WTO, international firms are excited about the huge opportunity to enter the potentially largest consumer market in the world, as one in five of the world's consumers is Chinese. Marketers, both foreign and local, are racking their brains for marketing strategies that will attract more customers. Many companies failed because of their lack of knowledge of the people and the market or have failed to conduct effective market research after their entries into China. At the same time, consumers in China are quickly adopting new values and western ideas because of their increased exposure to global media and western lifestyles, which lead to a new wave of consumerism.

The Pricing Strategy

Most Chinese consumers are sensitive to price and will usually choose less expensive products. In China, price competition is the practice most frequently employed by enterprises to compete for market share.

Many Chinese companies believe in the strategy of low profit margin and volume sales based on the assumption that lower price will increase the speed of turnover and eventually generate higher profit.

While the low-price strategy is widely adopted, some marketers use a high-price strategy, taking advantage of the conventional wisdom that "pian yi wu hao huo (cheap is no good)" and "yi fen qian yi fen huo (each additional cent paid is associated with additional value)." Foreign branded products or imported products are generally high priced and perceived as superior products.

It is interesting to observe the unique characteristics of psychological pricing practices in China, which go beyond simple considerations. Some Chinese people have a superstitious belief in lucky numbers and marketers price their products in such a way that the numbers can denote good luck. For example, a piece of furniture may be priced at 1199 to indicate "chang chang jiu jiu (long and lasting)," or 4451 meaning "shi shi ru yi (everything is as you wish)."

The Sales and Negotiation Practices

The old days when products were produced and allocated according to government plans have gone. Companies have to rely on their own marketing teams now to face multiple choices of ways to market their products, including direct and indirect marketing.

Direct selling used to be commonly exercised by both domestic and foreign firms in China.

Unfortunately, criminal exploitations and abuses of this system such as price frauds, sales of fake and smuggled products, seriously affected the interests of the consumers and the normal economic order and led the Chinese government to issue a ban on direct selling. Recently, direct marketing tools such as telemarketing, TV sales and internet marketing, are relatively new to Chinese consumers and have not yet proved to be very successful. Indirect marketing channels are all used in China where there are over 1.36 million wholesalers and nearly 14 million retailers of consumer products. Manufacturing enterprises are using diversified channels of distribution to get their products to the consumers.

Foreign managers easily agree that negotiating a contract with Chinese is definitely not the same as in the West. Moreover, Chinese negotiators are now behaving much more like their Western counterparts.

Negotiations tactics most often used by Westerners are cooperation (win-win situation) and defensiveness (standing firm) while, the negotiating style of Chinese are cooperation and sudden demands or changes.

This confirmed that China representatives are tough negotiators.

Advertising Practices

Many Chinese enterprises believe that advertising will automatically generate sales. A recent example is the exorbitant advertising expenditure of Qinchi Liquor, who spent US$38.55 million for prime time advertising on CCTV (China Central

Television), but failed to increase its sales.

Advertising theory seems to be unfamiliar to the most local advertising decision-makers. For many years, most advertising dollars have gone to television media, as they are seen as the most effective channels of communication to create product awareness among potential consumers in China.

The lack of reliable ratings data is another problem that makes it difficult for advertisers to make decisions and evaluate the effectiveness of their advertising efforts.

Promotion Practices

Both retailers and producers use consumer oriented promotion techniques. These practices range from coupons, premiums and deals to prizes, lucky draws, and contests. Obviously, these practices reflect the level of intensity in consumer market competition. When employing promotion techniques, it is important to develop appropriate consumer insights, which are extremely critical in a market that is large in territory, diverse in consumer preferences across regions.

Some research results have indicated that consumers are pragmatic in their attitudes toward promotion exercises. Buy one and get one free, price reduction or discount, discount coupons and premiums seem to be favored by consumers.

However, marketers need to be very careful when designing promotion strategies and extreme situations should be taken into consideration.

The practice of free product offers has caused chaos in some instances when unexpected numbers of people come to claim free products that could not be supplied.

Influences on Brand Building

The lack of well-known brands may be one of the weaknesses of Chinese manufacturers. The government is actively promoting national brands to drive domestic consumption and home grown businesses but the majority have not yet made much progress in breaking away from the images of a local brand. Some brands have established national recognition, like TCL, which is now one of the world's largest mobile phones manufacturers.

Local marketers have a tendency, as they do with numbers, to favor brand names that convey luck, happiness, longevity and prosperity. While some local marketers are trying to use brand names that have a foreign touch, foreign marketers are struggling to find a proper Chinese name for their brands.

Indeed, it is often very difficult to translate a western brand name into Chinese. Ideally, a brand should both have phonetic similarity and good meaning. A classical example of this is Coca-Cola, which is phonetically translated as "Ke Kou Ke Le" with the meanings of "deliciously enjoyable" and "bringing about happy laughter." Brands such as Philips, Nokia, or Sony, recognizing the difficulties in translating their brands, avoided the effort of associating the name with any particular Chinese meaning and successfully established brand recognition.

Reading Comprehension

Choose the best answers to the following questions.

1. The concept of marketing has only recently been introduced to China as _____.
   A. China entered into the WTO
   B. a tool in supporting sales efforts
   C. international firms enter into Chinese market
   D. a university course

2. In China, consumers are quickly adopting new values and western ideas because of _____.
   A. marketing strategies of western firms
   B. China's entry into the WTO
   C. increased exposure to global media and western lifestyles
   D. traveling to foreign countries

3. In China, _____ is the practice most frequently employed by enterprises to compete for market share.
   A. sales promotion
   B. price competition
   C. advertisement
   D. brand building

4. Which is true about promotion practices?
   A. When employing promotion techniques, it is not important to develop appropriate consumer insights.
   B. The practice of free product offers would cause chaos in some instances.
   C. Consumers are always pragmatic in their attitudes toward promotion exercises.
   D. Only the producers use consumer oriented promotion techniques.

5. What can we learn about the brand building in our country?

A. It is often very difficult to translate a western brand name into Chinese.
B. The majority of home grown business have made much progress in breaking away from the images of a local brand.
C. One of the weaknesses of Chinese manufacturers is the lack of well-known brands.
D. A & C.

VI. Assignment
1. Collect information about Chinese national brands which become internationally famous. Discuss how they succeed and what other home brands can learn from them.
2. Form small groups and each group starts your own business. Try to describe the process of your entering the market and some major marketing strategies.

Unit 11
Financial Management

 Learning Objectives

After learning this unit, you should be able to:
1. Know the meaning of financial management.
2. Understand the functions of financial management.
3. Understand the objectives of financial management.
4. Know the four parts of financial management.
5. Understand accounting and financial management systems.

 Lead-in

Financial management is the management of monetary resources. It involves planning accurately, directing the monetary resources at correct time and controlling the financial activities of a firm. Financial management is very important for a business to ensure it can run smoothly. Finance is an aspect which, if neglected, can lead to severe losses and closure of a firm.

Warm-up Questions/Discussion:
1. In your opinion, what activities in a company can be considered as financial management?
2. How can companies raise money for production? Discuss with your classmates.
3. What measures can be taken to improve the financial management?

Financial Management[①]

The present age is the age of industrialization. Large industries are being established in every country. It is very necessary to arrange finance for building, plant and working capital, etc. for the establishment of these industries. How much of capital will be required, from what sources this much of finance will be collected and how will it be invested, is the matter of financial management.

1. The Functions of Financial Management

Financial management is a business process that allows a company to record operating transactions and then prepare financial statements that are accurate, complete and in compliance with generally accepted accounting principles (GAAP) and industry practices. Financial management often may be useful in financial planning and decision-making processes.

A financial management specialist prepares fair and complete financial statements and then ensures that internal controls, policies and procedures around financial reporting mechanisms[②] are adequate and functional. A financial management specialist also may analyze operating data and business performance to recommend investment ideas to a firm's senior management.

Generally speaking, the functions of financial management fall into three categories:

(1) Financial Planning

It is the duty of the management to ensure that adequate funds are available to meet the needs of the business. In the short term, funds are required to pay the employees or to invest in stocks. In the middle and long term funds are required to make additions to the productive capacity of the business.

(2) Financial Control

Financial control helps the business to ensure that it is meeting its goals. Through financial control the firm decides how much to invest in short term assets and how to raise the required funds.

(3) Financial Decision Making

The three primary aspects of financial decision making are investment, financing

---

① The text is excerpted from www.ehow.com, www.economics.about.com, and www.svtuition.org with abridgment.

② mechanism（机制）: A system of parts that operate or interact like those of a machine.

and dividends①. Investment must be financed in some way for which various alternatives are available. A financing decision is to retain the profits earned by the business or be distributed among the shareholders via dividends.

2. Financial Management Objectives

Financial management objectives give an overview of how an organization will allocate and monitor its income, expenditures② and assets. Typically, financial management objectives are used to create practical policies and procedures. Proven ability to meet your objectives is a sign of good practice and a reputable business.

(1) Budget creation and management

One of the main objectives of financial management is to create, and stick to, a budget. This is imperative③ if you are going to make a profit in business. Budget projections should be tailored to fit in with the organization's financial year and should be regularly reviewed. Financial resources should only be used for the purposes that have been set out in the budget and expenditures should be monitored to ensure that departments across the company are keeping to their allocated funds.

(2) Income

Financial management objectives should include aims for your organization's income. For example, all income (both cash and bank credits) should be properly recorded and banked and invoices should be raised in a timely manner with clear recovery action policies in place for overdue④ accounts or payment failure. Once your income objectives have been created, you need to develop policies and procedures to allow the objectives to be met.

(3) Accountability⑤ procedures

Financial management objectives should include systems of accountability for finances. The best way to achieve this is to appoint authorized personnel who have to approve all transactions (typically by signing a document) before the funds can be released. This makes it easier to trace financial irregularities in the accounts to a specific individual or department who may simply have mistakenly entered figures

---

① dividend（股息，红利）: A share of profits received by a stockholder or by a policyholder in a mutual insurance society.
② expenditure（消费，支出）: Something expended, such as time or money.
③ imperative（势在必行的，急需的）: Extremely urgent or important; essential.
④ overdue（过期的，未兑的）: Not paid at the scheduled time.
⑤ accountability（承担责任）: Responsibility to someone or for some activity.

or, in more extreme cases, might be embezzling① funds. For larger organizations, accountability-related objectives include having an annual audit② of accounts. Audits are typically undertaken by an external organization and, for some businesses, are a legal requirement.

(4) Inventories

To be comprehensive, financial management should not just focus on the tangible annual income and expenditure, but should include the organization's assets as well. Consequently, one financial management objective should be to keep accurate and up-to-date records of all items of value, such as furniture and vehicles. It should also be made clear who has ownership and responsibility for these assets; for example, an organization might not have ownership of its office building but it might be responsible for its upkeep for the duration of the lease. Allowances for the maintenance of assets should be included in the budget.

3. Contents of Financial Management

In general, financial management consists of four kinds of management: investment management, capital raising management, working capital③ management and profit distribution.

(1) Investment management

Investment management is the professional management of various securities (shares, bonds and other securities) and assets (e.g., real estate) in order to meet specified investment goals for the benefit of the investors. Investors may be institutions (insurance companies, pension funds, corporations, charities, educational establishments etc.) or private investors (both directly via investment contracts and more commonly via collective investment schemes e.g. mutual funds or exchange-traded funds).

(2) Capital raising management

Large corporations could not have grown to their present sizes without being able to find innovative ways to raise capital to finance expansion. Corporations have five primary methods for obtaining that money.

① Issuing bonds.

A bond is a written promise to pay back a specific amount of money at a

---

① embezzling（盗用，挪用）：To take others' money for one's own use in violation of a trust.
② audit（审计）：An examination of records or financial accounts to check their accuracy.
③ working capital（营运资金）：The assets of a business that can be applied to its operation.

certain date or dates in the future. In the interim①, bondholders receive interest payments at fixed rates on specified dates. Holders can sell bonds to someone else before they are due.

<u>Corporations benefit by issuing bonds because the interest rates they must pay investors are generally lower than rates for most other types of borrowing and because interest paid on bonds is considered to be a tax-deductible business expense. However, corporations must make interest payments even when they are not showing profits.</u> If investors doubt a company's ability to meet its interest obligations, they either will refuse to buy its bonds or will demand a higher rate of interest to compensate them for their increased risk. For this reason, smaller corporations can seldom raise much capital by issuing bonds.

② Issuing preferred stock②.

A company may choose to issue new "preferred" stock to raise capital. Buyers of these shares have special status in the event the underlying company encounters financial trouble. If profits are limited, preferred-stock owners will be paid their dividends after bondholders receive their guaranteed interest payments but before any common stock dividends are paid.

③ Selling common stock③.

If a company is in good financial health, it can raise capital by issuing common stock. Typically, investment banks help companies issue stock, agreeing to buy any new shares issued at a set price if the public refuses to buy the stock at a certain minimum price. Although common shareholders have the exclusive right to elect a corporation's board of directors, they rank behind holders of bonds and preferred stock when it comes to sharing profits.

Investors are attracted to stocks in two ways. Some companies pay large dividends, offering investors a steady income. But others pay little or no dividends, hoping instead to attract shareholders by improving corporate profitability—and hence, the value of the shares themselves. In general, the value of shares increases as investors come to expect corporate earnings to rise. Companies whose stock prices rise substantially often "split" the shares, paying each holder, say, one

---

① interim（中间时期）：An interval of time between one event, process, or period and another.

② preferred stock（优先股）：Stock whose holders are guaranteed priority in the payment of dividends but whose holders have no voting rights.

③ common stock（普通股）：Stock other than preferred stock; entitles the owner to a share of the corporation's profits and a share of the voting power in shareholder elections.

additional share for each share held. This does not raise any capital for the corporation, but it makes it easier for stockholders to sell shares on the open market. In a two-for-one split, for instance, the stock's price is initially cut in half, attracting investors.

④ Borrowing.

Companies can also raise short-term capital—usually to finance inventories—by getting loans from banks or other lenders.

⑤ Using profits.

As noted, companies also can finance their operations by retaining their earnings. Strategies concerning retaining earnings vary. Some corporations, especially electric, gas, and other utilities, pay out most of their profits as dividends to their stockholders. Others distribute, say, 50 percent of earnings to shareholders in dividends, keeping the rest to pay for operations and expansion. Still other corporations, often the smaller ones, prefer to reinvest most or all of their net income in research and expansion, hoping to reward investors by rapidly increasing the value of their shares.

(3) Working capital management

Decisions relating to working capital and short term financing are referred to as working capital management. It is related to manage ment of current assets① and current liabilities. The goal of working capital (i.e. short term) management is therefore to ensure that the firm is able to operate, and that it has sufficient cash flow to service long term debt, and to satisfy both maturing short-term debt and upcoming operational expenses. In doing so, firm value is enhanced when, and if, the return on capital exceeds the cost of capital.

Working capital is that part of company's capital which is used for purchasing raw material and involves in sundry debtors. There are four types of working capital:

① Total or gross working capital is that working capital which is used for all the current assets. Total value of current assets will be equal to gross working capital.

② Net working capital is the excess of current assets over current liabilities.

③ Permanent working capital is that amount of capital which must be in cash or current assets for continuing the activities of business.

④ Temporary working capital. Sometimes, it may be possible that we have to pay fixed liabilities, and at that time we need working capital which is more than permanent working capital, then this excess amount will be temporary working

---

① current asset (流动资产): Cash or assets convertible into cash at short notice.

capital. In normal working of business, we don't need such capital.

Policies are the guidelines which are helpful to direct business. Finance manager can also make working capital policies. Here are the main capital policies of business:

① Liquidity[①] policy.

Under this policy, finance manager will increase the amount of liquidity for reducing the risk of business. If business has high volume of cash and bank balance, then business can easily pay its dues at maturity. But finance manger should not forget that the excess cash will not produce, and earning and return on investment will decrease. So liquidity policy should be optimized.

② Profitability policy.

Under this policy, finance manger will keep low amount of cash in business and try to invest maximum amount of cash and bank balance. It will ensure that profit of business will increase due to increasing of investment in proper way but risk of business will also increase because liquidity of business will decrease and it can create bankruptcy position of business. So, profitability policy should be made after seeing liquidity policy and after this both policies will be helpful for proper management of working capital.

(4) Profit distribution

The specific way that a company distributes profits varies from company to company. Some companies distribute a greater share of profits to investors, while others retain earnings within the company. In a general sense, corporate profits are used to satisfy both the operations necessary within the company and the demands of investors who own shares in the company.

① Operating needs.

The most immediate use of profits in most corporations is for upkeep[②] and expansion of corporate properties. When a company is profitable, it is likely to build additional plants, expand its sales force, or undertake other actions that expand its ability to generate additional profits. Depending on the structure of the company, the decision on where to allocate these profits can lie with the CEO, the board of directors or other company officers.

② Dividends.

Dividends are a physical distribution of the cash profits of a company to its shareholders. In times of rising profits, a corporation may declare an increased

---

① liquidity（流动性）：The quality of being readily convertible into cash.
② upkeep（保养，维修）：Maintenance in proper operation, condition, and repair.

dividend to allow shareholders to directly participate in the company's growing profit. A high dividend may also attract additional investors to a company's stock, which in turn could drive the share price higher. Companies that pay high dividends are generally not in a high-growth phase and therefore do not need all the cash generated from operations to fuel additional growth.

③ Bonuses[①].

Some corporations tie the compensation of certain employees to the profit performance of the company itself. When the company generates a higher profit, these employees get higher pay in the form of a bonus. This compensation structure allows the corporation to avoid paying high salaries to employees unless it has already booked the underlying profits.

④ Profit-sharing plans.

Profit-sharing plans are a type of retirement benefit that some companies offer as a perk for employees. Company contributions to profit-sharing plans are not mandatory but are based on the amount of profit that a company earns in any given year. Employees benefit by having funds available for distribution at retirement, without having had to contribute their own money along the way.

4. Accounting and Financial Management Systems

Accounting and financial management systems help businesses, small and large, with reports and queries. These systems provide managers with information to make good decisions based on facts, not gut feelings. Accounting and financial management systems serve the various needs of a firm, such as manufacturing cost information and the development and control of budgets.

(1) Types

Accounting and management accounting systems can be manual or computerized. Basically, these systems help businesses in many processes, such as paying bills, controlling expenses and recording revenues. Often these systems give management required reports and analysis with the focus on timeliness and reliability of information.

(2) Advantages

A business without an accounting or financial system in place is functioning without a compass, with decisions based on gossip, memory and biased data. The

---

① bonus (红利，额外津贴): A sum of money or an equivalent given to an employee in addition to the employee's usual compensation.

main advantage of a financial and accounting system is that data is objective and unbiased. Managers can rely on the system to get data based on actual business events, not hear-say. Another advantage of an accounting system is that it organizes your data, making it easy to find information without going through many files. For example, if you want to know how much a client owes you, you can look it up in the accounting system, which often stores many kinds of data.

(3) Internal controls

A financial and accounting management system is not perfect—it may contain errors. Internal controls can prevent or identify mistakes, making the financial system more accurate and reliable. <u>One common feature of internal controls is to segregate the duties of accounting personnel if more than one employee is involved in conducting accounting tasks from the beginning to the end of a process. For example, internal controls in paying bills include a person approving the bill and another one processing payment. This setup makes it harder for errors to go undetected.</u>

Exercises

I. Reviewing Questions

Answer the following questions according to the text.

1. What is financial management?
2. What are the functions of financial management?
3. What are the objectives of financial management?
4. List the four kinds of financial management.
5. How do corporations raise money?
6. What is the goal of working capital management?
7. How do corporations distribute their profits?
8. What are the types of accounting and financial management systems?
9. What are the advantages of accounting and financial management systems?
10. What can prevent or identify mistakes in the financial system?

II. Cloze

Read the following passage and fill in the blanks with the words given below. Change the form where necessary.

address	acquire	operation	alternative	paying
cash	track	accurate	management	subset

Unit 11 Financial Management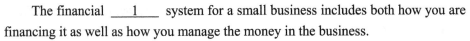

The financial ___1___ system for a small business includes both how you are financing it as well as how you manage the money in the business.

In setting up a financial management system, your first decision is whether you will manage your financial records yourself or whether you will have someone else do it for you. There are a number of ___2___ ways you can handle this. You can manage everything yourself; hire an employee who manages it for you; keep your records in-house, but have an accountant prepare specialized reporting such as tax returns; or have an external bookkeeping service that manages financial transactions and an accountant that handles formal reporting functions. Some accounting firms also handle bookkeeping functions. Software packages are also available for handling bookkeeping and accounting.

Bookkeeping refers to the daily ___3___ of an accounting system, recording routine transactions within the appropriate accounts. An accounting system defines the process of identifying, measuring, recording and communicating financial information about the business. So, in a sense, the bookkeeping function is a ___4___ of the accounting system. A bookkeeper compiles the information that goes into the system. An accountant takes the data and analyzes it in ways that give you useful information about your business. They can advise you on the systems needed for your particular business and prepare ___5___ reports certified by their credentials. While software packages are readily available to meet almost any accounting need, having an accountant at least review your records can lend credibility to your business, especially when dealing with lending institutions and government agencies.

Setting up an accounting system, collecting bills, ___6___ employees, suppliers, and taxes correctly and on time are all part of running a small business. And, unless accounting is your small business, it is often the bane of the small business owner. Setting up a system that does what you need with the minimum of maintenance can make running a small business not only more pleasant, but it can save you from problems down the road.

The basis for every accounting system is a good bookkeeping system. What is the difference between that and an accounting system? Think of accounting as the big picture of how your business runs—income, expenses, assets, liabilities—an organized system for keeping track of how the money flows through your business; keep ___7___ that it goes where it is supposed to go. A good bookkeeping system keeps track of the nuts and bolts—the actual transactions that take place. The bookkeeping system provides the numbers for the accounting system. Both accounting and bookkeeping can be contracted out to external firms if you are not comfortable with managing them yourself.

Even if you outsource the accounting functions, however, you will need some type of Recordkeeping Systems to manage the day-to-day operations of your business—in addition to a financial plan and a budget to make certain you have thought through where you are headed in your business finances. And, your accounting system should be producing Financial Statements. Learning to read them is an important skill to ___8___.

Another area that your financial management system needs to ___9___ is risk. Any good system should minimize the risks in your business. Consider implementing some of these risk management strategies in your business. Certainly, insurance needs to be considered not only for your property, office, equipment, and employees, but also for loss of critical employees. Even in businesses that have a well set up system, ___10___ flow can be a problem.

Clearly, financial management encompasses a number of crucial areas of your business. Take time to set them up right. It will make a significant difference in your stress levels and in the bottom line for your business.

III. Translation

1. A financial management specialist prepares fair and complete financial statements and then ensures that internal controls, policies and procedures around financial reporting mechanisms are adequate and functional. A financial management specialist also may analyze operating data and business performance to recommend investment ideas to a firm's senior management.

2. Corporations benefit by issuing bonds because the interest rates they must pay investors are generally lower than rates for most other types of borrowing and because interest paid on bonds is considered to be a tax-deductible business expense. However, corporations must make interest payments even when they are not showing profits.

3. Profit-sharing plans are a type of retirement benefit that some companies offer as a perk for employees. Company contributions to profit-sharing plans are not mandatory but are based on the amount of profit that a company earns in any

given year. Employees benefit by having funds available for distribution at retirement, without having had to contribute their own money along the way.

4. Accounting and financial management systems help businesses, small and large, with reports and queries. These systems provide managers with information to make good decisions based on facts, not gut feelings. Accounting and financial management systems serve the various needs of a firm, such as manufacturing cost information and the development and control of budgets.

5. One common feature of internal controls is to segregate the duties of accounting personnel if more than one employee is involved in conducting accounting tasks from the beginning to the end of a process. For example, internal controls in paying bills include a person approving the bill and another one processing payment. This setup makes it harder for errors to go undetected.

IV. Case Study

Why GM Failed

by Karen Berman and Joe Knight

Karen Berman is a founder and co-owner of the Business Literacy Institute, with Joe Knight. Joe is CFO at Setpoint Companies. They are the authors of *Financial Intelligence*.

Here's a question from a reader.

Rammohanpotturi asks:

I have a very specific question for both of you. Why do you think GM collapsed? A company which was started in 1909 and went on to stay well ahead in the automobile industry for 100 years collapsed. I understand it is not all of sudden. What happened to their financial management?

GM is a very interesting case. Yes, it is certainly one of the great titans of U.S. industry and it's not any fun to see them go into bankruptcy.

There have been several opinions put forward at to why this all happened:
- GM makes cars people don't want
- GM is too slow to innovate because of its size
- GM is too bureaucratic and unable to adjust to changing markets

- GM's dealer network is too large
- GM sold off its formerly profitable financing business GMAC

To us the problem with GM is very simple. GM stopped making a profit. The reason any company exists is to make a profit. When companies stop making a profit they fail. We measure profit using the income statement. The income statement simply takes what you sold in a period and subtracts the costs in the business during the same period. If sales are greater than costs or expenses then there is profit. If sales are less than costs then there is a loss.

GM stopped making profit in 2005. Since that time GM lost more than $90 billion through the 1st quarter of 2009. The next question, then, is, "why did those losses happen"? From our perspective, even though all of the above may be good points, the key to GM's losses has to do with sales and fixed costs.

I (Joe) have owned a small business with partners for several years. We have learned that to survive in tough times (BTW the definition of tough times in business is a drop in sales) we had to cut costs. Cutting cost is the most painful thing you have to do as an owner because it usually means having to cut jobs.

The problem for GM was that when the sales slowed down, they had trouble cutting costs because most of their costs were fixed. In other words, a lot of their costs did not go down as their sales went down. GM has tremendous fixed costs related to their union contract. Closing a plant, for example, did not necessarily mean the workers lost their jobs. Company pensions and legacy health care costs were fixed as well. So when sales went down, many costs stayed fairly constant. And that led to losses.

As the losses mounted and the economy struggled, these losses became so significant that GM could not survive as a viable business. In spite of billions of dollars of government support, the only solution for GM is to declare bankruptcy and try to lower those fixed costs through a court process.

Questions for discussion:
1. According to the text, what are the reasons for GM's failure?
2. If you were the CFO of GM, what measures will you take to solve the problem?
3. In your opinion, what should be done in a company when the sales are trending downward?

V. Supplementary Reading

Jobs Related to Financial Management

A financial manager is responsible for supervising and handling financial reports, investment portfolios, accounting, and all kinds of financial analysis for an organization. Additionally, he oversees cash management strategies and financial legislation and regulation. He manages the cash flow for an organization by supervising balance sheets, income statements, and the costs and revenue model.

1. What Does a Financial Manager Do?

The job responsibilities of a financial manager also involve supplying an efficient financial blue print and elucidating all the financial data for an organization, while minimizing costs and maximizing profits. The primary objective is to generate future revenue streams for an organization, while effectively managing the existing investments. He is also responsible for budgetary decisions and planning. Additionally, he must be well versed in the technical aspects of all kinds of financial decisions. This requires an in-depth knowledge of various statuary litigation and legal regulations.

Financial management jobs greatly vary in terms of a specific job description. Generally, the types of businesses that require the services of a financial manager are in the private sector, financial institutes, banking, charities, and governmental institutes. Financial manager jobs can be divided into two broad categories: managerial finance and corporate finance.

Managerial finance involves assessment and appraisal for all kinds of financial activities happening in an organization. Managerial finance does not involve drafting and implementation of financial techniques or strategies. Rather, its primary focus is on the regulation and administration of the existing projects.

Corporate finance, on the other hand, delegates a task to maximize corporate value to a financial manager. A financial manager in such a job position has to deal with decisions involving capital investment, equity, and debt, along with paying dividends to shareholders. In addition, a corporate finance manager deals with decisions related to investment banking to raise capital for the company. He achieves this by trading in securities and bonds.

A financial manager might also work in the capacity of a treasurer or controller. A job position in this capacity involves provision of directives for the preparation of financial reports, balance sheets, income reports, and analysis of present and future costs and revenues.

2. How to Become a Financial Manager?

(1) Education

A bachelor's degree in finance, accounting, economics, or business administration is often the minimum education needed for financial managers. However, many employers now seek candidates with a master's degree, preferably in business administration, finance, or economics. These academic programs help students develop analytical skills and learn financial analysis methods and softwares.

(2) Certification

Professional certification is not required, but some financial managers still get it. The CFA Institute confers the Chartered Financial Analyst (CFA) certification to investment professionals who have at least a bachelor's degree, have 4 years of work experience, and pass three exams. The Association for Financial Professionals confers the Certified Treasury Professional credential to those who pass a computer-based exam and have a minimum of 2 years of relevant experience.

(3) Work experience

Financial managers usually have experience in another business or financial occupation, such as loan officer, accountant or auditor, securities sales agent, or financial analyst.

In some cases, companies provide formal management training programs to help prepare highly motivated and skilled financial workers to become financial managers.

(4) Advancement

Because financial management is so important in keeping business operations efficient, experienced financial managers who display a strong grasp of the operations of various departments within their organization may be promoted to management positions. Some financial managers transfer to closely related positions in other industries. Those with extensive experience may start their own consulting firms.

(5) Important qualities

① Analytical skills. Financial managers increasingly assist executives in making decisions that affect the organization, a task for which they need analytical ability.

② Communication skills. Excellent communication skills are essential because financial managers must explain and justify complex financial transactions.

③ Detail oriented skills. In preparing and analyzing reports such as balance sheets and income statements, financial managers must pay attention to detail.

④ Math skills. Financial managers must be skilled in math, including algebra. An understanding of international finance and complex financial documents also is important.

⑤ Organizational skills. Financial managers deal with a range of information and documents. They must stay organized to their jobs effectively.

(6) Job outlook

The median annual wage of financial managers was $103,910 in 2010. The median wage is the wage at which half the workers in an occupation earned more than that amount and half earned less. The lowest 10 percent earned less than $56,120, and the top 10 percent earned more than $166,400.

Employment among financial managers is expected to grow 9 percent from 2010 to 2020, slower than the average for all occupations. However, growth will vary by industry.

Services provided by financial managers, such as planning, directing, and coordinating investments, will continue to be in demand as the economy grows. The United States remains an international financial center, meaning that the economic growth of countries around the world will likely contribute to employment growth in the U.S. financial industry.

Employment of financial managers in management of companies and enterprises is expected to grow by 3 percent from 2010 to 2020, slower than the average for all occupations. However, employment of self-employed financial managers is expected to grow at 20 percent from 2010 to 2020, faster than the average for all occupations.

Overall growth of employment for financial managers will be limited by expected employment declines in depository credit intermediation. This industry includes commercial banking and savings institutions, and employs the largest percent of these managers. From 2010 to 2020, employment of financial managers is expected to decline 14 percent in the depository credit intermediation industry.

As with other managerial occupations, jobseekers are likely to face competition because the number of job openings is expected to be fewer than the number of applicants. Candidates with expertise in accounting and finance—

particularly those with a master's degree or certification—should enjoy the best job prospects. An understanding of international finance and complex financial documents is important.

(7) Similar occupations

① Accountants and auditors. Accountants and auditors prepare and examine financial records. They ensure that financial records are accurate and that taxes are paid properly and on time. Accountants and auditors assess financial operations and work to help ensure that organizations run efficiently.

② Budget analysts. Budget analysts help public and private institutions organize their finances. They prepare budget reports and monitor institutional spending.

③ Financial analysts. Financial analysts provide guidance to businesses and individuals making investment decisions. They assess the performance of stocks, bonds, and other types of investments.

④ Insurance sales agents. Insurance sales agents help insurance companies generate new business by contacting potential customers and selling one or more types of insurance. An agent explains various insurance policies and helps clients choose plans that suit them.

Reading Comprehension

Choose the best answers to the following questions.

1. Which of the following is not the responsibility of a financial manager?
   A. supervising financial reports
   B. handling investment portfolios
   C. analyze financial data
   D. accounting

2. What are the two broad categories that financial manager jobs can be divided into?
   A. corporate finance and government finance.
   B. banking and finance of private sector.
   C. managerial finance and corporate finance.
   D. investment and managerial finance.

3. Which one below is not true towards the qualities for a qualified financial manager?
   A. Financial managers must be skilled in math, including algebra.
   B. Financial managers must know how to give orders.

C. Financial managers must explain and justify complex financial transactions.

D. Financial managers must pay attention to detail.

4. As the economy grows, what services by financial managers will continue to be in demand?

A. Directing.

B. Coordinating investment.

C. Planning.

D. All of the above.

5. According to the text, which one below is not true?

A. Budget analysts provide guidance to businesses and individuals making investment decisions.

B. Insurance sales agents help insurance companies generate new business by contacting potential customers and selling one or more types of insurance.

C. Financial analysts assess the performance of stocks, bonds, and other types of investments.

D. Accountants and auditors ensure that financial records are accurate and that taxes are paid properly and on time.

VI. Assignment

1. Interview some shopkeepers of the small businesses on your campus. Ask them about their methods of financial management. Write a report with about 200 words.

2. Collect information of three companies who have been troubled by poor financial management. Analyze the reasons of their problems and how they get out of the trouble. Make a presentation in class.

Unit 12
Financing

 Learning Objectives

After learning this unit, you should be able to:
1. Understand the concept of financing.
2. Know the nature and the main types of sources of financing.
3. Describe the main contents of debt and equity financing.
4. Show awareness of the risks of venture capital.
5. Describe the main considerations for a firm when financing.

 Lead-in

Whether you want to start a new business or run an existing one, you have to find money to finance its operations. Financing is just the commercial activity of providing funds for business activities, making purchases or investing. Financial institutions and banks are in the business of financing as they provide capital to businesses, consumers and investors to help them achieve their goals.

Warm-up Questions/Discussion:
1. How can you get the money when you need it in an emergency?
2. What are the financing options available to start-up businesses?
3. What is the cost of borrowing money from banks or other investors?

Financing[①]

Financing, generally speaking, is a means of currency transactions and an entity whose income exceeds its expenditure can lend or invest the excess income. On the other hand, an entity whose income is less than its expenditure can raise capital by borrowing or selling equity claims, decreasing its expenses, or increasing its income. The lender can find a borrower, a financial intermediary such as a bank, or buy notes or bonds in the bond market. The lender receives interest, the borrower pays a higher interest than the lender receives, and the financial intermediary earns the difference for arranging the loan.

1. Types of Sources of Financing

Businesses need finance sources to meet payroll[②] deadlines, acquire equipment, and expand or make business acquisitions[③], like buying land or other businesses. The time frame can dictate which type of finance source works best for funding. Bank is an obvious choice and works well for covering many short-term, medium-term and long-term financial requests. However, venture capital[④], private funding and trade credit are also sources of business financing.

(1) Short-term financing sources

Short-term financing solutions are needed on a daily, weekly and monthly basis to pay for office supplies, rent, utilities, equipment and payroll. Credit cards and trade credit (credit established with local trades and businesses) can assist a business in managing cash flow—the use of itemized statements allows for a clear visual representation of where the cash is being spent and a single payment can be made instead of multiple payments. Many businesses arrange for short-term lines of credit with their bank, referred to as the working capital, used to manage everyday business operations. Lines of credit are typically 90-day loans obtained through a commercial bank to assure that payroll and vendors[⑤] are paid on time, every time.

---

① The text is excerpted from http://www.smallbusinessnotes.com/business-finances with abridgment.
② payroll (工资单): A list of employees receiving wages or salaries, with the amounts due to each.
③ acquisition (收购): The act of contracting or assuming or acquiring possession of something.
④ venture capital (风险资本): Money made available for investment in innovative enterprises or research, especially in high technology, in which both the risk of loss and the potential for profit may be considerable. Also called risk capital.
⑤ vendor (供应商): A person who sells something, esp real property.

(2) Medium-term financing sources

Medium-term financing is used to fund a special business project or expansion that will increase production and revenue. Banks are a first stop when searching for this type of financing. Through letters of credit and equipment leases, banks can help with some of the financial risks involved with medium-term funding. Venture capital is also a finance source for expansion and special projects. Businesses offer venture capitalists a level of ownership in the business when they contribute funding. Another medium-term finance source is capital contributed by the existing owners—this is an additional investment the business owners make directly to the business coffers① and is called owners' equity. Owners' equity is considered a debt owed by the business to the owners of the business.

(3) Long-term financing sources

Any financial need requiring very large amounts of cash receives long-term funding. These sources of finance are generally designed to be paid off in one or more years and not in a few months. Businesses using this type of financing do so to purchase other businesses or buildings or to invest in long-term product development. Bank loans, venture capital and private financing are sources for long-term funding. Long-term business financing can be a combination of funding sources that together cover overall costs. For example, a private finance source (such as a car manufacturer like Ford or Honda) could cover the cost of the initial purchase of fleets of vehicles needed for a business expansion. <u>In addition, a local commercial bank loan could cover the purchase of the buildings to house the vehicles, and a line of credit could be used to cover payroll during the training of all the employees needed to run the expanded business.</u>

2. Debt Financing

Debt financing includes both secured and unsecured loans②. Security involves a form of collateral③ as an assurance the loan will be repaid. If the debtor defaults④ on the loan, that collateral is forfeited to satisfy payment of the debt. Most lenders

---

① coffers (库房): A chest, esp. for storing valuables.

② secured and unsecured loans (有担保和无担保贷款): A secured loan is a loan in which the borrower pledges some asset (eg. a car or a property) as collateral for the loan. Unsecured loans are monetary loans that are not secured against the borrowers assets.

③ collateral (抵押品): Security pledged for the repayment of a loan.

④ default (不履行义务): Failure to perform a task or fulfill an obligation, especially failure to meet a financial obligation.

will ask for some sort of security on a loan. Few, if any, will lend you money based on your name or idea alone.

You can also try to acquire debt financing through an unsecured loan. In this type of loan, your credit reputation is the only security the lender will accept. You may receive a personal loan for several thousand dollars-or more-if you have a good relationship with the bank. But these are usually short-term loans with very high rates of interest.

Most outside lenders are very conservative and unlikely to provide an unsecured loan unless you've done a tremendous amount of business with them in the past and have performed above expectations. Even if you do have this type of relationship with a lender, you may still be asked to post collateral on a loan due to economic conditions or your present financial condition.

The most common source of debt financing for startups often isn't a commercial lending institution, but family and friends. When borrowing money from your relatives or friends, have your attorney draw up legal papers dictating the terms of the loan. Why? Because too many entrepreneurs borrow money from family and friends on an informal basis. The terms of the loan have been verbalized but not written down in a contract.

<u>Lending money can be tricky for people who can't view the transaction at arm's length; if they don't feel you're running your business correctly, they might step in and interfere with your operations. In some cases, you can't prevent this, even with a written contract, because many state laws guarantee voting rights to an individual who has invested money in a business.</u> This can, and has, created a lot of hard feelings. Make sure to check with your attorney before accepting any loans from friends or family.

One of the most popular avenues of obtaining startup capital is credit cards. Although most charge high interest rates, credit cards provide a way to get several thousand dollars quickly without the hassle① of paperwork, as long as you don't overextend your ability to pay back the money in a timely fashion. Interest payments on credit-card debt add up quickly.

If you have three credit cards with a credit line of $5,000 on each card and you want to start a small business that you think will require approximately $8,000, you could take a cash advance on each card and start that business. Within six months, if you build up a profitable business and approach your local bank for a $10,000 loan

---

① hassle（麻烦）: A great deal of trouble; difficulty; nuisance.

at about 10 percent interest, you could use this money to pay off your credit-card balances (which most likely have 18-percent annual rates). After another six months, you could pay off the bank loan of $10,000.

A small-business loan usually costs a little more than a loan at the regular prime rate, which is the rate that banks charge their most favored customers. Small businesses usually pay one to three percentage points above that prime rate. Most small-business owners are more concerned with finding the right loan at the right terms than with the current interest rate. Be sure to shop around.

Banks tend to shy away from small companies experiencing rapid sales growth, a temporary decline or a seasonal slump①. In addition, firms that are already highly leveraged (a high debt-to-equity ratio) will usually have a hard time getting more bank funding.

3. Equity Financing

Equity financing is a method of financing in which a company issues shares of its stock and receives money in return. Depending on how you raise equity capital, you may relinquish② anywhere from 25 to 75 percent of the business.

Most small or growth-stage businesses use limited equity financing. As with debt financing, additional equity often comes from non-professional investors such as friends, relatives, employees, customers, or industry colleagues. However, the most common source of professional equity funding comes from venture capitalists. These are institutional risk takers and may be groups of wealthy individuals, government-assisted sources, or major financial institutions. Most specialize in one or a few closely related industries. The high-tech industry of California's Silicon Valley is a well-known example of capitalist investing.

Venture capital is one of the more popular forms of equity financing used to finance high-risk, high-return businesses. The amount of equity a venture capitalist holds is a factor of the company's stage of development when the investment occurs, the perceived risk, the amount invested, and the relationship between the entrepreneur and the venture capitalist.

Venture capitalists usually invest in businesses of every kind. Many individual venture capitalists, also known as angels, prefer to invest in industries that are familiar to them. The reason is that, while angels don't actively participate in the

---

① slump (暴跌): A sudden or marked decline or failure, as in progress or achievement.
② relinquish (放弃): To give up.

daily management of the company, they do want to have a say in strategic planning in order to reduce risks and maximize profits.

On the other hand, private venture capital partnerships and industrial venture capitalists like to invest primarily in technology-related industries, especially applications of existing technology such as computer-related communications, electronics, genetic engineering, and medical or health-related fields. There are also a number of investments in service and distribution businesses, and even a few in consumer-related companies, which attract venture capitalists.

In addition to the type of business they invest in, venture capitalists often define their investments by the business' life cycle: seed financing, startup financing, second-stage financing, bridge financing, and leveraged buyout①. Some venture capitalists prefer to invest in firms only during startup, where the risk is highest but so is the potential for return. Other venture capital firms deal only with second-stage financing for expansion purposes or bridge financing where they supply capital for growth until the company goes public. Finally, there are venture capital companies that concentrate solely on supplying funds for management-led buyouts.

Generally, venture capitalists like to finance firms during the early and second stages, when growth is rapid and cash out of the venture once it's established. At that time, the business owner either takes the company public, repurchases the investor's stock, merges with another firm; or in some circumstances, liquidates② the business.

Before approaching any investor or venture capital firm, do your homework and find out if your interests match their investment preferences. The best way to contact venture capitalists is through an introduction from another business owner, banker, attorney or other professional who knows you and the venture capitalist well enough to approach them with the proposition.

While poor management is cited most frequently as the reason businesses fail, inadequate or ill-timed financing is a close second. Whether you're starting a business or expanding one, sufficient ready capital is essential. It is not, however, enough to simply have sufficient financing; knowledge and planning are required to manage it well. These qualities ensure that entrepreneurs avoid common mistakes

---

① leveraged buyout（融资收买）: A buyout using borrowed money; the target company's assets are usually security for the loan.

② liquidate（清算）: Eliminate by paying off (debts).

like securing the wrong type of financing, miscalculating the amount required, or underestimating the cost of borrowing money.

4. Financing tips

Before inquiring about financing, ask yourself the following:

• Do you need more capital or can you manage existing cash flow more effectively?

• How do you define your need? Do you need money to expand or as a cushion① against risk?

• How urgent is your need? You can obtain the best terms when you anticipate your needs rather than looking for money under pressure.

• How great are your risks? All businesses carry risks, and the degree of risk will affect cost and available financing alternatives.

• In what state of development is the business? Needs are most critical during transitional stages.

• For what purposes will the capital be used? Any lender will require that capital be requested for very specific needs.

• What is the state of your industry? Depressed, stable, or growth conditions require different approaches to money needs and sources. Businesses that prosper while others are in decline will often receive better funding terms.

• Is your business seasonal or cyclical? Seasonal needs for financing generally are short term. Loans advanced for cyclical industries such as construction are designed to support a business through depressed periods.

• How strong is your management team? Management is the most important element assessed by money sources.

• Perhaps most importantly, how does your need for financing mesh with your business plan? If you don't have a business plan, make writing one your first priority. All capital sources will want to see your business plan for the startup and growth of your business.

 Exercises

I. Reviewing Questions
Answer the following questions according to the text.
1. What is financing?

---

① cushion(起缓冲作用之物): Something resilient used as a rest, support, or shock absorber.

2. How many types of sources of financing are there? What are they?
3. What do businesses use long-term financing to do?
4. What is only accepted by the lender in unsecured loan?
5. Why does the author ask people to draw up legal papers when borrowing money from relatives and friends?
6. What kinds of companies do the banks probably refuse to fund?
7. Why do most individual venture capitalists prefer to invest in industries that are familiar to them?
8. What is business life cycle?
9. Why do venture capitalists like to finance firms during the early and second stages of the life cycle?
10. What risks does financing bring to businesses?

II. Cloze
Read the following passage and fill in the blanks with the words given below. Change the form where necessary.

appealing	trust	generate	mainstream	accountable
promissory	covert	liquidity	belly-up	frequent

When it comes to the financing popularity contest, equity funding is currently in vogue. Articles in the ___1___ media about venture capital have glamorized the concept of selling stock in your startup, and entrepreneurs across the board would much prefer to raise money in the form of equity rather than debt.

Why is equity so ___2___? Because it feels like you're getting "free" money during the startup stage. There are usually no repayment obligations and no interest payments due to equity investors. You'll also have some say in negotiating the price of your stock, any dividend payments and the position the investor will have in your company. If your business goes ___3___, it's their loss (unless, of course, your investors can prove in court that you didn't disclose critical information that would have influenced their decision to invest).

Besides providing funding, equity investors can be helpful in other ways as well. They bring their business experience and lessons learned to bear on your company, and they can become a ___4___ advisor, mentor or board member. The best equity investors are those with expertise in your industry, experience launching a business, a cool temperament and deep pockets. Some say choosing an equity investor is like getting married—you're making yourself ___5___ to this person through thick and thin, so choose carefully.

Before you go investor shopping, though, you should carefully think about just what you're selling and what having equity investors really means for you and your business. Very few businesses will ever be able to deliver a decent return on investment (ROI) for equity investors. The typical restaurant or retail store, for example, is unlikely to have any ___6___ for its shares. And even if you plan to have a high-growth tech business, the chance of reaching liquidity for your early investors is low. You must be honest with yourself about whether your investors expect to be paid back.

Assuming you won't have a glamorous initial public offering, you'll need to find a way to allow your investors a graceful exit. One option is to find a new wave of investors willing to buy out the old ones at a share price that feels like a win-win for all. Another option for investors—especially friends and family who want to stay involved—is to ___7___ equity positions into loans. In my role as president of Circle Lending, I've encountered these loan conversions quite ___8___, even though equity investors typically have no legal recourse in the event the business fails. This is one of hidden secrets of startup financing—that equity investments from relatives, friends and other startup investors often morph into loans if the businesses fail.

But what about good, old-fashioned loans? If the sheen of equity capital is tarnished by the reality of having to ___9___ a respectable ROI, you can fall back on the old familiar friend: a loan. The good news about debt financing is that you're still completely in charge of your business—your only duty to your lender is to make your payments on time, as spelled out in your ___10___ note. As long as you do that, your lender has no right to meddle in your business. Interest payments are typically a deductible business expense, and if your lender is someone you know well, you may be able to get favorable repayment terms that can make the loan walk and talk much like an equity investment.

III. Translation

1. Credit cards and trade credit (credit established with local trades and businesses) can assist a business in managing cash flow—the use of itemized statements allows for a clear visual representation of where the cash is being spent and a

single payment can be made instead of multiple payments.

2. In addition, a local commercial bank loan could cover the purchase of the buildings to house the vehicles, and a line of credit could be used to cover payroll during the training of all the employees needed to run the expanded business.

3. Lending money can be tricky for people who can't view the transaction at arm's length; if they don't feel you're running your business correctly, they might step in and interfere with your operations. In some cases, you can't prevent this, even with a written contract, because many state laws guarantee voting rights to an individual who has invested money in a business.

4. However, the most common source of professional equity funding comes from venture capitalists. These are institutional risk takers and may be groups of wealthy individuals, government-assisted sources, or major financial institutions. Most specialize in one or a few closely related industries.

5. Some venture capitalists prefer to invest in firms only during startup, where the risk is highest but so is the potential for return. Other venture capital firms deal only with second-stage financing for expansion purposes or bridge financing where they supply capital for growth until the company goes public. Finally, there are venture capital companies that concentrate solely on supplying funds for management-led buyouts.

IV. Case Study

How to Restart a Company

Robin Sauve was growing increasingly anxious. She and her husband, John, had started Barkley Logistics, based in Enfield, Connecticut, last June, shortly after buying the assets of her former employer, Premier Logistics, which had shut down after running out of financial options. Now, four months into the life of the new business, orders were slowly picking up for Barkley, which arranges merchandise shipments and deliveries of time-sensitive materials, such as coupons and promotional fliers. Though not nearly as much business as Sauve had hoped for, the flurry of new jobs was nonetheless straining her ability to finance operations, and

Sauve's financial adviser had told her she would soon need to get a line of credit to finance the company's growth.

But the idea of going deeper into debt put both Robin and John, who heads sales and marketing, into a panic. They had already taken on $40,000 in credit card debt, a tolerable level, they figured. Though Robin believed in the business, she reasoned that if things didn't work out, she could still sell the company's assets, find a new job, and pay off her credit cards. Taking on even more debt with a line of credit—her financial adviser had said she would need at least $75,000—was a leap she felt she just couldn't make, as she would possibly be putting everything at risk, including her house. "In my head, this was huge," Robin says. "I thought, if you do this, there is no turning back."

Buying the business was the easy part. The fallout from Premier's implosion was another matter. Premier contracted with trucking companies to move material for its customers. But when the logistics firm ran into cash-flow problems and couldn't pay those carriers, the carriers turned around and tried to collect from Premier's customers. (Girard Robitaille, Premier's former president, declined to comment except to say, "We were in business for almost 10 years and served our customers well.") And even though Barkley was not affiliated with the former owners of Premier, Sauve knew former Premier clients would be wary of doing business with her. At the same time, she needed to contract with some of the very trucking firms Premier had shortchanged. And she feared they might think her firm was just an extension of Premier and refuse to deliver shipments until she covered their losses from Premier. "That would have collapsed us before we got off the ground," she says, "It was nerve-racking."

As she got her start-up off the ground, Sauve realized she needed some help. Though she knew the operations side of the business, Sauve wasn't as strong as in finance. An accountant friend introduced her to Robert Perry, a retired partner at her friend's firm. Perry agreed to oversee her books and counsel her on strategy. His very first bit of advice: Sauve would need access to outside capital. But he said a bank would want to see several months of revenue before it would even consider funding the company.

After months of troubled nights filled with anxious dreams, Robin started gaining more confidence. Barkley completed 30 jobs in October, and doubled the business in September. For the first time, revenue covered operating expenses (though the Sauves still weren't and aren't, paying themselves or their employees).

Sauve was also encouraged that some former clients who had been gun-shy about giving her business seemed to be coming around. One former customer wrote Sauve an e-mail explaining that the fallout from Premier's failure made Barkley "a bit toxic around here," but he didn't see it as "a long lasting problem" and admired her "chutzpah" in starting the new business.

Given the pace of new contracts, Barkley was on track to hit $100,000 a month in sales by the end of April—a trajectory that gave Sauve confidence in putting her personal assets on the line wasn't as foolhardy as she originally feared. After a conversation with her husband, she decided to move ahead with an application for the line of credit. "I knew this was the make-or-break moment," she says. "We need to either go for it or stop operating the business."

(The text is excerpted from www.inc.com)

Questions for discussion:
1. Why did Sauve and John succeed in their business? What was the core element that made them succeed?
2. If you run into this situation, what will you do? Why?
3. Do you think that what Sauve did would work in China? Why?

V. Supplementary Reading

Angel Investors

Angel investors are individuals who invest in businesses looking for a higher return than they would see from more traditional investments. Many are successful entrepreneurs who want to help other entrepreneurs get their business off the ground. Usually they are the bridge from the self-funded stage of the business to the point that the business needs the level of funding that a venture capitalist would offer. Funding estimates vary, but usually range from $150,000 to $1.5 million.

The term "angel" comes from the practice in the early 1900s of wealthy businessmen investing in Broadway productions. Today "angels" typically offer expertise, experience and contacts in addition to money. Less is known about angel investing than venture capital because of the individuality and privacy of the investments, but the Small Business Administration estimates that there are at least 250,000 angels active in the country, funding about 30,000 small companies a year. The total investment from angels has been estimated at anywhere from $20 billion to $50 billion as compared to the $3 to $5 billion per year that the formal venture capital community invests. In fact, the potential pool of angel investors is substantially larger. There are about two million people in the United States with the discretionary net worth to make angel investments.

The Center for Venture Research at the University of New Hampshire which does research on angel investments has developed the following profile of angel investors:

- The "average" private investor is 47 years old with an annual income of $90,000, a net worth of $750,000, is college educated, has been self employed and invests $37,000 per venture.
- Most angels invest close to home and rarely put in more than a few hundred thousand dollars.
- Informal investment appears to be the largest source of external equity capital for small businesses. Nine out of 10 investments are devoted to small, mostly start-up firms with fewer than 20 employees.
- Nine out of 10 investors provide personal loans or loan guarantees to the firms they invest in. On average, this increases the available capital by 57%.
- Informal investors are older, have higher incomes, and are better educated than the average citizen, yet they are not often millionaires. They are a diverse group, displaying a wide range of personal characteristics and investment behavior.
- Seven out of 10 investments are made within 50 miles of the investor's home or office.
- Investors expect an average 26% annual return at the time they invest, and they believe that about one-third of their investments are likely to result in a substantial capital loss.
- Investors accept an average of 3 deals for every 10 considered. The most common reasons given for rejecting a deal are insufficient growth potential, overpriced equity, lack of sufficient talent of the management, or lack of information about the entrepreneur or key personnel.
- There appears to be no shortage of informal capital funds. Investors included in the study would have invested almost 35% more than they did if acceptable opportunities had been available.

For the business seeking funding, the right angel investor can be the perfect first step in formal funding. It usually takes less time to meet with an angel and to receive funds, due diligence is less involved and angels usually expect a lower rate of return than a venture capitalist. The downside is finding the right balance of expert help without the angel totally taking charge of the business. Structuring the relationship carefully is an important step in the process.

What does an angel investor expect?

There are almost as many answers to what angels expect as there are angels. Each has their own criteria and foibles because they are individuals. Almost all want a board position and possibly a consulting role. All want good communication although for some that means quarterly reports, while for others that means weekly updates. Return objectives range from a projected internal rate of return of 30% over five years to sales projections of $20 million in the first five years to the potential return of five times investment in the first five years. Most are looking for anything from a 5 to 25 percent stake in the business. Some want securities-either common stock or preferred stock with certain rights and liquidation preferences over common stock. Some even ask for convertible debt, or redeemable preferred stock, which provides a clearer exit strategy for the investor, but also places the company at the risk of repaying the investment plus interest. Additionally, the repayment may imperil future financing since those sources will not likely want to use their investments to bail out prior investors.

Some angels ask for the right of first refusal to participate in the next round of financing. While this sounds eminently reasonable, some venture capitalists will want their own players only or certain investment minimums so this strategy may limit who future participants might be.

Future representation of the board of directors also needs to be clarified. When a new round of financing occurs, do they lose their board right? Or should that could be based on a percentage ownership—when their ownership level drops below a certain level, they no longer have board representation.

In order to protect their investment, angels often ask the business to agree to not take certain actions without the angel investors approval. These include selling all or substantially all of the company's assets, issuing additional stock to existing management, selling stock below prices paid by the investors or creating classes of stock with liquidation preferences or other rights senior to the angel's class of security. Angels also ask for price protection which is anti-dilution provisions that will result in their receiving more stock should the business issue stock at a lower price than that paid by the angels.

To prepare to solicit an angel, several critical factors will aid in making the approach successful. First, assemble an advisory board that includes a securities accountant and an attorney. Two important functions of the board are to recommend angels to contact and to work with the management team to develop a business plan to present to the angel. The business plan itself should define the reason for financing, how the capital will be spent and the timetable for going public or seeking venture capital funding. It should include: an executive summary (description of the business, opportunity and strategy, target market, projections and competitive advantages); the industry, the company and its products and services (including entry and growth strategies); market research and analysis (customers, market size and trends, competition, estimated market share and sales); the economics of the business (including gross and operating margins and break-even analysis); marketing plan (overall strategy, pricing, advertising, promotion, and distribution); design and development plans (product/service improvement and new products/services); manufacturing and operations plans (geographic location, facilities and capacity improvements); management team (organization overview, biographies and compensation plans for key employees); financial plan (tax returns, profits and loss forecasts, pro-forma cash flow analysis and balance sheets, 5-year projections); and proposed company offering (desired financing, securities offering, capitalization, timetable).

Most of all, take your time in forming a relationship with an angel. You are going to be spending a number of years together at a critical time in your business' life. Take the time to assure yourself that this is a person who you are comfortable with through both the ups and downs the future will bring.

Reading Comprehension

Choose the best answers to the following questions.

1. Angel investors are individuals who invest in businesses looking for _____ than they would see from more traditional investments.

    A. a higher return

    B. a lower return

    C. not higher return

    D. not lower return

2. Today "angels" typically offer _____ in addition of money.

    A. expertise

    B. experience

C. contacts

D. All of the above

3. All of the following are what angels expect except _____.

   A. a board position and possibly a consulting role

   B. privileges of purchasing

   C. good communication

   D. anything from a five to 25 percent stake

4. Angels often ask the owner of the company not to do some actions not including _____ in order to protect their investments.

   A. selling all or substantially all of the company's assets

   B. issuing additional stock to existing management

   C. selling stock higher prices paid by the investors

   D. creating classes of stock with liquidation preferences

5. When you decide to solicit an angel for your business, what are the most important factors you should consider?

   A. An executive summary and market research and analysis

   B. The industry, the company and its products and services

   C. The economics of the business and marketing plan

   D. All above and some other factors

VI. Assignment

1. Interview some corporate owners who ran into the problem of finance before and came through it by financing via banks or other investors. Ask them about the brief steps and specific situation of the financing process. And write a report with about 200 words.

2. Please prepare a ten-minute presentation to introduce the current situation of global finance and stock markets.

Unit 13
Corporate Social Responsibility

 Learning Objectives

After learning this unit, you should be able to:
1. Know the basic ideas of CSR.
2. Describe the development course of CSR.
3. Tell the importance of social responsible actions for a business.
4. Know how a business can shoulder its social responsibility.
5. Discuss the relation of social responsible actions and economic performances.

 Lead-in

While most people demand ethical conduct for their idols and political leaders, few do so for businessmen. Ever since their coming into being, businessmen have been regarded as creatures which are by nature profit-thirsty, unscrupulous and unethical. As an old Chinese saying goes, "No businessman is not unscrupulous." But as the economy develops and businessmen have been exerting ever-growing influence, more and more people demand businesses to behave more ethically and become more responsible toward the society.

Warm-up Questions/Discussion:
1. How much do you know about corporate social responsibilities?
2. What do you think is the most important factor for a business? Profits or reputation?
3. Can you list any companies which are both socially responsible and committed to profits?

Corporate Social Responsibility

Definition of Social Responsibility in Business

Social responsibility is defined as a theory that obligates① individuals and groups to act in a way that benefits the greater good of the society. Applied to businesses, it means that a company can be defined as socially responsible if its main objectives, practices and processes not only respect laws and regulations, but also contribute to the growth and well-being of the community.

Corporate Social Responsibility

Conducting socially responsible business can bear many other names, including corporate social responsibility (CSR), social performance and sustainable responsible business. CSR, the most common term, was first used in the late 1960s by multinationals. It is defined as a form of self-regulated social responsibility within a business model. The objective of CSR is to encourage actions that promote activities that have a positive impact on employees, stakeholders, clients and the environment.

Community-based Development

The community-base development approach to CSR encourages business to work with local communities to better themselves. A good example of this is Tyson Food, the biggest producer and marketers of chicken, beef and pork products in the world. The food giant practices community-based development through its KNOW Hunger program. By collaborating with the Food Research and Action Center, the Tyson initiative helps raise awareness of hunger in America.

Philanthropy

Another common approach to social responsibility in business is through philanthropy②. This can include financial aid and donations of time, gifts or expertise. When companies decide to make donations to a community that is faced with a natural disaster such as a flood or an earthquake, they are exercising philanthropic social responsibility.

---

① obligate (使负义务): To bind, compel, or constrain by a social, legal, or moral tie.
② philanthropy (慈善事业): The effort or inclination to increase the well-being of humankind, as by charitable aid or donations.

Creating Shared Value

The shared value model is based on the belief that a company and its community's well-being are interdependent. This approach encourages businesses to create economic and social value toward the community by focusing on social issues it can help resolve through its own specialization. For example, car manufacturers have been introducing hybrid and electric cars to the benefit of a healthier environment.

Laws and Regulations

A particular feature of CSR is that it is a self-governing principle. Although this means no law or regulation makes CSR obligatory, ISO 26000 was put in place in November 2010. ISO 26000 is a recognized international standard put in place to provide guidelines and encourage voluntary commitment to social responsibility. It targets a wide range of organizations in both the public and private sectors.

About Corporate Social Responsibility

As early as 1969, corporations have been paying attention to their impact on the local community and the world. Arising from the social justice movement of the 1960s, companies have found that it is good for their bottom line to be involved, to invest in their local community, to pay living wages and offer health benefits to their employees, to provide safe and sanitary[①] work environments, to take care to avoid child or slave labor when purchasing parts and materials from overseas suppliers, to reduce pollutants produced by their products and to promote responsible business practices worldwide. Rather than bending laws or asking for exceptions, these companies strive to go beyond the law to ensure that what they do to make a profit is not at the expense of quality of life, sustainability or fairness to community members, suppliers, employees, investors or customers.

History

The earliest example of a corporate social and environmental responsibility report, according to professors Alice and John Tepper Marlin, was made in 1972 by Abt and Associates[②]. There were no standards set at this time. The professors

---

① sanitary（卫生的）: Of or relating to health or the protection of health.

② Abt and Associates（美国 Abt 公司）: Abt Associates was ranked as one of the top 20 global research firms in 2011 and also named one of the top 40 international development innovators. The company has multiple offices in the U.S. and program offices in nearly 40 countries.

helped develop standards of accountability① for future reports in 1973, including the recommendation that the auditors for those reports should be certified by a third party. Ben and Jerry's used five categories in their report in 1989. Shell Oil② followed with its own report in 1991, and has sometimes erroneously③ been credited with originating the social responsibility report movement. The Body Shop④, also credited with originating corporate social responsibility, followed soon after. Social Accountability International was founded in 1997 to certify corporate responsibility auditors. Avon Corporation was certified under its standards in 1998.

Features

Corporate social responsibility includes making certain that suppliers are treating their workers well, paying a living wage, providing opportunities for education and advancement, investing in their communities and protecting the environment. This is not always an easy standard to meet. Efforts to change practices overseas do not always have these results. Poverty relief efforts, such as securing a clean water supply for the community, providing access to public health clinics and ensuring that area children get needed food and vaccines⑤ must take place before pressure can be put on local governments to enforce worker health, safety and wage laws. The benefit to the company is a new group of loyal customers for its products, resulting in dollars spent being at least partially returned to company coffers.

Considerations

Not all companies agree on the value of corporate social responsibility efforts as they apply to the bottom line. Philanthropy that does not produce a return of some kind becomes malfeasance⑥ if it drives the company out of business. If consumers are unaware of the efforts the company has made and how those efforts affect costs of production, they may buy a competing product at a lower price.

Companies must make sure that consumers know about their socially responsible efforts, and this can be tricky. Striking the right note between informing

---

① accountability（有义务）: Responsibility to someone or for some activity.
② Shell Oil（壳牌石油公司）: One of the world's leading energy companies, based in the Netherlands and the UK.
③ erroneously（错误地）: In a mistaken manner.
④ The Body Shop（化妆品连锁店）: A chain of cosmetics stores.
⑤ vaccine（疫苗）: A biological preparation that improves immunity to a particular disease.
⑥ malfeasance（渎职）: Misconduct or wrongdoing, especially by a public official.

the consumer and corporate bragging can be difficult. Depending upon the product, the company could even find itself fielding accusations of hypocrisy. Tobacco companies in particular face this issue, as their products are a delivery system for a substance that is known to cause health problems, fetal abnormalities and death. No amount of fair trade practices can make up for that.

Consumers must take the responsibility to inform themselves about the practices of the companies whose products they buy most often. Switch brands when you find a company whose ethics match your own. Use products from companies that practice fair and sustainable trade, and that do their best to limit pollution and other environmental damage.

Benefits

Let responsible companies know why you are buying from them. This increases the likelihood that the company will continue its efforts to create safer products free of chemicals, genetically altered materials, antibiotics or hormones. Workers at fair trade companies will have more money available, much of which will return to the local economy. This helps raise the standard of living in an area, and puts pressure on companies that do not practice corporate responsibility to raise wages and offer better benefits to prevent workers from leaving to join the other company.

Potential

If every consumer buys from responsible companies, other companies would have to become more socially responsible in order to compete. Lower pollution levels would result in fewer visits to the doctor or emergency room for people with asthma and environmental allergies. Workers would have fewer absences due to injury and illness. Families could afford to buy homes, cars and other items needed. <u>Schools would have more money to spend on improvements, through a combination of income tax and corporate taxes, rather than relying solely on real estate taxes as they do now.</u> Forests would be planted rather than mowed down and chewed into paper and siding.

Importance of Social Responsibility in Business

Social responsibility is so important to current and long-term business success that corporate social responsibility, CSR, has become a widely recognized business

Unit 13 Corporate Social Responsibility

process in the early 21st century. Entrepreneurs point out that CSR is an evolution of corporate ethics because it involves balancing the social expectations of all stakeholders, including shareholders, citizens, providers and customers, along with environmental responsibility.

Basic Integrity

Most experts and CSR analysts agree that this broad business concept is an evolution of basic business ethics and integrity. Entrepreneur and business strategist Robert Moment "The Seven Princes of Business Integrity" agree that treating stakeholders with respect and earning trust of customers through ethical business operations is the CSR foundation. Leading advocate of corporate accountability, the As You Sow Foundation, also stresses the importance of internal business controls that mandate ethics from corporate leaders and employees.

Community Relations

The word "social" is key to understanding how CSR goes beyond basic integrity. Moment states in one of his seven principles that as a CSR adherent, you must "remain involved in community-related issues and activities thereby demonstrating that your business is a responsible community contributor." This community involvement and participation shows your marketplace that you are interested in more than just taking money from their pockets. In the long run, this strategy leads to a stronger public reputation and more profitable business relationships.

The Environment

Another reason CSR is much broader than conventional business ethics is its necessary inclusion of environmental responsibility. Once an opportunity for companies to add value and enhance their brand images, green-friendly operations are now a societal requirement with CSR. As You Sow discusses the importance of preserving the environment, optimizing efficient use of natural resources, such as renew, reuse and recycle, and reduction of waste as important to the environmental component of CSR. Companies that do not consider these initiatives draw the ire[①] of the government, public and consumer watch groups.

---

① ire（愤怒）：Anger; wrath.

Bottom Line

The underlying question is whether CSR operations improve a company's bottom line performance. David Vogel argues in his 2008 Forbes article that "CSR Doesn't Pay." Vogel argues that operating under CSR guidelines is not likely to produce higher tangible profits for a company throughout time. Now that socially responsible behavior is expected, it goes largely unnoticed, argues Vogel. He does agree, though, that companies that ignore CSR may experience public backlash① and negative business consequences. Still, many advocates of CSR believe that companies can still profit in the long run through stronger business and customer relationships.

How Business Can Be Socially Responsible

For a business to be socially responsible it means that the business is conscious of the environment in which it operates. The environmental conditions that influence the activities of a business define the society that the business is indebted to. Therefore, social responsibility is a way of giving back and in so doing businesses aim at improving the welfare of the society in general.

Businesses exist for the sole purpose of making profits and creating wealth for the owners. But for them to return profits, they must provide goods and services. The provision of goods and services is itself a form of responsibility. Once they make profits, business must pay taxes which the government uses to provide essential services to the society at large. This setup does not exonerate② businesses from voluntary corporate social responsibility. They should go further and serve the society because it allows them to use scarce resources. Social responsibility is all about being ethical. Businesses should view the society as the host of the factors of production, the source of profits and as shareholders to the scarce resources.

Some of the reasons why businesses are indebted to the society include the fact that they are part of the society's problems. Secondly they have a moral duty to help. As an entity, a business should mind the welfare of everyone in society. Thirdly, businesses expect that they will continue operating in the society in future. This calls on them to protect the host society. Fourthly, business contributes to social ills in many ways and so they must act to correct them where possible and finally,

---

① backlash（对抗）: An antagonistic reaction to a trend, development, or event.
② exonerate（使免责）: To free from a responsibility, obligation, or task.

social responsibility improves the image of the business and endears① it to the society even more.

The stakeholders in the society include the consumers, the workers, the shareholders, the local authorities and the general public. Ways that a business can give back to these groups of stakeholders include:

Give preference to the immediate public when it comes to hiring. This makes the public feel attached. Give fair wages and never be seen to be exploiting workers. Set fair prices for the goods and services provided. Again exploiting the consumers is irresponsible. Aim at quality production and customer satisfaction which are the pillars of establishing good relationships and gaining respect. Set up social welfare facilities. For example, businesses can use part of their proceeds to build schools and health care facilities.

Participate in social activities. One way of doing this is by sponsoring sporting events and tournaments that involve the host society. Share ideas and intelligence. Organizing community forums is one way of enhancing interactions with the society with an aim of helping them come up with plans and strategies on how to solve common problems. Communicate your actions to the public. Give periodic assessment reports so that your activities and achievements are not a mystery to the public. Use part of your businesses resources to fund research and development that is aimed at creating solutions for problems that affect the entire society. For example, a business can fund a research on how to find a cure for a common disease. This mainly works in developing countries where governments can not take care of such needs on their own. Participate in setting up social amenities②. This keeps the society happy and one aim of being socially responsible is to keep the society happy. Recognize minorities such as the disabled. It is good to come up with a program that encourages and promotes equity among all members of the society. It is the contemporary way of being responsible. In some places such as Africa, people are increasingly becoming aware of the role of Multi-National corporations in environmental degradation. Businesses in these areas have therefore a duty to show respect to the environment by leading the way in its conservation.

The examples above do not exhaust ways that businesses can participate in corporate social responsibility. They can device many ways of being helpful by seeking to protect all the stakeholders' interests. Besides, the key to social

---

① endear (使受喜爱): To cause to be beloved or esteemed.
② amenity (愉快): The fact or condition of being pleasant or agreeable.

responsibility is giving back.

Exercises

I. Reviewing Questions
Answer the following questions according to the text.
1. What is corporate social responsibility?
2. How can the companies do to shoulder the corporate social responsibility?
3. What was the first example about corporate social responsibility?
4. What is the content of corporate social responsibility?
5. Why should a company make their consumers know its efforts in CSR?
6. Why is the corporate social responsibility important?
7. How will consumers respond to a company's social responsible actions?
8. What was Vogel's argument on CSR?
9. Does a company still have any social responsibilities apart from paying taxes?
10. What should a company do to pay back the society?

II. Cloze
Read the following passage and fill in the blanks with the words given below. Change the form where necessary.

result	imply	dynamic	precede	performance
distinct	expectation	mutual	conflict	principle

Although economic and legal responsibilities embody ethical norms about fairness and justice, ethical responsibilities embrace those activities and practices that are expected or prohibited by societal members even though they are not codified into law. Ethical responsibilities embody those standards, norms, or __1__ that reflect a concern for what consumers, employees, shareholders, and the community regard as fair, just, or in keeping with the respect or protection of stakeholders' moral rights.

In one sense, changing ethics or values __2__ the establishment of law because they become the driving force behind the very creation of laws or regulations. For example, the environmental, civil rights, and consumer movements reflected basic alterations in societal values and thus may be seen as ethical bellwethers foreshadowing and __3__ in the later legislation. In another sense, ethical responsibilities may be seen as embracing newly emerging values and norms society expects business to meet, even though such values and norms may reflect a higher standard of ___4___ than that currently required by law. Ethical responsibilities in this sense are often ill-defined or continually under public debate as to their legitimacy, and thus are frequently difficult for business to deal with.

Superimposed on these ethical expectations emanating from societal groups are the ___5___ levels of ethical performance suggested by a consideration of the great ethical principles of moral philosophy. This would include such ___6___ as justice, rights, and utilitarianism.

No metaphor is perfect, and the CSR pyramid is no exception. It is intended to portray that the total CSR of business comprises ___7___ components that, taken together, constitute the whole. Though the components have been treated as separate concepts for discussion purposes, they are not ___8___ exclusive and are not intended to juxtapose a firm's economic responsibilities with its other responsibilities. At the same time, a consideration of the separate components helps the manager see that the different types of obligations are in a constant but ___9___ tension with one another. The most critical tensions, of course, would be between economic and legal, economic and ethical, and economic and philanthropic. The traditionalist might see this as a ___10___ between a firm's "concern for profits" versus its "concern for society," but it is suggested here that this is an oversimplification. A CSR or stakeholder perspective would recognize these tensions as organizational realities, but focus on the total pyramid as a unified whole and how the firm might engage in decisions, actions, and programs that simultaneously fulfill all its component parts.

In summary, the total corporate social responsibility of business entails the simultaneous fulfillment of the firm's economic, legal, ethical, and philanthropic responsibilities. Stated in more pragmatic and managerial terms, the CSR firm should strive to make a profit, obey the law, be ethical, and be a good corporate citizen.

III. Translation

1. This approach encourages businesses to create economic and social value toward the community by focusing on social issues it can help resolve through its own specialization. For example, car manufacturers have been introducing hybrid and electric cars to the benefit of a healthier environment.

2. Poverty relief efforts, such as securing a clean water supply for the community, providing access to public health clinics and ensuring that area children get needed food and vaccines must take place before pressure can be put on local governments to enforce worker health, safety and wage laws.

3. Schools would have more money to spend on improvements, through a combination of income tax and corporate taxes, rather than relying solely on real estate taxes as they do now.

4. Another reason CSR is much broader than conventional business ethics is its necessary inclusion of environmental responsibility. Once an opportunity for companies to add value and enhance their brand images, green-friendly operations are now a societal requirement with CSR.

5. They should go further and serve the society because it allows them to use scarce resources. Social responsibility is all about being ethical. Businesses should view the society as the host of the factors of production, the source of profits and as shareholders to the scarce resources.

IV. Case Study

Corporate Social Responsibility at Apple

by Rosa Chun

News of Steve Jobs's death sent shockwaves through the technology industry, a world that he, in large part, shaped with his career. Apple's executives are now left with the challenge of how to lead a company, whose identity has been inextricably linked to Jobs' for decades. The task is formidable, especially when Apple's fanatically loyal customer base is considerably less certain about what to expect from CEO Tim Cook.

What makes leading Apple difficult to maintain is the fact that the company is not selling a product as much as it is a vision, the founder's vision. Apple products are undeniably cutting edge, well built and beautiful to look at, but ultimately they are commodities that now face tough competition. Samsung is gnawing into iPhone sales by offering technically superior product for comparable price.

According to recent media coverage, it would seem that Apple is interested in developing a new vision, one which includes CSR. Jobs never showed much interest in public "do-gooding." He always maintained that equipping the public with the best technology is worth more than cash grants to charities. But earlier this month Cook announced that Apple would embrace a new corporate charity matching program, using a model much like those of other major companies—a dollar for dollar match for employee donations of up to $10,000 a year. Cook clearly wants to send the message that Apple is evolving in the way it perceives CSR, a major differentiating factor between himself and his charismatic predecessor.

Developing a CSR strategy around neither a sense of obligation nor calculation but rather around certain well-defined character virtues is highly effective. In particular, integrity, empathy and zeal, among others, are critical during times of uncertainty; they need to be well coordinated and implemented from the inside-out—not the other way around.

Integrity: Any major organizational change is accompanied by insecurity. The transition from Jobs' approach to hiring and firing is bound to create uncertainty among employees, and in corporate environments uncertainty inevitably creates pernicious maneuvering and second guessing at middle management levels. The new CSR initiatives should present both the company and its new CEO with a unique opportunity to promote an image of integrity and to differentiate the new leadership from that of the Jobs era. However, philanthropy is not a good place to start. It should start from inside, promoting trust and openness, the internal integrity.

Empathy: Empathy creates emotional bonding between the company and stakeholders allowing companies to endure a difficult time. Apple is currently embroiled in lawsuits that are likely to restrict consumer choices in the future if it carries on. Publishers are frustrated by Apple's hammerlock over apps and magazine subscriptions on the iPad. There have been indications that Samsung, Apple's most threatening competitor, angered by patent law suits, will finally fight back to counter sue Apple. While from Apple's point of view, taking legal action against competitors may seem necessary as a means of protecting innovation, public opinion works differently. For multinational companies the legal victory can often end with a kind of zero sum game, leaving it with a reputation for arrogance and insecurity. Apple will have to worry about its reputation all the more so if it wins the battles against competitors.

Zeal: Zeal is perhaps the virtue most-embedded at Apple's core and is represented by their continuous innovation and excitement in terms of products and customer experience. By emphasizing CSR, Tim Cook would need to bring that famous Apple zeal to social issues, offering an innovative approach, as competitor Google did, when it famously began encouraging its employees to spend 20% of their time on their own projects.

Questions for discussion:
1. Jobs maintained that equipping the public with the best technology is worth more than cash grants to charities. Do you agree with his opinion? Why?
2. The Apple executives have carried out a series of new strategies to cope with the potential threats from competitors. What do you think of them?
3. After Jobs's death, what do you think Apple would do to the society in the future?

V. Supplementary Reading

Responsible Business Conduct in China

All countries are facing the challenges of promoting sustainable development and conditions which facilitate responsible conduct on the part of business. As the world economy becomes more integrated, China, together with other industrialized countries and emerging countries, have a shared responsibility to meet these challenges.

China Can Benefit from Policies to Encourage Responsible Business Conduct (RBC)

China can benefit from adopting and implementing effective policies to encourage responsible business conduct (RBC). Problems have arisen in the course of the country's rapid industrialization, some of them capable of threatening social stability or damaging relations with other countries. While the Chinese government has primary responsibility for solving such issues, enterprises can contribute to solutions, both by complying with laws and regulations and also by striving to meet societal expectations that are not expressed as legal obligations. RBC is to be encouraged on economic as well as societal grounds, as it can render investment by Chinese enterprises more competitive and sustainable both at home and abroad. More broadly, it can play a key role in the government's initiative to create a harmonious society. The Chinese government strongly encourages enterprises to comply with the law and to behave responsibly, both in China and in their overseas activities.

Effective Policies to Encourage RBC Can Help Address Serious Problems

The Chinese government's decision in recent years to adopt policies to encourage business to behave more responsibly came after more than two decades of rapid economic development resulting from reforms initiated in 1978. Since then, rapid economic growth has raised living standards nationwide. As in other countries, this rise in living standards has been accompanied by unwelcome side-effects such as environmental degradation and increasing inequality. While at an earlier stage of development many people expressed a willingness to tolerate these as the inevitable costs of social progress, a new generation of Chinese people is now calling for the rise in incomes to be matched by improvements in other areas of life. Some newly affluent city dwellers, for example, are campaigning to protect the country's architectural heritage from property developers, or to breathe clean air and eat clean food. At the other end of the social spectrum, farmers resist land seizures by officials and workers protest against non-payment of wages. As a result, the government is concerned that illegal and/or anti-social behavior of officials and companies may threaten the social and political order.

Such problems are not unique to China. OECD countries faced similar challenges in an industrialization process that, for many, started early several centuries before that in China. The Industrial Revolution brought rises in living standards only at terrible social cost. Countries that have now adopted enlightened standards of corporate conduct took many years to address such challenges as slavery, child labor, racial and religious discrimination, sexism, differential social class access to education and healthcare, slum housing, sub-standard—often dangerous—consumer products, and poisoned air and water. Older citizens in these countries can attest to great improvements during their lifetimes. Nevertheless, such problems, though massively diminished, still persist in some form.

China is today under international and internal pressure to move far faster in addressing these challenges than the industrialized countries did. Now that China, with one of the most open economies in the world, is integrating into an increasingly globalized world economy, it has become dependent on international investment and trade. Its exporters must take heed of consumer concerns in overseas markets just as its large enterprises must learn the rules to be observed in countries in which they wish to invest. China's rapid industrialization is causing it to become a large and wasteful user of energy and raw materials and to rank among the world's leading polluters. At the same time, China's internal social strains (one indication of which is the alarming rise in the Gini coefficient) have inevitably become a major focus of government attention.

OECD countries have found that business can play an important role in helping to address the challenges resulting from economic growth and development. Laws are important, but so is a culture of compliance. These countries are happy to share the lessons learned from decades of policy development with countries that are now industrializing, so that they may have an opportunity to avoid or at least alleviate the harsh by-products of economic change. At the same time, they are ready to learn from the good experiences of non-OECD countries, including China, that is facing up to common challenges.

Below are cited examples of major problems on both domestic and international levels to which the Chinese government seeks assistance from business in implementing its chosen solutions. This is indicative, not exhaustive.

China Is Adopting Policies to Encourage Responsible Business Conduct

The Chinese government is strongly encouraging companies to adhere to high standards of behavior. RBC is enshrined in the latest version of the Company Law, which requires companies to comply with laws and regulations, social morality and business morality. A code of conduct has been established for the textiles sector which may be extended to cover other sectors and the government has reportedly prepared RBC guidelines for all industries. The proponents of RBC are making a business case for it based on the notion of soft competitiveness.

At the same time, the Chinese government is developing framework conditions to enable RBC in China. It has put in place a series of measures to ensure disclosure by enterprises of both financial and non-financial information. It has enacted laws to protect the rights of workers, including women workers and children, and is taking measures to protect the environment. Responding to concerns of domestic and international consumers, the Chinese government is taking measures to improve product safety.

The Chinese government is striving to ensure corporate compliance with laws relating to RBC. Further development of the capacities of the legal system that better ensures judicial competence and independence would facilitate these efforts. Stakeholder and public consultation in the development of legislation is improving. Consultation and arbitration procedures are available. The Chinese government is using RBC as an instrument to ensure legal compliance.

Remaining Challenges

While the Chinese government has made efforts to encourage responsible business conduct, Chinese enterprises are still largely unaware of what RBC entails and have not organized themselves to promote it. This is not surprising, considering the short history of RBC initiatives in China, but the situation is not enhanced by the disparate nature of these initiatives. The lack of co-ordination of government agencies' approaches hinders communication of the government's expectations to Chinese companies. One result of the amorphous nature of RBC work in China at present is the lack of a set of nationally-recommended standards of corporate conduct and of effective reporting systems at enterprise level. However the central government is understood to be preparing a set of such standards and is also considering designating a government department as the national coordinating body for RBC. Such steps to improve co-ordination of RBC policy are to be encouraged. Legislation and regulations establishing framework conditions for responsible business conduct, for example, in such areas as environmental protection and occupational health and safety, have been put in place in recent years, but have yet to be consistently and effectively implemented at local level.

Reading Comprehension

Choose the best answers to the following questions.

1. Chinese enterprises can contribute to solutions by the following ways of _____.
   A. complying with laws and regulations
   B. striving to meet societal expectations that are not expressed as legal obligations
   C. both A and B
   D. neither A nor B
2. With the development of economy and the rise in living standards, many people are inclined to pay attention to those things except _____.
   A. protecting the country's architectural heritage from property developers
   B. tolerating environmental degradation as the inevitable costs of social progress
   C. that farmers resist land seizures and workers protest against non-payment of

wages

D. breathing clean air and eat clean food

3. Responsible business conduct (RBC) in China can help _____.

   A. address domestic challenges and relieve concerns of international consumers

   B. facilitate sustainable overseas investment by Chinese enterprises

   C. produce both tangible and intangible net benefits for Chinese enterprises

   D. All of the above.

4. All of the following are correct policies that China has carried out to encourage RBC except _____.

   A. formulating regulations and laws to force companies to comply with RBC

   B. encouraging companies to adhere to high standards of behavior

   C. developing framework conditions to enable RBC in China

   D. striving to ensure corporate compliance with laws relating to RBC

5. In the last paragraph of this essay, the author is _____ to the Chinese current situation of the implementing of RBC.

   A. positive

   B. negative

   C. objective

   D. indifferent

VI. Assignment

1. Interview the managers of some companies which are doing well in the CSR. Ask them about the advantages and benefits from CSR, and the disadvantages and problems they met. Write a report with about 200 words.

2. Please prepare a ten-minute presentation to introduce how the governments of different countries encourage the businesses to comply with CSR and why it is so important for both the businesses and the society.

Unit 14

Going to the International Market

 Learning Objectives

After learning this unit, you should be able to:
1. Understand the meaning of globalization.
2. Know the international market environment.
3. Understand the reasons of going international.
4. Describe the challenges and opportunities of going to the international market.
5. Know the principal modes of going international.

 Lead-in

International business refers to a wide range of business activities undertaken across national borders. Along with rapidly increasing globalization, international business has become a popular topic that has drawn the attention of business executives, government officials and academics. International business is different from domestic business. At the international level, the globalization of the world economy and the differences between countries present both opportunities and challenges to international businesses. Business managers need to take account of the global business environment when making international strategic decisions and managing ongoing international operations.

Warm-up Questions/Discussion:
1. What foreign products or services have you used?
2. Which countries are China's major trade partners?
3. What do you think of economic globalization?

Going to the International Market

1. The Background: Globalization

The international business is developing rapidly under the background of globalization. Globalization refers to the increasingly global relationships of culture, people, and economic activity. It is generally used to refer to economic globalization: the global distribution of the production of goods and services, through reduction of barriers to international trade such as tariffs, export fees, and import quotas① and the reduction of restrictions on the movement of capital and on investment. Globalization may contribute to economic growth in developed and developing countries through increased specialization and the principle of comparative advantage②. The term can also refer to the transnational circulation of ideas, languages, and popular cultures.

(1) The globalization of markets

A powerful force drives the world toward a converging commonality, and that force is technology. It has facilitated international communication, transport, and travel. It has made isolated places and impoverished people eager for modernity's allurements③. Almost everyone everywhere wants all the things they have heard about, seen, or experienced via the new technologies.

The result is a new commercial reality—the emergence of global markets for standardized consumer products on a previously unimagined scale of magnitude. Corporations geared to this new reality benefit from enormous economies of scale in production, distribution, marketing, and management. By translating these benefits into reduced world prices, they can decimate④ competitors that still live in the disabling grip of old assumptions about how the world works.

(2) The globalization of production

The globalization of production means that the world has become the global village and now the producers can get the benefit from different cultures and cheap labors all around the world. Now the companies move to other parts of the world where they get the product at low cost. There is another reason for this. This

---

① import quota（进口配额）：A type of protectionist trade restriction that sets a physical limit on the quantity of a good that can be imported into a country in a given period of time.

② comparative advantage（比较优势）：It refers to the ability of a party (an individual, a firm, or a country) to produce a particular good or service at a lower opportunity cost than another party.

③ allurement（诱惑物）：The things causing attraction.

④ decimate（成批杀死，大量毁灭）：To destroy or kill a large part of (a group).

happens due to the natural resources the countries have and how much they facilitate the foreign investment to come to their countries and invest their money in those countries. By keeping various actions the company can reduce cost of the production, can produce innovative produce and can compete in the market in the better way.

Now the whole scenario has changed the manufacturing companies who are producing things in different countries. <u>We can take Honda as an example, which is making the spare parts in China, assembling the products in Pakistan and designing the engine in Japan. So the production is distributed into three places.</u> This term is more widely used as the globalization of products. The production which needs high technological knowledge is given to those countries where the people are highly skilled.

2. The International Market Environment

Although firms marketing abroad face many of the same challenges as firms marketing domestically, international environments present added uncertainties which must be accurately interpreted. Indeed, there are a host of factors that need to be researched and evaluated when preparing an international marketing strategy. Key aspects of any potential foreign market include: demographic and physical environment; political environment; economic environment; social and cultural environment; and legal environment.

(1) Demographic and physical environment

Elements that need to be assessed and fit under this category include population size, growth, and distribution; climate factors that could impact on business; shipping distances; time zones; and natural resources.

(2) Economic environment

Factors in this area include disposable income and expenditure patterns; per capita income[①] and distribution; currency stability; inflation; level of acceptance of foreign businesses in economy; Gross Domestic Product (GDP); industrial and technological development; available channels of distribution; and general economic growth. Obviously, the greater a nation's wealth, the more likely it will be that a new product or service can be introduced successfully. Conversely, a market in which economic circumstances provide only a tiny minority of citizens with the

---

① per capita income (人均收入): Per capita income or income per person is the numerical quotient of national income divided by population, in monetary terms.

resources to buy televisions may not be an ideal one for a television-based marketing campaign.

(3) Social and cultural environment

This category encompasses a wide range of considerations, many of which can—if misunderstood or unanticipated— significantly undermine a business's marketing efforts. These include literacy rates; general education levels; language; religion; ethics; social values; and social organization. Attitudes based on religious beliefs or cultural norms often shape marketing choices in fundamental ways as well. Cultures differ in their values and attitudes toward work, success, clothing, food, music, sex, social status, honesty, the rights of others, and much else. Even business practices can vary tremendously from people to people. <u>For instance, haggling① is never done by the Dutch, often by Brazilians, and always by the Chinese. The company that does not take the time to make itself aware of these differences runs the risk of putting together an international marketing venture that can fail at any number of points.</u>

(4) Legal environment

This includes limitations on trade through tariffs or quotas; documentation and import regulations; various investment, tax, and employment laws; patent and trademark protection; and preferential treaties. These factors range from huge treaties that profoundly shape the international transactions of many nations to trade barriers erected by a single country.

(5) Political environment

Factors here include system of government in targeted market; political stability; dominant ideology; and national economic priorities. This aspect of an international market is often the single most important one, for it can be so influential in shaping other factors. For example, a government that is distrustful of foreigners or intents on maintaining domestic control of an industry or industries might erect legal barriers designed to severely curtail② the business opportunities of foreign firms.

3. Reasons for Globalization

Most companies move their business operations to foreign countries by going global. They take their business esoverseas for different reasons. These companies

---

① haggling（讨价还价）：To bargain, as over the price of something.
② curtail（缩减，削弱）：To place restrictions on.

adopt the reactive or defensive approach to stay ahead of the competitions. A few of them take the proactive① or aggressive approach to accomplish the same purpose. A majority of them choose to adopt both approaches to avoid a decrease in their competition. In order to remain competitive, companies move as quickly as possible to secure a strong position in some of the key world or emerging markets with products customized for the need of the people in such areas in which they plan to establish. Most of these world markets are attracting companies with new capital investments with very good incentives. Some of the reactive or defensive reasons for going global are:

(1) Trade barriers

(2) Customer demands

(3) Globalization of competitors

(4) Regulations and restrictions

In the case of trade barriers, companies move from exporting their products to manufacturing them overseas in order to avoid the burden of tariffs, quotas, the policy of buy-local and other restrictions that make export too expensive to foreign markets. Companies respond to customer demands for effective operations and product assurance and reliability, or/and logistical problem solutions. Most foreign customers, who seek accessibility to suppliers may request that supply stay local in order to enhance the flow of production. Companies usually follow that request to avoid losing the business. For the globalization of competitors, companies are aware that if they leave companies overseas too long without challenge or competition, their investments or foreign operations in the world market may be so solid that competition will be difficult. Therefore, they try to act quickly. Most companies' home government may have regulations and restrictions that are so inconvenient and expensive, thus limiting the expansion, encroaching② in the companies' profits, and making their costs uncontrollable. Hence the reason for the companies moving to different market environment with few foreign restrictive operations. The proactive or aggressive reasons for going global are:

(1) Growth opportunities

(2) Economies of scale

(3) Incentives

(4) Resource assess and cost savings

---

① proactive (先发制人的，积极的): Acting in advance to deal with an expected difficulty.

② encroach (侵占): To take others' possessions or rights gradually or stealthily.

Many companies will prefer to invest their excess profits in order to expand, but sometimes they are limited because of the maturity of the markets in their area. Therefore, they seek the overseas new markets to provide such growth opportunities. So, these companies, in addition to investing their excess profits, also try to maximize efficiency by employing their underutilized resources in human and capital assets such as management, machinery and technology. Companies seek economies of scale in order to achieve a higher level of output spread over large fixed costs to lower the per-unit cost. They also want to maximize the use of their manufacturing equipment and spread the high costs of research and development over the product life cycle. Some of the developing countries that need improvement and development through capital infusion, skills, and technology voluntarily provide incentives such as fixed assets, tax exemptions, subsidies, tax holidays, human capital, and low wages. These incentives seem attractive to these companies due to their increase in profits and reduction of risks.

4. The Challenges and Opportunities of Going to the International Market

International markets can offer technology companies significant opportunities to expand and diversify their product and service offerings, increase brand awareness and drive revenues. But companies contemplating international expansion also face daunting[①] risks and uncertainties, along with operational challenges that can be difficult to anticipate.

Meeting international rules and regulations is considered the biggest challenge to growth in international markets. Local safety and quality tests, for example, are two challenges preventing China's auto and pharmaceutical[②] industries from growing as fast as they might like in overseas markets.

Adapting to a new business environment is also considered a major challenge. Many companies are seeking local partners in an effort to better understand local consumer tastes and needs, effective marketing methods, and other issues such as local business customs. However, many firms are currently over-reliant on partners such as distributors to help them "learn the ropes" in international markets, when they should be seeking advice from more qualified third parties such as a PR[③], marketing, or law firm.

---

① daunting（使人气馁的）：Discouraging through fear.
② pharmaceutical（制药的）： Of or relating to drugs used in medical treatment.
③ PR（公共关系）：Public relations.

One benefit of going international of the companies is that it can diversify its consumer base and revenue streams①. A company that markets only to local consumers is especially vulnerable to domestic economic trends. With consumers in other countries buying products and services from the international division, the company can maintain revenue streams in foreign markets. The company can stay afloat even when the local economy fails to provide enough consumers.

When a company is going global, it increases the ability of the business to attract large corporations as clients. These companies already have their own global operations, and they need to give their business to globalized companies diversified and structured to accommodate their needs. If the company is trying to market products and services to large companies, globalization will get their attention, showing big clients that the company aggressively pursues in foreign markets.

5. Mode of Going to the International Market

After the decision of going global has been made, the exact mode of operation has to be determined. The risks concerning operating in the international market are often dependent on the level of control a firm has, coupled with the level of capital expenditure outlayed. The principal modes of going global are as follows:

(1) Exporting

Direct exporting involves a firm's shipping goods directly to a foreign market. A firm employing indirect exporting would utilize a channel or intermediary, who in turn would disseminate② the product in the foreign market. From a company's standpoint, exporting consists of the least risk. This is so since no capital expenditure, or outlay③ of company finances on new non-current assets, has necessarily taken place. Thus, the likelihood of sunk costs, or general barriers to exit, is slim. Conversely, a company may possess less control when exporting into a foreign market, due to not control the supply of the good within the foreign market.

(2) Joint ventures

A joint venture is a combined effort between two or more business entities, with the aim of mutual benefit from a given economic activity. Some countries often mandate that all foreign investment within it should be via joint ventures. By

---

　　① revenue streams (收入来源): Revenue streams refer specifically to the individual methods by which money comes into a company.
　　② disseminate (传播): To spread abroad.
　　③ outlay (花费): The spending or disbursement of money.

comparison with exporting, more control is exerted; however, the level of risk is also increased.

(3) Direct investment

In this mode, a company would directly construct a fixed asset within a foreign country, with the aim of manufacturing a product within the overseas market.

Assembly denotes the literal assembly of completed parts, to build a completed product. An example of this is the Dell Corporation. Dell possesses plants in countries external to the United States of America, however it assembles personal computers and does not manufacture them from scratch. In other words, it obtains parts from other firms, and assembles a personal computer's constituent parts (such as a motherboard, monitor, CPU, RAM[①], wireless card, modem, sound card, etc.) within its factories. Manufacturing concerns the actual forging of a product from scratch. Car manufacturers often construct all parts within their plants. Direct investment has the most control and the most risk attached. As with any capital expenditure, the return on investment (defined by the payback period, Net Present Value, Internal Rate of Return, etc.) has to be ascertained, in addition to appreciating any related sunk costs with the capital expenditure.

Exercises

I. Reviewing Questions

Answer the following questions according to the text.

1. What is the definition of economic globalization?
2. What is the meaning of globalization of market?
3. What are the advantages of globalization of production?
4. What are the key factors need to be considered when going into the international market?
5. Why should we understand these factors correctly?
6. What is the most important aspect among the international market environment?
7. How can a company remain competitive according to the passage?
8. What is the biggest challenge for Chinese companies while going global?
9. What are the modes of going to the international market?
10. Which mode of going global is of the greatest amount of risk?

---

① RAM（随机存取存储器，内存）：Random Access Memory. Computer memory that can be read from and written to in arbitrary sequence in a very high speed for computer and laptop.

Unit 14 Going to the International Market

II. Cloze
Read the following passage and fill in the blanks with the words given below. Change the form where necessary.

remain	assess	inherent	resource	familiar
liability	negotiation	fit	feasible	targeted

The decision to go international must be made with care, as there are many risks and potential obstacles to consider. Cultural and language barriers are among the most obvious of these considerations. Variations in religious beliefs, societal norms, and business ___1___ styles all have an impact on how business needs to be conducted when dealing with foreign counterparts. Language barriers may present an obstacle when trying to communicate the benefits and advantages of a company's products and services overseas.

There are ___2___ political and economic risks when expanding into foreign markets. Instability of some foreign governments can pose a threat to the security of a business overseas. Even natural disasters happen. Foreign exchange might present a barrier to get paid when you sell abroad.

The benefits of going international often ___3___ an advantage, even with all of the risks carefully considered. An organization that wants to go overseas needs to be prepared by having developed a specific international marketing plan, and decide how to enter the ___4___ market. An international marketing plan should outline and define the product or service to be sold and the country or countries in which it will be sold. In doing so, it is essential to consider whether a product that works in China will work in other markets.

A company that wishes to expand internationally needs to be ___5___ with the target country's culture and determine the feasibility of marketing its product or service in that environment. Market conditions must be ___6___ to ensure that a new company can win a share of the foreign market. Tariffs, duties and compliance with China's export administration regulations are other important issues to consider as well. These considerations require some expertise in the financial and legal aspects of exporting.

Developing the required organizational processes and allocating appropriate ___7___ to an international effort often requires creating a separate export department within an organization that is responsible for all aspects of dealing with foreign markets. Many companies attempt this by having a single sales manager and his or her assistants responsible for setting a budget, shipping goods and developing international growth. However, this can be an expensive alternative when overhead and ___8___ costs are considered.

If a company chooses going alone it may need three to five years to develop a sizeable market share. In many cases, assistance from an outside source can dramatically reduce the time it will take to become established in foreign markets.

The use of a consultant or a company with the "Know Who" and the "Know How" is often the most ___9___ way to break into an international market. In effect, these marketing authorities can manage your entire international sales effort more quickly and efficiently. They can also provide localization services, starting but going beyond, simply translating materials to the desired language. Localization refers to adapting a company's entire image to ___10___ another culture. Export management companies offer working capital, clearing customs paperwork, and trade insurance for a fee and commission. Beyond the obvious value of intimate know-how and access to extensive overseas contacts that they can provide is the benefit of having after sales support. A good export management consultant has years of specialized experience in knowing or negotiating with governments, freight forwarders and banks.

III. Translation

1. We can take Honda as an example, which is making the spare parts in China, assembling the products in Pakistan and designing the engine in Japan. So the production is distributed into three places.

2. For instance, haggling is never done by the Dutch, often by Brazilians, and always by the Chinese. The company that does not take the time to make itself aware of these differences runs the risk of putting together an international marketing venture that can fail at any number of points.

3. Most foreign customers, who seek accessibility to suppliers may request that supply stay local in order to enhance the flow of production. Companies usually follow that request to avoid losing the business.

4. However, many firms are currently over-reliant on partners such as distributors to

help them "learn the ropes" in international markets, when they should be seeking advice from more qualified third parties such as a PR, marketing, or law firm.

5. Thus, the likelihood of sunk costs, or general barriers to exit, is slim. Conversely, a company may possess less control when exporting into a foreign market, due to not control the supply of the good within the foreign market.

IV. Case Study

Coca Cola's Global Marketing

by Bilaras

Coca-Cola is one of the most widely used soft drink in the world. The company has very efficient and extensive distribution system in the world. There is a great variety of brands offered by Coca-Cola throughout the world like Diet coke, sprite, Fanta, Rc cola, Minute made etc. You can find the Coca-Cola soft drinks anywhere in every country of the world.

The "Coca-Cola" brand has adopted the strategy of global marketing. It is considering the whole world as single market place and uniform marketing strategy was being used by Coca-Cola for many years, but now the trend is changing and different marketing campaigns are being designed for different regions of the world.

Coca-Cola has got such an intensive distribution and bottlers system that its products are available everywhere in the world, starting from Middle East to Australia. You can find Coca-Cola product on every retail outlet.

There are many reasons why company decided to sell its product on international market. The prospect exists to sell "Coca-Cola" worldwide, because "Coca-Cola" is a product which can be used by everyone irrespective of age and gender, all over the world. Marketing globally demands the company to have a marketing team in line with a country's consumers so effective sales can be made and good relations with the abroad key employees can be maintained.

If we look on advertising perspective of Coca-Cola, advertising has created a demand for "Coca-Cola" worldwide. However, advertising has to be in line with the domestic culture. An adapted marketing mix means adjusting the mix with the prevailing culture, geographic, economic and other differences in different countries.

Different languages and cultures cause problems.

In addition, Coca-Cola's bottling system is one of their greatest strengths. It permits them to do their business on a global scale while at the same time maintaining a national approach. The bottling companies are domestically owned and operated by independent business people who are authorized to sell products of the Coca-Cola Company. Because Coke does not have complete ownership of its bottling network, its main source of revenue is the sale of concentrate to its bottlers.

Brand image is the significant factor affecting Coke's sale. Coca-Cola's brand name is very well known all over the world. Packaging changes have also affected sales and industry positioning, but in general, the public has tended not to be affected by new products. Coca-Cola's bottling system also allows the company to take advantage of infinite growth opportunities around the world. This strategy gives Coke the opportunity to service a large geographic, diverse area.

The increasing health consciousness and emphasis of healthy lifestyle not only in developed nations, but also in developing nations, have slowed down the sales of Coca-Cola's carbonated soft drinks. In response to this health consciousness issue, the company introduced Diet Coke in 1982. Such change of consumer life style had also led to the introduction of its bottled purified water.

Coca-Cola's brand personality reflects the positioning of its brand. The process of positioning a brand or product is a complex managerial task and must be done over time using all the elements of the marketing mix. Positioning is in the mind of the consumer and can be described as how the product is considered by that consumer.

It is of a lot importance to create the right brand image that closely in lines with the consumers' life experiences and feelings. Sponsorship is one way of building these associations. Through events such as Coca-Cola's Form and Fusion Design Awards and sporting events' a brand manager can ensure that its product image is made relevant to the target audience. An element of the marketing mix involves making aware the customers. The promotional mix will often include sales promotion, advertising, direct selling and public relations elements.

Questions for discussion:
1. Why did Coca-Cola decide to go global in 1919?
2. What are the important factors that made Coca-Cola succeed in the global market?

3. Currently what is the biggest challenge that Coca-Cola faces when expanding its business in the world?

V. Supplementary Reading

The Challenges for International Courier Giants in the China Market

In China, where the courier market is flourishing amid the backdrop of a fast-growing economy, international courier giants such as UPS are not as aggressive as they are in international markets. Due to persistently high costs and difficulties in developing networks, they are either on the sidelines or are exploring the market on a small scale. Some have even seen declines in business.

Slower Expansion

Since the 1990s, China's international courier market has gradually been taken over by the four international giants—DHL, TNT, UPS and FedEx, which have been growing by more than 20% to 40% per annum. EMS, the courier service by China Post, has been declining by 4% year-on-year.

The domestic courier market has a lot of potential. According to World Trade Organization (WTO) requirements, the Chinese courier market had to be fully opened up to competition by the end of 2005. But in most regions, especially central cities such as Beijing and Shanghai, private courier companies command 80% of market share.

Today, if one calls the customer service departments of FedEx, UPS, DHL and TNT to courier documents from Guangzhou or Shanghai to Beijing, UPS would respond that it only serves clients with whom it has contracts; FedEx, DHL and TNT would take the business, but the quote would be more than 100 RMB from FedEx and DHL; TNT emphasizes medium-to-high end clients, and would actively persuade the customer to sign a long-term contract.

TNT, which at one point aggressively offered domestic courier services, signed up 50 new partners in 2005. But it announced recently that it would no longer develop new partners. In addition, TNT has stopped some regional development programs. At the same time, TNT (China) has overhauled its structure and merged its international and domestic courier services.

Currently, TNT's domestic courier services cater mainly to multinationals—offering them both international and domestic courier services. Fees are settled weekly or even monthly. And single parcels are seldom processed. TNT has a network of 4,500 stores, 1,300 mail boxes and 17,000 franchisees in the U.S., its home country. In contrast, in China, TNT only signs contracts with a few clients.

High Costs and Difficult Acquisitions

According to Ken McCall, former CEO of TNT China, TNT had analyzed and planned the domestic courier business after having developed partners in China for a year. TNT found that the scale of Chinese courier services is not big and the market is not mature. As a result, TNT considered a low-key approach. "The domestic courier business is very small– an infant in our big family," he notes.

Chen Xianbao, executive vice president of ZJS Express, a private courier service company, says that DHL had suffered huge losses since it started domestic courier services due to small volume and high operating costs. Daily courier volume originating from Shanghai, for example, was just tens of kilograms. Private courier companies tend to have several times larger sales. EMS of China Post delivers more than 100,000 pieces a day.

Considering the Shanghai to Beijing courier route as an example. S.F. Express and Tian Tian Express charge 20 RMB and 15 RMB per kg respectively and 10 RMB for every extra kg. EMS charges 26 RMB per kg and 12 RMB for every extra kg. In contrast, FedEx's Next-Morning Delivery charges 135 RMB for 2kg, and 90 RMB for Next-Day Delivery.

High operating costs might be a major reason for these high fees. According to Xu Yong, former operating director with FedEx East China and former president of Tian Tian Express, human resources, management and operating expenses for international courier companies are three to five times higher than those of their private counterparts.

Furthermore, international giants hope to acquire domestic courier companies to quickly fill the gaps of their domestic coverage. But there are not many candidates for acquisition. Large private courier companies are mostly alliances of small franchisees. The headquarters have limited managerial control over franchisees, which fight for their regional turfs. If international giants acquire these franchisees, they have to inject a lot of capital and energy to remedy this situation.

Opportunities and Challenges

Not all international courier giants are pessimistic about making money in the

China market, however. FedEx recently entered the market on a high note.

When FedEx entered the China courier market, Chen Jiangliang, president of its China operations, noted in public that although FedEx didn't have any pricing advantage compared with domestic courier companies, it catered to high-end customers demanding timely delivery and reliability. According to him, "90% of our existing international clients in the China market told us they needed reliable limited delivery-time services in China, expecting us to deliver parcels for them in China while conducting international business." Indeed, UPS pointed out in its recent report that China would have a very large middle class in the next 20 to 30 years. Chinese business and economic development means that demand for high-end services has huge potential.

Alan Graf, CFO of FedEx, said on June 20 that the courier business in China would negatively impact on its quarterly earnings and 2008 profits.

Many large private courier companies are mulling over transformations. Low-end business accounts for 60% of the total market, and has long bid farewell to the high-margin period to enter into a thin-margin era instead. From 1992 to the present, courier costs from Shanghai to Hangzhou dropped to between 3 and 5 RMB, a reduction of 100 times. It is imperative for courier companies to look for new areas of profits, the experts note.

"We can no longer fight for business at each distribution points," says Xu Jianguo, the head of a private courier company. "We need to drive the network by products and customers." Having experienced failure once, Xu Jianguo has overhauled his business model completely. Today, he no longer targets the low-end market of delivering documents, samples and gifts, but targets parcels under 300 kg and small-scale logistics businesses over 300 kg. His main clients are big companies such as DHC and Procter&Gamble.

Delivering high-value goods and even providing warehousing and storage services in the medium-to-high-end markets are areas of focus for private courier companies reinventing themselves for breakthroughs. Currently, Shentong Express, ZJS Express and Yuantong Express, well-known private courier companies, are expanding into logistics and even e-commerce. For example, Shentong and Yuantong have been appointed courier companies for taobao.com, the largest C-C e-commerce website in China.

Regulatory Risks

For private and foreign courier companies, the uncertainty of the Postal Law of PRC has been their number one headache.

The current Postal Law was issued in 1986. In recent years, the Postal Law has been amended but not passed yet. The main issue is the range of weights under the monopoly of China Post and the administrative qualification standards for conducting courier business. China Post wishes to limit the competitive pressure on EMS from private and foreign courier services companies by setting the range so that it can continue its monopoly.

The Postal Law under revision has already seen nine drafts, and the latest one even bans foreign companies from delivering letters in China. Currently, four international courier giants have all entered the domestic courier market, and business letters are part of their businesses. If the ban takes effect, the business of the international courier companies will be dwelt a serious setback.

Reading Comprehension

Choose the best answers to the following questions.

1. When Jim Casey first started his business on courier services in 1907, _____ were his main tools for delivery.
   A. cars
   B. bicycles
   C. planes
   D. tracks

2. Now TNT's domestic courier services mainly cater to _____ courier services.
   A. domestic
   B. international
   C. no
   D. both domestic and international

3. Of the following factors, _____ is the major reason for the high fees of the courier services in China.
   A. high operating costs
   B. high prices of oil
   C. high costs of labor
   D. high costs of vehicles

4. According to Chen Jiangliang, president of FedEx's China operations, the

company inclined to meet the demands of _____ customers requiring timely delivery and reliability.

A. normal

B. special

C. high-end

D. most

5. For private and international courier companies, the uncertainty of the Postal Law of PRC is their number one headache because _____.

A. China Post wishes to limit the competitive pressure by regulatory

B. they can not enter the courier market

C. China does not like them

D. the law is often revised and China wants to protect market for the China Post

VI. Assignment

1. Please do some researches of Chinese products on the international market, and make a list of the products that sell well and the products that have fewer sales. Write a report with about 200 words.

2. Please prepare a ten-minute presentation to introduce why some companies are very successful in the international market and explain their strategies when going global.

Unit 15

E-business

 Learning Objectives

After learning this unit, you should be able to:
1. Explain the concept of E-business.
2. Know the development process of E-business.
3. Describe the advantages and disadvantages of E-business.
4. Get some tips of creating your own E-business.

 Lead-in

Electronic business, commonly referred to as "eBusiness" or "e-business," or an internet business, may be defined as the application of information and communication technologies (ICT) in support of all the activities of business. Commerce constitutes the exchange of products and services between businesses, groups and individuals and can be seen as one of the essential activities of any business. Electronic commerce focuses on the use of ICT to enable the external activities and relationships of the business with individuals, groups and other businesses.

Warm-up Questions/Discussion:
1. Do you often do shopping online? Share some experience with each other.
2. What is your opinion on e-business?
3. Have you ever thought of starting your own e-business?

Introduction to E-business[①]

There is no universal accepted definition of the word e-business. IBM launched a theme activity and built a term called e-business in 1996, and it was the first time to use this word. However, e-commerce was the widely used buzzword[②] by then. The shift in nomenclature meant a paradigm shift as well. As the internet continues to grow and expand, the term e-business can be allowed for more types on the web. E-business can be defined as the conduct of automated business transactions by means of electronic communications networks end-to-end.

1. History of E-business

With the advent of the World Wide Web (WWW), or the "web," traditional business organizations that had relied on catalog sales had a new sales vector. Other businesses found that the web was a good place to put customer service information, such as manuals and drivers, as well as a place to help create a consistent corporate image. As the web developed, a number of Internet-based businesses developed, including companies like eBay and Amazon, and web-based information repositories like eHow.

(1) Early use of the web for business

Business began using websites for marketing shortly after graphical-based web design became available in the early 1990s. Most of these websites served to provide visitors basic information about a company's products and services, and included contact information, such as phone numbers and email addresses, to assist consumers in contacting a company for services. The move from providing simple business information to soliciting business[③] via the web occurred almost as soon as marketing departments realized that company websites were available to millions of people. Online sales began in 1994 with the ability to encrypt[④] credit card data.

(2) Early online sales

With the advent of the Secured Socket Layer (SSL), developed by Netscape in

---

① The text is excerpted from www.ehow.com
② buzzword（流行词）: A word or phrase connected with a specialized field or group that usually sounds important or technical and is used primarily to impress laypersons.
③ soliciting business（招揽生意）: To seek to obtain businesses.
④ encrypt（加密）: To put into code or cipher.

1994, websites developed the ability to encrypt sessions, thus making credit card transactions over the Internet safer. With an encrypted connection between a company's server and a client computer, credit numbers could be masked so they could not be intercepted by a third party, thus making theft of card information less likely. This security led to an increased number of businesses offering products for sale via the web.

(3) Birth of modern web sales

Developments in server technology, including the ability to build websites from product databases, resulted in creation of large Internet-only businesses like eBay and Amazon. In previous product-sales websites, each product had to be manually posted on a web page. With database-driven sites, companies could use web-page templates① to display tens of thousands of products on-the-fly②. As the number of available products increased, so did traffic and sales on these websites.

(4) Payment system advances

Early SSL implementations were good, but many people still did not trust them to secure credit card payment information. In addition, it was too expensive to process micropayments—payments of less than a dollar—through traditional credit card systems. As a result, a number of micropayment sites came and went. One has remained and has done very well because of its ability to transfer money from a variety of funding sources, including credit cards and bank accounts, without revealing the payer's credit card information to the merchant. That company is PayPal. PayPal has enabled credit card processing by many small businesses that would otherwise not be eligible for a traditional credit card merchant account.

(5) Dot-com bubble of 2001

Problems with customer confidence began in the late 1990s. Notable denial of service (DOS) attacks on prominent websites made customers worry that their credit card data might not be safe. Throughout this period, online businesses received large capital investments via Initial Public Offerings (IPOs), and saw their stock selling at prices far above the actual value of their companies. Many companies had good ideas but poor business plans, and speculators bid up③ the prices of stocks in Internet companies. The initial blows came as some on-line companies began reporting large losses and investors began examining the viability

---

① template（模板）：A model or standard for making comparisons.
② on-the-fly（即时）：On the run or in a hurry.
③ bid up（抬价）：To cause (a price) to rise by increasing the amount bid.

of online business plans. Fearful investors started to sell their stocks, causing the overinflated stock prices to plummet below their actual value. A number of well-known companies closed, such as eToys. Many other companies that lacked solid business plans failed between 2001 and 2002.

(6) The current state of e-business

Currently, e-business ranges from simple sites providing corporate information to sites offering goods and services for sale online. Innovative uses for new voice and video communication technologies include online language tutoring. Large commercial information repositories are growing and the use of the Internet for research is now common. Online sales from web-based storefronts① continue to grow. Sales of digital information, in the form of eBooks and digital music files, are more recent offerings by e-businesses like Apple, Amazon, and Barnes & Noble.

2. E-business Advantages & Disadvantages

E-business has transformed the way companies function in today's economic marketplace. The technological advances of the past few decades have given businesses the ability to grow and expand beyond their local market. The Internet allows small businesses to reach national or global consumers with their products and services, increasing their sales and profits. Along with these advantages come some disadvantages, creating higher levels of economic challenges not previously seen.

(1) Low business costs

One big advantage of e-business is the low startup costs needed to begin business operations. Many small companies today simply start via the Internet, expanding into traditional brick and mortar stores② once they have increased their working capital. Depending on their business success, companies may choose to simply expand their Internet footprint rather than creating a physical storefront. Internet storefronts are relatively cheap, with businesses needing a computer, website hosting service and Internet connection as their main operating equipment.

(2) Multiple market segments

E-business allows companies to expand into new markets, both nationally and internationally. Entry barriers to these new markets are relatively low, depending on

---

① web-based storefronts (网络店面): A virtual store existing on the internet.

② brick and mortar stores (实体店面): It is a traditional "street-side" business that deals with its customers face to face in an office or store that business owns or rents.

the type of goods or services sold via the e-business website. Government regulation may also be easier when conducting e-business as local and national governments have not imposed heavy regulations on many or all sectors of e-business. Goods may also be purchased by consumers for uses other than originally intended, creating a new secondary market for the e-business's products.

(3) More competition

A major disadvantage of e-business is the increased levels of competition. Because individuals and traditional businesses may enter the e-business marketplace, sellers must find a competitive advantage over more competitors than usual. Foreign companies may also be entering the e-business marketplace flooding the market with cheap or inferior goods. Companies may also offer substitute goods at a cheaper price, giving consumers more purchasing options than before. These types of competition can limit a new e-business from getting off the ground, much less succeeding in the marketplace.

(4) Difficult customer relations

Another major disadvantage of e-business is the difficulty of creating positive goodwill through a website and computer. <u>Consumers traditionally place high value on customer service in the brick and mortar business environment. Creating this same type of positive customer service is difficult for e-businesses, considering that their customers may be hundreds or thousands of miles away from the e-business's operations.</u> Consumers may also have difficulty in understanding mistakes or errors since impersonal email is a common form of communication in e-business.

3. Important Factors in E-businesses

The act of doing business via the Internet e-business has exploded in recent years, accounting now for many billions of dollars annually in sales. While many people love the idea of being able to shop without ever leaving their homes, e-businesses can offer problems, both for buyers and sellers, which need to be considered.

(1) Security

The biggest concern for both buyers and sellers with e-business often is security; hackers are always on the prowl① for unsecured websites, where they can steal credit card information and other data. While improvements have been made in recent years with the advent of complex encryption techniques, there still are many e-businesses out there with gaping holes in its online security.

---

① on the prowl (徘徊): Actively looking for something.

(2) Connection issues

Traffic on the Information Superhighway can sometimes get snarled①, resulting in long waits for shoppers as they flip through web pages; a broken connection can lead to orders not getting processed, or a customer accidentally paying for the same item twice. Many e-businesses could solve some of these problems with improvements to their websites or increased bandwidth, but they may not be able to afford to do so.

(3) Getting the goods

When a person buys something at a local store, they can often take it home or have it delivered the same day. Items purchased online, however, must be mailed; some businesses process orders quickly and use delivery services that will get items to purchasers the next day. Others, however, may be slow in getting orders out the door, and in an effort to keep down costs they may rely on slower delivery methods, resulting in delays of several days—and at times, weeks, or items being lost.

(4) Reputation

Developing a good reputation can be a long and tedious process for an e-business, no matter how long they have been doing business in a traditional manner; many customers, not being able to learn about fledgling e-businesses due to a lack of reviews, make their business elsewhere. Such caution is justified: There are many disreputable businesses online that have no intention of giving a customer an honest shake, keeping customers from doing business with them.

4. How to Create an E-business

Electronic business ventures, or e-businesses, are a popular method for starting and running a company. Typically done over the Internet, an e-business can operate as a standalone online storefront, or it can be an additional component to a brick-and-mortar company that operates in the real world. Although it is possible to purchase an existing e-business, it is relatively easy to start one on your own. With a nominal investment and a little time, you can have an e-business up, running and accepting customers. Here are some tips of running an e-business:

(1) Determine the concept for the business you wish to start

Decide if you would like to have an online storefront to sell products, operate a social network or dating site, or maybe even just report the news and earn revenues from advertising. There are limitless types of e-businesses available. Choose the

---

① snarled（混乱）：In a confused mass.

type of electronic business you would like to operate.

(2) Write a business plan that will serve as a guide for your e-business

Cover the details about what your business will be and how it will operate. Identify your strengths and weaknesses, your competitors and how you will market your business. Also include a budget that covers your fixed assets, marketing and operational costs.

(3) Secure the investment you need for your e-business

Most start up companies get their seed capital from cash advances on credit cards or from loans that come from family and friends. You can also take out a small business loan from your bank. If you fail to meet the qualifications for the loan, your bank loan officer can help you apply for a loan backed by the Small Business Administration. If your e-business requires a significant investment, you may require the aid of a private investor or venture capital firm.

(4) Register a company so that a legal entity will own the e-business

Business registrations are done with the secretary of state in the state in which you will be conducting business. You can also find the proper paperwork at your local city clerk or county clerk. Fill out the appropriate forms and pay the related fees to open your company. The amount of the fee will vary depending on what state you are in and whether your company is a **sole proprietorship**[①] or a partnership.

(5) Obtain a domain and hosting account

An Internet domain name provides you with a private web address that directs customers to your e-business. The domain is backed by a web hosting account, which provides you with a place to store the files for your e-business. Web hosting is paid on a monthly or annual subscription plan, with the price depending on how much server space and **bandwidth**[②] you require.

(6) Construct a website for your e-business

The website serves as the primary point of contact between the e-business and its customers. The type of website you build will depend primarily on the primary purpose of your e-business. If you are building a storefront, you will need to build a shopping cart website, while a dating website would require an entirely different

---

① sole proprietorship（个体工商户）: A business entity that is owned and run by one individual and in which there is no legal distinction between the owner and the business.

② bandwidth（带宽）: The amount of data that can be passed along a communications channel in a given period of time.

Unit 15 E-business   243

design. Consider the purpose of your website and create a design that is specific to those needs.

 Exercises

I. Reviewing Questions
Answer the following questions according to the text.
1. What is e-business?
2. When did e-business come to emerge?
3. What were the functions of the websites at early stage of e-business?
4. Why did the company PayPal remain doing very well when so many micropayment sites came and went?
5. Could you give a brief introduction to "dot-com bubble"?
6. What are the main advantages and disadvantages of e-business?
7. Why are e-businesses very competitive?
8. What should we pay attention to when shopping online?
9. What are the important factors for an e-business?
10. How can we do when establishing an e-business?

II. Cloze
Read the following passage and fill in the blanks with the words given below. Change the form where necessary.

| air-conditioned | ensure | authorized | contain | access |
| separate | employees | location | failover | confidential |

Despite e-business being business done online, there are still physical security measures that can be taken to protect the business as a whole. Even though business is done online, the building that houses the servers and computers must be protected and have limited ___1___ to employees and other persons. For example, this room should only allow authorized users to enter, and should ___2___ that "windows, dropped ceilings, large air ducts, and raised floors" do not allow easy access to unauthorized persons. Preferably these important items would be kept in an ___3___ room without any windows.

Protecting against the environment is equally important in physical security as protecting against unauthorized users. The room may protect the equipment against flooding by keeping all equipment raised off the floor. In addition, the room should __4__ a fire extinguisher in case of fire. The organization should have a fire plan in case this situation arises.

In addition to keeping the servers and computers safe, physical security of __5__ information is important. This includes client information such as credit card numbers, checks, phone numbers, etc. It also includes any of the organization's private information. Locking physical and electronic copies of this data in a drawer or cabinet is one additional measure of security. Doors and windows leading into this area should also be securely locked. Only __6__ that need to use this information as part of their jobs should be given keys.

Important information can also be kept secure by keeping backups of files and updating them on a regular basis. It is best to keep these backups in a __7__ secure location in case there is a natural disaster or breach of security at the main location.

"Failover sites" can be built in case there is a problem with the main location. This site should be just like the main __8__ in terms of hardware, software, and security features. This site can be used in case of fire or natural disaster at the original site. It is also important to test the "__9__ site" to ensure it will actually work if the need arises.

State of the art security systems, such as the one used at Tidepoint's headquarters, might include access control, alarm systems, and closed-circuit television. One form of access control is face (or another feature) recognition systems. This allows only __10__ personnel to enter, and also serves the purpose of convenience for employees who don't have to carry keys or cards. Cameras can also be placed throughout the building and at all points of entry. Alarm systems also serve as an added measure of protection against theft.

III. Translation

1. Most of these websites served to provide visitors basic information about a company's products and services, and included contact information, such as phone numbers and email addresses, to assist consumers in contacting a company for services. The move from providing simple business information to soliciting business via the web occurred almost as soon as marketing departments realized that company websites were available to millions of people.

2. Developments in server technology, including the ability to build websites from

product databases, resulted in creation of large Internet-only businesses like eBay and Amazon. In previous product-sales websites, each product had to be manually posted on a web page. With database-driven sites, companies could use web-page templates to display tens of thousands of products on-the-fly.

3. Depending on their business success, companies may choose to simply expand their Internet footprint rather than creating a physical storefront. Internet storefronts are relatively cheap, with businesses needing a computer, website hosting service and Internet connection as their main operating equipment.

4. Consumers traditionally place high value on customer service in the brick and mortar business environment. Creating this same type of positive customer service is difficult for e-businesses, considering that their customers may be hundreds or thousands of miles away from the e-business's operations.

5. Electronic business ventures, or e-businesses, are a popular method for starting and running a company. Typically done over the Internet, an e-business can operate as a standalone online storefront, or it can be an additional component to a brick-and-mortar company that operates in the real world.

IV. Case Study

E-business Development of Intel

by Dien D. Phan

Intel Corp. located in Santa Clara, California, is the world's largest producer of Integrated Circuits Chips today. Incorporated in 1968, Intel supplies the computing and communications industries with chips, boards and systems building blocks that are integral to computers, servers, and networking and communications products. Today, the company has evolved from a processor maker into a supplier of network and server hardware, Internet hosting services, and other e-business components. Its technological leadership ranges from microprocessor design to advanced manufacturing and packaging.

In 1997, Intel began to investigate the feasibility of building an e-business system. The project started with the forming of a Virtual Worldwide E-Business

Project Team. Because the project strongly emphasized customer market needs, Intel's sales and marketing was given overall management responsibility.

From pressure exerted by many value chain partners who wanted Intel to play a leadership role, Intel's management decided to advise customers that Intel was serious about e-business. It created an "e-business program" (a self-service extranet) which focused on procurement and customer support for Intel products. Access to the site was restricted to Intel's authorized business partners and customers.

Project teams that participated in the early development of the e-business system included:

A project planning team that consisted of customer, technical and logistical representatives was created to define the scope and objective of the project.

Business analysts were brought in during the early stages to help define the business workflow and to assess how information was given to customers.

Intel's sales and marketing staff were told to study and define how to work with customers via the e-business system.

Intel's Planning and Logistics Group was included on the planning team to help the IT department to develop the solutions to integrate the new e-business with existing business activities.

The IT department was positioned as an "enabler" of business. Its role was to implement the solutions from the Planning and Logistic Groups.

With over 50% of its revenues and many customers coming from outside the US, the benefits of a global e-business system for Intel were too great to be ignored. To support over US$ 25 billion annual sales in 1998 and a worldwide network of business partners, resellers, and original equipment manufacturers (OEM), Intel had to improve its efficiency by automating its business to business processes. Traditional business processes at Intel at that time were too slow and thus a decision was made to deploy a web-based order management system.

On July 1st, 1998, Intel officially began taking orders from OEM and distribution customers using its new personalized websites. This system enabled approximately 200 of Intel's customers in almost 30 countries to place orders for Intel products, check product availability and inventory status, receive marketing and sales information, and obtain customer support in real-time, 24 h a day, 7 days a week. Major successes are:

Intel moved US$ 1 billion dollars in revenue to its on-line e-business system in the first 15 days, surpassing the company's initial goal of doing this in the first 3 months. After the first month of deployment, Intel continued to receive US$ 1 billion value of orders on-line each month for the rest of 1998. Independent customer surveys rated Intel's e-business at a 94% satisfaction level. Intel became the eighth most profitable company in the US in 1999 and climbed to the fifth in 2000.

Many of Intel's employees who participated in the development of the e-business system continue to receive promotions many years after its successful deployment. Sandra Morris was promoted to the CIO position.

Questions for discussion:
1. How can Intel Corp. succeed in the fierce competition of the PC market? What methods did they adopt to overcome the difficulties?
2. What were the Virtual Worldwide E-Business Project Team's main tasks to solve the problems of business online?
3. Do you think it is necessary to develop e-business and deploy problems and challenges when running small enterprises?

V. Supplementary Reading

It's a Big Deal

This is a typical day for a group-buying enthusiast: she goes to work after giving herself a little refresher—a Burberry perfume that she bought a few days ago with 59 percent off. At lunch, she and several colleagues have a spicy hotpot in a nearby restaurant, 70 percent off. After work, she decides to have her car washed for Spring Festival with a coupon entitling her to 83 percent off. Midnight is the most exciting moment for her when all the group-buying websites display new offers of the day. Sometimes she cannot get to sleep until she places a couple of orders and marks the deadline of each coupon on a sticker.

Group buying, a business model borrowed from the United States-based Groupon.com, is enjoying increasing popularity in China among people like this enthusiast. The popularity, in turn, is shaping the way companies reach out to customers.

Letao.com, a Chinese online shoe retailer, said it has cooperated with group-buying websites "many" times. At least 11 group-buying activities on these websites were major ones that attracted a large number of consumers. "It's an easy way to grab users in a short time, and the cost is low compared with other marketing tools," said Chen Hu, vice-president of the e-commerce website. He added that of the 11 major group-buying sales, the biggest attracted 81,659 people. "More than 80 percent of the users that have taken part in group buying eventually come to Letao," he said, adding that the cost to get a new user through group buying is less than one third of traditional advertising. Chen said Letao, which hasn't spent anything on advertising since it started selling shoes in May 2009, will continue with the group-buying strategy as a way to publicize itself to potential customers.

The number of Chinese group-buying websites, which have been springing up since last March, quickly rose to 1,880 by the end of last year, driven by the country's e-commerce boom, according to China e-Business Research Center. Large Chinese Internet companies, such as Sina Corp, Tencent Holdings Ltd, and Alibaba Group, all opened their own group-buying websites to cash in.

The country's group-buying users hit 18.75 million, accounting for 4.1 percent of China's 457 million Internet users, said a recent report by China Internet Network Information Center. The craze is spreading from first-tier cities to second-tier and third-tier cities, and "there will be rapid growth in 2011," the report said.

"I think China's group-buying market may surpass that of the US by the end of this year," said Wu Bo, chief executive of the major group-buying website, lashou.com. He said that although Chinese group-buying prices are lower than those in the US, Chinese users tend to buy more, which makes it possible for the total group-buying transaction volume to exceed that of the US. He estimated that group-buying users might account for up to half of China's online shoppers by the end of this year from the current 11.7 percent.

It's not just domestic websites that are pinning their hopes on this business. Groupon, the group-buying pioneer, has also decided to enter the Chinese market. "China is such an important market... you'll likely see us there," Rob Solomon, president and chief operating officer of Groupon, said in an earlier interview with China Daily.

Groupon is going to partner the Chinese Internet giant Tencent to offer its services in the country, a well-placed source told China Daily. The source said their group-buying website will employ 1,000 people within three months.

As more and more players enter the fray, group-buying websites will have to differentiate themselves to stand out from the increasingly fierce competition. "The group-buying websites may develop in different ways in the future: some may focus on user data analysis, some may gradually develop into more of an advertising platform, and others may stick on as an e-commerce website with improved functions," said Feng Xiaohai, chief executive officer of another popular group-buying website, manzuo.com.

Lashou.com has introduced a social networking feature onto its website, which enables strangers to interact with each other and go to the same group-buying activity, such as a movie or a lunch. Wu, from Lashou, said the function is not meant to generate revenue, but to make the website more interesting. He added that a local-based function will soon come online, which will allow users to "check in" in different places and gain coupons from local service providers.

But both group-buying websites and analysts said the industry will undergo an overhaul in the coming years, during which a large number of small players will fade as they find it increasingly difficult to compete with big players, whether in terms of financing, marketing, or user service. "A time for fast expansion is over in some cities, for example, Beijing, and the market has begun to adjust among different players," said a research note by domestic research company Analysys International.

Problems Facing The Market

Behind the boom, problems are also arising with the fast-growing group-buying market, such as user experience and after-sale service. Users sometimes find what they order from the group-buying websites is not what they actually get at local shops, and some consumers said they were not happy with their experience.

Zheng Xin, a 27-year-old in Wuhan, Hubei province, bought a BBQ meal coupon from group-buying website nuomi.com on Jan 7. More than 18,000 consumers bought the same deal. But after she paid the website announced that the deal had been canceled. Like most of the buyers, Zheng felt she was let down by the website. "If they could not make the BBQ real, why do they list it as a group-buying activity? I paid already," she said. According to Nuomi.com, it was the BBQ restaurant that canceled the deal; while the restaurant said what Nuomi posted on its website contradicted their contract.

Regardless of who was responsible, according to Hover Xiao, a senior analyst at the market research firm International Data Corporation, such occurrences are inevitable in a fast-growing market.

Most of the stores that are willing to participate in group buying are small-size and medium-size stores or companies, as group buying helps them to widen their sales channels and promotes their brand effectively, he said. "But most of the group-buying websites in China are small ones so quality problems easily occur," he said.

Even though the number of group-buying websites will increase over the next two years, only the bigger companies will survive in the long run, he said. Group-buying categories in the future will not be restricted to local shops and services, and more and more online merchandise will dominate the industry, he added. To regulate the group-buying industry, he said that government involvement is necessary, and regulation should be established by legislation.

Reading Comprehension
Choose the best answers to the following questions.
1. Midnight is the most exciting moment for group-buying enthusiasts, because all the group-buying websites _____.
   A. sell cheaper goods
   B. offer new goods for group-buying
   C. open for sales
   D. close to have a rest
2. Letao.com, a Chinese online shoe retailer, said it has cooperated with group-buying websites for many times and _____ has attracted many people.
   A. beautiful shoes
   B. interesting ads
   C. cheaper prices
   D. the brand
3. According to Wu Bo, chief executive of the major group-buying website, lashou.com, what is his attitude toward China's group-buying market?
   A. Optimistic
   B. Negative
   C. Indifferent
   D. Ironic
4. According to the passage, all of the following are problems when facing the fast-growing group-buying market except _____.

A. user experience
B. after-sale service
C. quality problems
D. insufficiencies of choices

5. Most of the group-buying websites in China are all of the following except _____.
A. small companies
B. facing fierce competition
C. hard to survive in two years
D. happy to offer cheaper goods

VI. Assignment

1. Interview some people who have online shopping experience. Ask about their opinions of the e-business and the trouble they have met in online shopping. Write a report with about 200 words.
2. Please prepare a 15-minute presentation to introduce the development process of three famous E-commerce companies of the world and analyze the reasons for their success.

部分练习参考答案

Unit 1 Business Environment

Ⅱ. Cloze
1. adopt   2. confusing   3. categories   4. affect   5. scanning
6. dynamic   7. framework   8. more competitive   9. operations   10. predict

Ⅲ. Translation
1. 就像大学要制定政策维持纪律一样,公司应该制定政策去指导那些常常要做出决策的管理者。公司的政策就是一个企业个性的指针,应该与其经营宗旨保持一致。
2. 一个企业的正式组织结构就是对工作任务和人员的一种系统安排。这个结构决定着信息在企业内如何传递,每个部门负责什么工作,由谁来做出决策。一些企业用组织结构图来简单地说明其正式组织结构。这种组织结构图是对企业内部职权系统和沟通渠道的一个图示说明。
3. 管理理念就是管理者对员工和工作及其他管辖范围内事务的一套个人信念和价值观。管理理念会对员工的行为产生影响,使其产生自我应验的预言。因此,企业宗旨和管理理念必须协调一致。
4. 在人们都喜欢单色直筒裤的环境里,一个设计出条纹喇叭裤的时装设计师不可能成功。一个倾向于保守的社会环境不会接受看上去非常时髦的风格。如果这个设计师不改变他的服装风格,他的事业将遭受挫折。同样的道理也适用于那些生产销售产品的厂商和店铺。
5. 当计算机刚被发明的时候,它有一个房间那么大。人们必须利用打孔卡片才能使用它最基本的功能。今天的计算机更加强大了,但只有手掌那么小。如果企业不能跟上技术发展的步伐,将会面临生产成本增加和产品价格提高的风险。如果一个企业的生产成本高于其他竞争者,它将很快被淘汰。

Ⅴ. Supplementary Reading
1. D   2. D   3. C   4. D   5. A

Unit 2　Entrepreneurship

Ⅱ. Cloze
1. agreement　2. traditional　3. traits　4. willingness　5. made
6. Despite　7. foundation　8. ranked　9. Prior　10. vital

Ⅲ. Translation
1. 成功的企业家精神取决于多种因素。首要因素是一个专注的、有才华的和有创造力的企业家。他应该有办法、有精力也有眼光去创造一个新的企业，这是任何一个新创建企业的基石。但是，他也应该有能力去获取各种重要资源以创造出一个新企业，而不是让它仅仅是一个想法。
2. 在研究企业家精神时，这些研究者主要关注的是各种行为，而不是组织结构。他们认为，企业家精神表现在个人或团队的创新行为、资源的获取、自主决策和承担风险等方面。从理论上，他们给出的定义可以包括各种具有不同职能和目标的，不同种类和规模的企业。
3. 德鲁克给企业家精神下的定义是：一个系统的、专业的、对企业所有员工都适用的纪律。这个定义把我们对企业家精神的理解带入了一个新的高度。他曾做过解释，他认为企业家精神是任何企业在任何时候都可以战略性地运用的东西，不论是一家新企业还是历史悠久的企业。
4. 企业家被认为是拥有"优良的特质"。但是，要准确定义哪种特性和素质能够使人创业成功是一个非常难的事情。因为当今的企业家高矮胖瘦都有。他们来自于不同的行业、种族，有着不同的年龄、性别和教育背景。企业家没有统一的模子。企业家们自己塑造了自己。
5. 例如，有的人认识了一些成功的企业家就会受到激发，去自己着手创办企业。成功的企业家能够成为那些想创业的人的楷模，他们证明了创业不是都意味着破产。

Ⅴ. Supplementary Reading
1. B　2. A　3. D　4. C　5. D

Unit 3　Discovering Business Opportunities

Ⅱ. Cloze
1. franchise　2. eventually　3. talents　4. consideration　5. untapped
6. demand　7. served　8. suffering　9. introduce　10. formula

III. Translation

1. 显然，当你发现市场中存在效率低下的现象，又知道怎么样去改进，并且具有或者能够获取到进行这种改进的资源和能力，这就可能是一个非常有趣的商业创意。
2. 理解顾客没有被满足的需要是不可替代的。这将让你清楚你是否有能力以一个既能让顾客满意，又能让你获利的价格去满足这些需要。
3. 当一个准备创业的人发现了一个很有前景的未被满足的需要，他应该去发现和评估风险，进而决定是否抓住这个商机。
4. 当你能够回答这些问题，并且发现了顾客需求，了解了市场竞争和管理规定，你将有机会针对市场情况去设计你的产品或者服务。
5. 世界各地的研究都表明，企业家和普通人、成功的企业家和失败的企业家之间在性格特征上并没有很大的不同。

V. Supplementary Reading
1. D   2. A   3. B   4. A   5. C

Unit 4 Establishment of a Business

II. Cloze
1. launching   2. survive   3. traction   4. commit   5. viability
6. rush   7. potential   8. identified   9. refine   10. encourage

III. Translation

1. 商业不是诡计，不是输赢交易，不是欺诈。它是行动，是坚持，是耐心，是真诚，是信念，是勤奋。它建立长期的关系并让这种关系带来共赢的效果。商业为这个世界创造价值，并且会因为让人们的生活变得更好而得到回报。商业就是通过给予他人而得到自己所要的。
2. 你的商务活动越是可预测、可重复和可靠，你就会越高效。通过学习、流程再造，进而制订一套系统方法的文件来指导客户服务、财务管理、团队沟通和市场营销等。你将不必再为企业中程序化的事务花费脑筋，而把时间集中花在思考更加具有创新性的方法去为你的顾客创造更多价值。
3. 另一方面，有限合伙人承担有限的责任，这意味着他们的责任仅限于他们在企业的投资。有限合作人无权管理企业。他们投资企业，然后按照合伙协议约定的方式分享利润或者承担损失。
4. 如果你想在网上开办企业，要检查一下你的企业名称是否已经被注册为一个域名。选择一个以.com 或者.net 结尾的域名，不要使用以其他后缀结尾的域名，因为它们不符合商业的严肃性，除非是.org 和.gov，而这两个通常是用于非盈利组织和政府机构。
5. 创业时撰写商业计划书就如同画一个关键的路线图。有人曾说过："当你不去计划的时候就意味着你计划失败了。"没能写计划的最大原因就是认为自己没有足够的时间。不幸的是，这样想的人，比起他们撰写商业计划的时间，日后要花的时间会更多。

V. Supplementary Reading
1. A   2. C   3. D   4. B   5. D

Unit 5　Organizational Structure

II. Cloze
1. scene   2. maximize   3. achieved   4. coordinates   5. criticisms
6. demands   7. inefficiency 8. evolved   9. staffing   10. flaws

III. Translation
1. 组织结构也许会与企业运行中不断变化的实际情况不相符合，当这种分歧继续增长的时候就会降低企业的绩效。例如，一个不当的组织结构可能会妨碍合作，因此而妨碍订单在规定的时间内和有限的资源与预算内完成。
2. 一些理论家建立起后官僚主义组织，其中的决策都基于对话和共识，而不是职权和命令。这种组织呈网络状，而不是层级状，并且边界是开放的（与文化管理完全相反）；它强调超决策制定规则而不是决策制定规则。
3. 功能型结构的核心是任务的协调分配与专业化分工，这种结构能使生产有限数量的产品或者服务变得高效且可预测。而且，当功能型结构组织将其活动垂直合为一体时效率会更高，因此产品可以以更快的速度和更低的成本来出售和分销。
4. 另一种现代结构是网络型结构。大型企业有可能不能灵敏地采取行动做出反应，而新的网络型结构能够把一些商业项目外包出去，这样做能更好或者更便宜。实际上，网络型组织中的经理通常会花大部分时间用电子方式来协调和控制外部关系。
5. 实际上，商业专家列举了许多区分高效组织结构与低效组织结构的特点。认识这些因素对创业者和企业主尤其重要，因为这些人在决定他们企业最终组织结构中起着重要作用。

Ⅴ. Supplementary Reading
1. C   2. D   3. B   4. C   5. B

Unit 6　Recruiting and Training Employees

Ⅱ. Cloze
1. apply   2. goal   3. concentrates   4. communications   5. minimize
6. organization   7. meeting   8. preparing   9. link   10. enabling

Ⅲ. Translation
1. 员工推举制度就是通过咨询现有员工来聘请新员工，此种情形下，现有员工需提供那些他们认为能填补组织内某个空缺职位的人的名字和联系方式。
2. 需注意的是，在大学或者职业学院招聘员工往往是有局限性的，因为这些应聘者没有可供追查的记录来预测他们的表现，因此他们不适合较高层级的职位。
3. 另外，这种招聘方式可以降低招聘成本，大多数情况下也是一种节约时间的方式。因为只有几个应聘者被推荐给招聘公司选择。而运用其他招聘方式时招聘公司需要考虑大量的应聘者，并最终找出最优秀的那个人。这种方式既耗时间也需要大量人力。
4. 组织可以通过综合三种人力资源因素来确定新员工的培训需求，那就是：整个组织的需求，具体工作的特点和特定个人的需求。因此鉴别哪些培训内容能使员工更有效履行自己的职责是最为重要的，因为它能够帮助设计培训手册和评估方式。
5. 因此，员工入职培训是非常重要的，可以被当作员工培训的一种方式。它应该把重点放在各种人事规章制度，组织中的关键人员，以及企业的宗旨、历史和文化或者还有其他内容。

Ⅴ. Supplementary Reading
1. B   2. D   3. D   4. C   5. C

Unit 7　Employee Motivation

Ⅱ. Cloze
1. fulfilling   2. assumption   3. success   4. revolves   5. squelch
6. impact   7. fosters   8. accused   9. delivered   10. exhibit

Ⅲ. Translation
1. 激励 motivation 一词来自于拉丁文"movere"，意思是移动。激励的定义是：

确定行为的目的和方向的心理活动；为了达到某种未满足的需求而使用某种方法的倾向；一种满足未满足的需求的内在推动力；一种渴望得到的意愿。

2. 因此，管理层认为要严格监督，管理员工，建立一套系统全面的管理系统。如果没有一套足够吸引人的激励制度，员工将表现出极小的进取心，并且会抓住一切机会逃避责任。相信 X 理论的经理会相当依赖于用恐吓和强迫手段来使员工顺从。这会导致不信任、严格的监管及惩罚性的氛围。

3. 马斯洛需求的层次越高，就越不明显，且越不容易描述，但是它们又非常重要。社会需要是指我们想要成为我们所在集体的一部分。公司可以给员工创造机会来分享公司的共同目标和愿景。奖赏那些通过付出和努力为公司的成功做出贡献的员工，可以达到这个效果。

4. 为员工的自我管理和自我决策提供更多的自主权。在清晰的框架和有效的实时沟通的前提下，在规定范围、界限和需要向经理做出反馈的关键点后，授权员工做出决策。

5. 即使这些抱怨不能如员工所愿，得到恰当的处理。但你若去处理了这些抱怨，并向他们反馈了你对这些抱怨的看法和解决办法，他们将会感激你。处理员工所关心的问题并且做出相应的反馈是无比重要的。

V. Supplementary Reading
1. C   2. D   3. C   4. A   5. B

Unit 8 Corporate Culture

II. Cloze
1. adaptive   2. elements   3. speeches   4. colleagues   5. cost
6. sort   7. loyalty   8. capacity   9. succession   10. interest

III. Translation
1. 信念就是我们对什么是真实的、正确的事物的看法，以及对我们的行为可能造成的后果的预期。你越清楚你珍惜和相信的是什么，你就越快乐，越有效率。

2. 知识型的企业从个人和集体的不断学习中获得竞争优势。在一个拥有完善的知识管理系统的公司中，员工的学习就是公司自身的学习。人们态度的变化会在指导公司行为的正式和非正式规则之中有所反映。

3. 沟通使一个企业成长发展，它给了公司与员工交流，教育或指导员工的机会。双向沟通和自上而下的沟通在企业经营中都很重要。双向沟通使公司内部同一级别或职位的员工之间能够传递消息，而自上而下的沟通是上级向下级传达信息。这两种沟通形式在工作中都起着很大作用。
4. 然而，国家间文化的差异导致了管理上的意见分歧。国家文化之间的差异深深植根于各国的文化价值观中，而这些文化价值观可以决定人们对如何经营公司的期望，以及领导者和员工的关系会怎样影响雇主和雇员之间的预期关系。
5. 如果一个企业的文化和员工对企业的期望不一致，将会导致很多不良后果，例如，较低的工作满意度，较高的工作倦怠感，普遍的工作压力，以及跳槽意向等。

Ⅴ. Supplementary Reading
1. B 2. D 3. C 4. B 5. D

Unit 9　Production and Product

Ⅱ. Cloze
1. distinct　　2. design　　3. maturity　　4. release　　5. share
6. saturated　7. abandon　8. fluctuations　9. specifics　10. responding

Ⅲ. Translation
1. 人力资本是指劳动者通过教育、培训和实践而获取的技能。学生上大学是在获取人力资本，工人在从实践或培训中获取人力资本，学习识字的孩子也在获取人力资本。
2. 18世纪宾夕法尼亚州的农民发现他们的土地渗出了石油，他们十分恐慌而不是高兴。没人知道可以用石油做什么。直到19世纪中期，人们才发现了一种可以将石油精炼为能够提供能量的煤油的方法，从而使石油成为了一种自然资源。
3. 由于特殊品昂贵的特性，其购买者多来自社会的富有阶层。特殊品不是人们必需的，人们购买它是出于个人偏好或欲望。一个商品的品牌名称和独一无二的特性是吸引消费者购买的主要因素。
4. 同样，用于生产过程的机器和设备也属于工业产品，这其中包括重型设备如塑料和金属的模具、加热室和冷却室，甚至是对成品进行自动化包装的机器设备。
5. 因为多数厂商可以提供相同的产品，他们在竞争中更多依靠价格而不是产品差异化，这时，收入的涨幅就开始下降，利润开始减少。与此同时，激烈的竞争要求厂商增加对营销和销售的投入来保持其市场份额，从而增加了企业经营的总成本。

部分练习参考答案 259

Ⅴ. Supplementary Reading
1. B   2. C   3. D   4. A   5. C

Unit 10　Marketing

Ⅱ. Cloze

1. targeting　2. established　3. marketing　4. live　5. reduction
6. increase　7. benefit　8. purchases　9. promotions　10. inferior

Ⅲ. Translation

1. 这一时期，受科学技术创新的推动，社会急剧变化。其结果之一就是产品生产第一次与产品消费分离。批量生产，不断发展的交通设施以及日益增多的大众媒体意味着生产者有必要并且有能力开发更多更赚钱的商品分销途径。
2. 物品的价格是决定其销售额的重要因素。理论上来说，价格实际上是由顾客所感知到的待售商品价值决定的。调查顾客对价格的看法是很重要的，因为这样能够表明他们对想要购买的商品的重视程度以及他们想购买什么。一个公司的价格政策根据时间和环境的不同而有所差异。
3. 为商品和服务做促销或广告的相关成本通常在该商品生产总成本中占相当大的比例。但是成功的促销活动能够提高销售量，广告和其他费用就能分摊到更多的产品中去。虽然促销活动通常是为了应对激烈竞争等问题，但是这能够让公司获取一系列信息，是非常划算的。
4. 市场细分是将一个较大的市场根据消费者的相同需求和应用划分为更小市场的一种策略。不同的消费者群体可以根据不同的人口因素来确定，这取决于调查目的。
5. 公司也会进行"反市场定位"，即试图改变消费者对其他品牌的看法。直接攻击对手的品牌可能会引起人们的不满或者违法，但公司可以非常小心地去设计方案，比如用"与领先品牌相比"或"我们不像其他品牌"等语言。

Ⅴ. Supplementary Reading
1. D   2. C   3. B   4. B   5. D

Unit 11　Financial Management

Ⅱ. Cloze

1. management　2. alternative　3. operation　4. subset　5. accurate
6. paying　7. track　8. acquire　9. address　10. cash

III. Translation

1. 财务管理专家要准备公正完整的财务报表,并确保公司与财务报告机制相关的内部控制、公司政策和程序是充分且实用的。财务管理专家也可以分析经营数据和经营业绩,向企业高级管理人员提供投资理念方面的建议。

2. 公司可以通过发行债券获利,因为它们向投资者支付的利率一般低于大多数其他类型借贷的利率,并且支付债券的利息是作为免税的业务费用。然而,即使公司没有获取利润,也必须支付债券利息。

3. 利润分享计划是一些企业用以激励员工的一种退休福利。公司对利润分享计划的投入不是强制性的,而是基于公司任一年的利润额。员工退休后会从这部分公司投入中享有资金,而不用在工作期间自己出资。

4. 会计与财务管理体系能够为任何规模的企业提供报告和查询服务。这些系统能向管理者提供信息,使他们根据事实,而不是直觉做出正确的决策。会计与财务管理体系能满足公司各方面的需求,如生产成本信息和预算的制订和控制。

5. 内部控制的一个共同特点是如果不止一人参与进行会计任务,那么从开始到结束,会计人员的职责是分离的。例如,在支付账单的内部控制中,一人核准账单,另一人处理付款。这样的安排能使财务管理错误更容易被发现。

V. Supplementary Reading

1. D 2. C 3. B 4. D 5. A

Unit 12 Financing

II. Cloze

1. mainstream   2. appealing   3. belly-up   4. trusted   5. accountable
6. liquidity   7. convert   8. frequently 9. generate 10. promissory

III. Translation

1. 信用卡和贸易信贷(与当地的行业和企业建立的信贷)可以帮助一个企业管理现金流,如逐项报表的使用使得现金的开销变得清晰明确,并且可用一次性支付代替多种付款。

2. 此外,当地的商业银行贷款可用来购买楼宇以放置车辆,同时,信用额度可用于支付培训扩大业务所需员工期间的工资。

3. 如果人们无法近距离观察企业经营状况,那么贷款给你时会非常谨慎。如果他们觉得你没有正确地经营管理,他们可能会介入并且插手你的企业经营。在某些情况下,即使有书面合同你也无法防止这种情况,因为许多国家的法律保证了个人在对一个企业投资后就在企业中拥有投票权。
4. 然而,最常见的专业的股权融资资金来自于风险投资家。他们是机构式的风险承担者,可能是富裕人士的群体,受政府资助的,或者是主要的金融机构。他们中大部分专门投资一个或几个密切相关的行业。
5. 有些风险投资家倾向于只投资刚创建的公司,投资这类公司的风险最高,但潜在回报也是最高的。其他风险投资公司仅进行第二阶段以扩张为目的的融资,或为公司上市前的发展提供过渡性融资。最后,还有一些风险投资公司专门为管理层收购提供资金。

Ⅴ. Supplementary Reading
1. A   2. D   3. B   4. C   5. D

Unit 13 Corporate Social Responsibilities

Ⅱ. Cloze
1. expectations   2. precede   3. resulting   4. performance   5. implied
6. principles   7. distinct   8. mutually   9. dynamic   10. conflict

Ⅲ. Translation
1. 这种做法鼓励企业通过自身的专业化来帮助解决受关注的社会问题,从而为社会创造经济和社会价值。例如,汽车制造商推出的混合动力汽车和电动汽车有益于提供一个更健康的环境。
2. 扶贫工作包括确保社区清洁用水,为人们提供社会公共卫生诊所,确保该地区儿童获得必需的食物和疫苗。这些工作必须在政府因压力实施促进工人健康、安全和保证最低工资的法律之前完成。
3. 通过结合所得税和公司税,学校将有更多的钱进行改善提升,而不是像现在这样仅仅依靠房地产税。
4. 企业社会责任相对于传统企业道德来说更加广泛的另一个原因是它必须包括环保责任。在过去,企业为了增加价值和提高自己的品牌形象会去做绿色环保行动,而如今绿色环保行动是企业社会责任的内在要求。
5. 他们应该更进一步的去服务社会,因为是社会允许了他们使用其各种稀缺资源。社会责任则是道德的体现。企业应视社会为生产要素的主人,利润的来源,以及稀缺资源的共享者。

Ⅴ. Supplementary Reading
1. C   2. B   3. D   4. A   5. C

Unit 14 Going to the International Market

II. Cloze
1. negotiation   2. inherent   3. remain   4. targeted   5. familiar
6. assessed   7. resources   8. liability   9. feasible   10. fit

III. Translation
1. 我们可以以本田为例，本田在中国制造配件，在巴基斯坦组装产品，而在日本设计引擎。因此生产过程被分配到三个地方进行。
2. 举例来说，荷兰人从来不会讨价还价，巴西人时常会这样，而中国人却对之习以为常。一家公司如果没有花时间去了解这些差异，其国际市场营销行为是有风险的，各种问题都会让其经营失败。
3. 大多数寻求供应商的外国客户可能会要求本地供应产品，以便加速生产流程。而企业为了留住客户通常会满足其要求。
4. 然而，许多企业目前过度依赖分销商之类的合作伙伴来帮助它们在国际市场上"摸清门路"，实际上它们应该向更具资历的第三方咨询意见，比如公关公司、市场营销公司或者法律事务所。
5. 因此，沉没成本或一般的退出壁垒的可能性不大。反过来说，由于无法控制在国外市场的良好供应，一个公司出口产品到国外市场时可能控制权会更少。

V. Supplementary Reading
1. B   2. D   3. A   4. C   5. D

Unit 15 E-business

II. Cloze
1. access   2. ensure   3. air-conditioned   4. contain   5. confidential
6. employees   7. separate   8. location   9. failover   10. authorized

III. Translation
1. 这些网站大多向访问者提供有关公司的产品和服务的基本信息，包括联系方式，如电话号码和电子邮件地址，以协助消费者联系公司为其提供服务。当营销部门一意识到公司的网站可以为数以百万计的人所用时，马上从通过网络提供简单的商业信息转向通过网络招揽生意。
2. 服务器技术的发展，包括根据产品数据库建立网站的能力，导致了 eBay 和亚马逊等大型互联网企业的创建。在以前的产品销售网站，每个产品必须手动张贴在网页上。拥有数据库驱动的网站，企业可以使用网页模板即时显示数以万计的产品。

3. 根据它们成功的商业经验，企业可以选择简单地扩大它们在互联网上的业务，而不是创建一个实体店面。互联网店面相对便宜，企业仅需一台计算机，网站托管服务和互联网连接作为自己的主要经营设备。

4. 传统上，消费者对实体经营环境里的客户服务高度评价。对电子商务企业来说，要提供相同的良好客户服务比较困难，因为它们的客户使用的是电子商务操作，可能有数百或数千英里之遥。

5. 电子商务企业，或电子商务，是一种创建和经营公司的流行做法。电子商务通常是通过互联网作为一个独立的网上商店来经营，也可以是一家在现实世界中运行的实体公司的附属成分。

V. Supplementary Reading
1. B   2. C   3. A   4. D   5. D